The Washington Post

DINING GUIDE

BY
PHYLLIS C. RICHMAN

Washington's Top Criti
Rates Area Resto

INTRODUCTION

Y ou're given the chance to try on shoes before you buy them, and you can test-drive a car. But dinner at a restaurant? No matter that it sometimes might cost as much as a new suit. You've got to order blindly, with no more to go on than friends' often-limited experiences, the menu's vague and sometimes inaccurate descriptions, the advice of a waiter who may never have tasted the food, and any cues you can pick up from noticing the dishes at the next table. Little else that you spend your money on is bought so blindly.

That's why people turn to restaurant critics.

However, you should read any restaurant review with healthy skepticism. Here's why: While your movie ticket buys you the same experience as a movie critic, and a theater will warn you if the leading role is being played by an understudy, restaurants change all the time — without warning. A restaurant might have gained a new chef or a new owner since it was reviewed. The prices may have gone up, the menu may have been revised. Yet the old reviews — sometimes years old — still hang in the front window as if everything has stayed the same. And even if a review is fresh off the presses and the original staff is intact, each meal is different. The chef's or the waiter's mood affects your meal. The fisherman's weather conditions or the time elapsed since the corn was picked can make the difference between a good meal and a bad one. The lighting, the dining room temperature, who's at the next table, what was last cooked in the deep-fryer — much influences your dinner's quality.

Thus a review, like tomorrow's weather forecast, is only a prediction, and that's where the critic's expertise enters. A critic needs to do more than relate the particulars of his or her meals. From a few visits, a critic should be able to assess the restaurant's strengths and weaknesses, then pass guidelines along to the reader.

Over these 20 years I have had to put up with some unspeakably bad meals. But I've also had countless exciting meals — prepared by talented chefs and served by thoughtful and intelligent staffs. I owe them gratitude not only for delicious afternoons and evenings, but also for what their craft has taught me. I thank them.

I also owe two decades' worth of gratitude to *The Washington Post* — not just for bankrolling this expensive education but also for providing me with a platform and absolute freedom for my opinionated prose. The *Post's* publisher, Donald Graham, has been endlessly supportive and even, on occasion, an uncomplaining lunch companion. The legendary Ben Bradlee, Shelby Coffey and the late Howard Simons and Marion Clark hired me, and I've remained enormously grateful to them. The *Post's* current executive and managing editors, Len Downie and Bob Kaiser, have continued to challenge and reinforce me; particular thanks to Bob Kaiser for having somehow dissolved the barriers to the *Post* publishing its first restaurant guidebook.

Just as restaurants are group efforts, so are books. My thanks go to Noel Epstein, who became a one-man publishing company and transformed my reviews into the book you hold. Bob Barkin and Susan Davis designed and illustrated my first *Post* writings, and now, two decades later and to my great satisfaction, designed and illustrated this book. And in another reunion, Kathleen Stanley, who used to edit my column in *The Washington Post Magazine*, dropped everything — family and freelance life — to pitch in at the last minute and tie up all the loose ends so that we could meet our deadline.

There are so many others to thank as well: my constantly interesting and entertaining colleagues at the *Post*, the friends and family who have gone anywhere to eat anything in order to help me do my job, my three children — Joe, Matt and Libby — who are now able to make jokes about growing up with a refrigerator filled with nothing but little white carryout boxes and aluminum foil swans. And most of all, Bob Burton, who always remains ready at home with a tomato-onion-anchovy sandwich or a properly baked potato when I need an antidote to restaurant food. Nor can I forget the readers who call, write and send me e-mail messages to tell me about new restaurants they've found, to chime in with their agreement or to accuse me of having the tastebuds of a doorknob. I learn from them all.

Over the past 20 years American cooking has come into its own, no longer in the shadow of the French. Thus, instead of *bon appetit*:

Good appetite.
Phyllis C. Richman

A.V. RISTORANTE
607 New York Ave. NW, Washington, DC
(202) 737-0550

ITALIAN   ♿

Open: M-Th 11:30 am-11 pm, F 11 am-midnight, Sat 5-midnight
Entrees: $6.50-$15 **Closed:** Sun **Credit Cards:** All major
Reservations: Accepted for 12 or more **Dress:** Casual
Parking: Free lot **Metro:** Gallery Place-Chinatown

This big, bare, unlovely set of dining rooms is the great-grandfather of our real Italian red-sauce restaurants. It's loved and hated, famous and notorious. Its menu is immense, but many of the dishes are never (and maybe never have been) available. The regulars know to order from the long list of daily specials scrawled on a board in the entrance hall.

A.V. can be cheap or not, and if you don't ask prices ahead of time, you might find some surprises at the end. Another trick the regulars know: These are huge portions, so order accordingly. Mixed meat platters, mixed seafood platters, sauteed vegetables all tend to be plain and good. The pizza is for purists, not adventurers, and it's thin-crusted and savory enough to make diners from New York stop complaining for a while. Pastas are straightforward and hearty, none better than Spaghetti Caruso, heavy with whole chicken livers, peppers, onions and mushrooms in a full-flavored tomato sauce.

The dining room is as dark as a cave (even at lunch), the service is offhand, the mood is hectic. Don't look for refinements in the decor or the food. But look for aromas and bold flavors to remember.

> **"The pizza is for purists, not adventurers, and it's thin-crusted and savory enough to make diners from New York stop complaining for a while."**

2

AFGHAN
2700 Jefferson Davis Highway, Alexandria, VA
(703) 548-0022

AFGHAN   ♿

Open: M-Th 11 am-11 pm, F-Sun 11 am-midnight
Lunch Entrees: $6-$8 **Dinner Entrees:** $6-$13
Pre-Theater: Daily 4:30-6:30, $25 (for 2) **Credit Cards:** All major
Reservations: Recommended **Dress:** Casual
Parking: Free lot **Entertainment:** Afghan music F evening

Washington has several good Afghan restaurants, some far more attractive than this plain, warehouse-sized cavern, and most of my favorite Afghan dishes are done better elsewhere. But the bread — called *nan* — is what attracts me to this restaurant, and in an Afghan meal the bread is all-important.

You can see what I mean when you order a kebab. It's four long, flat skewers threaded with meat, piled on flat bread the size and shape of a skateboard. Blistered from being cooked right on the oven floor, the bread is browned and blackened in spots. It is wonderful bread, stretchy and chewy, with the flavor that a well-developed yeast dough should have. It tastes like pizza dough with soul. Scoop up a little of the tiny tomato-cilantro side salad and the cilantro-green yogurt dip, and eat the bread and the meat together. Think of campfires and of carrying your life's possessions in saddlebags.

Prices here are so low that even the extravagances cost hardly more than an appetizer elsewhere. So splurge on the rib chops. They are cut thin and cooked thoroughly so that the meat is crisp at the edges. Otherwise, there's boneless lamb or less meaty lamb ribs. The beef is ground, mildly seasoned meatballs alternating with bits of tomato on the skewers. But you can taste the seasonings most clearly on the chicken kebabs. They highlight the garlic and cumin and coriander, as well as the charcoal smoke. Also intriguing is *carrayee*, a mix of diced chicken or lamb sauteed with tomatoes, peppers and onions, smothered in coriander leaves and topped with a fried egg. The cooking here is rustic; some dishes are oily, some dull. Yet the surprise is not that AFGHAN serves some unsatisfying dishes but that, at its prices, the appetizers and kebabs are as good as they are and the bread is so distinctive.

"Think of campfires and of carrying your life's possessions in saddlebags."

AMAZONIA GRILL
4615 Wisconsin Ave. NW, Washington, DC
(202) 537-0421

BRAZILIAN

Lunch: M-F noon-3 **Entrees:** $8-$18
Dinner: M-Th 5:30-10:30, F 5:30-11:30, Sat-Sun noon-11:30
Dinner Entrees: $11-$18 **Brunch:** Sat-Sun noon-4, $12
Credit Cards: All major **Reservations:** Recommended
Dress: Casual **Parking:** Street **Metro:** Tenleytown-AU
Entertainment: Bossa nova Th evening

In good weather, the hub of this restaurant is the covered porch. The dining room inside is more dressed up, with stuccoed walls and large paintings of Brazilian life, forest-green tablecloths and vases of various red flowers. But the porch seems more innately tropical.

A large icy *caipirinha* also sets the scene. This is a jolting limeade made with clear Brazilian liquor, lots of lime wedges and a little sugar. It calls for immediate food to cushion the blow, particularly since this is one of the many restaurants where appetizers are the stars. *Carne seca* is chunks of cured dried meat cooked to crispness yet nearly falling apart. Mussels come drenched in garlic and dill and flamed with cognac — just right for dunking bread. Other seafood appetizers are flavored with coconut milk and palm oil, a theme that carries through the entrees. A nutritionist probably would recoil in horror, and many people find the strong palm oil an acquired taste. But if you've loved food in the tropics and haven't found any here that matches your memories, palm oil may be the missing link.

The star of a Brazilian restaurant is *feijoada*, a large pot of black beans crammed with ham, sausage and other varieties of pork. It's accompanied by a platter of toasted manioc meal, reminiscent of bread crumbs, with shredded collard greens and slices of orange. These unlikely components make a great amalgam. The less daring can have grilled steak or fried chicken, though with a Brazilian touch. More elaborate meat entrees run to chicken with pineapple; fried bananas and collard greens; duck with yucca leaves, cognac, olive oil and garlic; or *churrascada,* a mixed grill for two. Seafood dishes are variations on the palm oil theme. The colors are vivid, the aromas intense, the textures viscous and rich. This is Brazilian food made for Brazilians, not tamed for North American tastes. For some that's a drawback. For most it's an advantage.

ANATOLYA
633 Pennsylvania Ave. SE, Washington, DC
(202) 544-4753

TURKISH   ♿

Lunch: M-F 11:30-3:30 **Entrees:** $5.25-$9
Dinner: M-F 3:30-10, Sat 5:30-10 **Entrees:** $9-15 **Closed:** Sun
Credit Cards: AE, MC, V **Reservations:** Recommended
Dress: Casual **Parking:** Street **Metro:** Eastern Market

This is an intimate restaurant run by a husband-and-wife team, Tildikim and Dilek Mit. He's in the kitchen and she's in the dining room, charmingly greeting and serving. Neighbors drop by, children are fussed over. ANATOYLA is a hometown kind of place with a lacy tearoom look, its tables covered with pink and pastel green cloths (unfortunately protected with clingy plastic). On the walls are Turkish rugs and over the tables are hanging lamps, cleverly fashioned from upended copper kettles.

You can sample most appetizers in one fell swoop with a *mezze* platter, with its tangy hummus, refreshing baba ghanouj and dill-perfumed stuffed grape leaves. My favorite part of the mezze platter is roasted eggplant, thick slices so soft they nearly collapse under a blanket of yogurt sauce that has garlic, dill and mint competing at top pitch. That yogurt sauce — thick and rich, sometimes with shredded cucumber and mint as well as garlic and dill — is a recurring theme. Most important, it's the binding element in a wonderful appetizer of shredded, sauteed carrots. The yogurt sauce weaves its way among the entrees, too. It moistens the bed of cubed pita bread for *yogurtlu* kebab (beef or lamb, sliced and grilled) or the spiciest and best of the meat dishes, Adana kebab, long sausages of ground lamb, teasing the tongue with cumin and garlic. Plain grilled kebabs are better elsewhere.

> **"The greatest appeal of Anatolya is among the appetizers."**

In sum, the greatest appeal at ANATOLYA is among the appetizers: anything with eggplant, anything sauced with yogurt, certainly those stuffed grape leaves and that brilliant carrot mezze. At the other end of the menu, ANATOLYA'S baklava is sensational. Follow it with Turkey's most famous contribution to cuisine: coffee, boiled in a tiny pot to a foamy few tablespoons' worth, thick, dark and nearly syrup. It offers a sweet, quiet ending to a gently pleasant meal.

AQUARELLE
Watergate Hotel
2650 Virginia Ave. NW, Washington, DC
(202) 298-4455

AMERICAN

Breakfast: Daily 7-10:30 **Entrees:** $10.75-$16.75
Lunch: Daily 11:30-2:30 **Entrees:** $15.75-$19.75
Dinner: Daily 7-10:30 **Entrees:** $18.75-$26
Pre-Theater Menu: Daily 5:30-7, $35 **Credit Cards:** All major
Reservations: Recommended **Dress:** Casual except dinner
Parking: Free valet **Metro:** Foggy Bottom

Chef Robert Wiedmaier, now at the Watergate's renamed dining room, has an impossible task: He's supposed to be replacing Jean-Louis Palladin, long the city's most celebrated chef. Wiedmaier is a talented chef whose sauces are known for rich flavors and light textures and whose dishes combine American ingenuity with French finesse. Appetizers show Wiedmaier's talent to greatest advantage, and he makes much of such luxuries as foie gras and asparagus at prices that don't quite take your breath away.

The most exciting entrees are game such as pheasant or squab. And while he still needs to work on his vegetable accompaniments, he turns out superlative grilled and roasted meats and fish. Desserts are as colorful as the watercolors on the walls, and fruit tarts are exquisitely fragile.

At last look, though, most of the sophistication at AQUARELLE was in the chef's hands. The refinements on the plate weren't carried out in the dining room. Instead of flowers on the table, the centerpiece was a decanter of colored water. It doesn't need changing as often.

" . . . dishes combine American ingenuity with French finesse."

Service is well meaning, but the dining room staff is sorely in need of training. Except for the water view that a few of the tables offer, the front of the house is just another pretentious hotel dining room.

AROMA
1919 I St. NW, Washington, DC
(202) 833-4700

INDIAN

Lunch: M-F 11:30-2:30, Sat-Sun noon-2:30
Dinner: Sun-Th 5:30-10, F-Sat 5:30-10:30
Entrees: $5.50-$15 **Brunch:** Sat-Sun noon-2:30, $9
Pre-Theater: Daily 5:30-7, $12.50 **Credit Cards:** All major
Reservations: Recommended for lunch **Dress:** Casual
Parking: Street **Metro:** Farragut West

Once French, then Italian and now Indian, this small space has retained the pretty lace-curtain look of its European origins. And despite the formal tucked shirts and bow ties of its dining room staff, AROMA has a friendly homeyness. Tables are close enough together that, true to the restaurant's name, you can get a whiff of your neighbor's curry.

The highlight of the menu is the tandoori chicken, moist and tender under its neon-red spice rub. Vegetable dishes such as spinach and eggplant are also vividly flavorful. But much is not. Breads tend to be heavy, kebabs bland and dry, and lamb curry just a thick red stew, more sweet than spicy, though its meat is lean and plentiful.

In other words, AROMA is an Indian restaurant to know about if you're in the area, pleasant but inconsistent. Its prices are as mild as its seasonings, with the gala multi-course meal for two priced as meals for one might be elsewhere.

ARUCOLA
5534 Connecticut Ave. NW, Washington, DC
(202) 244-1555

ITALIAN   ♿

Lunch: M-Sat 11:30-2:30 **Entrees:** $9-$15
Dinner: Sun-Th 5-10, F-Sat 5-10:30 **Entrees:** $11-$21
Credit Cards: All major **Reservations:** No
Dress: Casual **Parking:** Free lot

What used to be the dark, cozy Chevy Chase Lounge has been replaced by a bright yellow restaurant that looks like a summer day in the Italian countryside. Its wood-burning oven in back produces pizzas, its wood-fueled rotisserie turns chickens, and an antipasto cart offers grilled and marinated vegetables as well as soft white mozzarella. The menu reads like Italian poetry.

The food these days, though, seems to plead for editing. *Pappardelle* with a sauce of arugula pesto is thick and chewy, the pasta uneven and its sauce minimally flavorful. And it's the best of the pastas I've tried. Atop others, the seafood has been shriveled and dry, and a spinach cream sauce with anchovies has tasted like green library paste. As for the antipasto, some of it is palatable, but much of it is exceptionally acidic. Probably the safest bets here are the fish specials, grilled fillets topped with something uncomplicated like good briny Italian black olives and capers.

"The food these days seems to plead for editing."

What brings the neighborhood to this once-intriguing trattoria? It's not the service, which is brusque and slapdash. In part it may be the more enticing decor. But the principal answer is the age-old cliche: location, location, location.

ASHBY INN
692 Federal St., Paris, VA
(540) 592-3900

AMERICAN   ♿

Dinner: W-Sat 6-9 **Entrees:** $16.50-$22
Brunch: Sun noon-2:30, $19 **Closed:** M-T
Credit Cards: MC, V **Reservations:** Required
Dress: Casual **Parking:** Free

This small inn has been the fulfillment of a typical Washington dream: Its proprietors, Roma and John Sherman, gave up jobs on Capitol Hill to run a country inn with a few rooms for overnight guests, yet close enough to Washington to draw those who merely want to dine. They change the menu daily, keeping it close to the season, and grow some of what they serve. John Sherman's passion for wine shows in the personalized and decently priced list.

You can dine on a terrace overlooking the garden, on an enclosed porch, or in rooms that look like colonial dining rooms or a tavern. The furnishings have a New England simplicity, turned romantic by hurricane lamps. The menu, too, shows restraint: not too many choices, nothing complicated. The vegetables

" . . . the fulfillment of a typical Washington dream."

shine on their own, in a roasted corn chowder or a buttery spinach accompaniment to a grill or a roast. A plain roast chicken is crackling and juicy, a memorable bird. And the region's local rockfish is served brown and crusty, silky inside.

This is not flashy cooking — it shows considerable reserve — and its plainness can highlight the flaws. But if you order whatever is most local, most seasonal and most simple, dinner is likely to be as satisfying as it is soothing.

ASIA NORA
2213 M St. NW, Washington, DC
(202) 797-4860

ASIAN

Dinner: M-Th 6-10, F-Sat 6-10:30 **Entrees:** $15-$23
Closed: Sun **Credit Cards:** MC,V
Reservations: Recommended **Dress:** Casual
Parking: Street **Metro:** Foggy Bottom

Chef Munehiro Mori brings Japanese expertise and American experience to this exquisitely beautiful fusion restaurant, and you can see it most clearly in his fish entrees. Sea bass decorated with fresh green herbs and wrapped in translucent rice paper becomes a crunchy, slightly chewy package with every nuance of flavor captured inside. Sesame-crusted tuna is cooked rare and delicately sweetened with a flowery ginger-orange sauce; it's Japanese even if its bed of saffron fettuccine is Italian.

But when Mori moves too far from Japan to India, Thailand or America, he gets lost (although the very Western spice-rubbed rack of lamb is excellent, as good as the best American restaurant might serve). The curries are wimpy, the pizza tastes like fast food, and the risotto misses by a continent. Even more disappointingly, only a few of the appetizers can compete with the entrees.

> **"When [Chef Munehiro] Mori moves too far from Japan . . . he gets lost."**

The environment could be considered worth the trip. Frog-skin-green walls and museum-quality artifacts make ASIA NORA one of the most serenely handsome rooms in which anyone could dine. The wine list remains interesting, if pricey. The service is soothing and intelligent. And the rectangular slab plates on which food is served are of spare magnificence, a proper background for the feathery green garnishes and the colorful sauces squiggled and striped on the food.

But given its top prices, ASIA NORA leaves itself little room for error. When its experiments work, it's worth every penny; when they don't, you'll wish for the return of Nora's old down-to-earth City Cafe.

ATILLA'S
2705 Columbia Pike, Arlington, VA
(703) 920-8255

TURKISH   ♿

Lunch: M-F 11-2:30 **Entrees:** $6-$7.45
Dinner: M-Sat 5-11 **Entrees:** $9-$15
Closed: Sun **Credit Cards:** DIS, MC, V
Reservations: For 6 or more **Dress:** Casual **Parking:** Free lot
Entertainment: F-Sat 9-midnight Middle Eastern music

S ome people are satisfied to find one outstanding dish on a menu and just come back when they have a hankering for that favorite. Whether other dishes are good or bad doesn't concern these loyalists. ATILLA'S is the place for them.

It's hardly necessary to order appetizers, because the waiter automatically brings you the best of them when you are seated. A basket of house-made pita, deeply browned and heavily sprinkled with sesame seeds, arrives with a plate of hummus — tart and spicy hummus, smooth but not pasty, light despite a slick of oil on top. Nobody in the area makes better pita or hummus, and the first round is free.

You're not just stuck with hummus, though. The Albanian liver is a revelation, the tiny cubes coated with spices that make them sharp and tangy, sauteed until they are crusty and tender and accompanied, like almost everything else, by a pile of shaved red onion and

"The doner kebab is enough to bring honor to Atilla's."

parsley. Fried eggplant with garlic and tomato sauce tastes much like Italian *caponata* (even without the olives and capers), and it's good despite its oiliness.

The entree list looks long, but it's mostly variations of grilled lamb. Forget everything but the *doner* kebab. This mixture of thinly cut lamb, beef and veal is formed into a giant meatloaf and grilled on a vertical spit. You've probably seen something similar called a gyro in local carryouts, but that factory-made frozen version is as much like ATILLA'S as a hot dog is like homemade sausage. It's available as a platter, piled on pita or on damp, soft rice. So you don't really need to find out whether the rest of the entrees are juicy or dry, over-marinated or under-seasoned that day. The *doner* kebab is enough to bring honor to ATILLA'S.

AUSTIN GRILL
2404 Wisconsin Ave. NW, Washington, DC
(202) 337-8080

AMERICAN/SOUTHWESTERN

Open: M 11:30 am-10:30, T-Th 11:30-11, F 11:30-midnight,
Sat 3-midnight, Sun 3-10:30 **Entrees:** $6.50-$14
Brunch: Sat-Sun 11-3, $5-$7 **Credit Cards:** All major
Reservations: No **Dress:** Casual **Parking:** Valet (fee) at dinner

One crunch of a chip and you know the food at the AUSTIN GRILL and SOUTH AUSTIN GRILL is far above ordinary, gummy, Tex-Mex cooking. These chips taste of corn, they're light, and they're fried in fresh oil. The two salsas on the table are not just hot, but flavorful.

But while all the cute stencils on the walls, the down-home decor and can't-keep-still music might lead you to expect that these are nothing more than taco palaces, the menu will convince you that these AUSTIN GRILLS are more serious than that. Along with the inevitable fajitas, burritos and enchiladas, the AUSTIN GRILLS serve awfully good grilled fish (though I'd skip the little dish of sweet orange tequila butter), as well as shrimp and scallops. There are chili-and-garlic-marinated pork chops *adobado* and a rib-eye version of *carne asada*. And some days you might find *posole* among the specials.

For me, though, the stars of the menu are the crab-meat quesadilla, which is delicate and subtle, and the green chili, a wonderful, slow-burning stew with roasted *poblanos* and cilantro fighting for prominence and plenty of diced chicken and potatoes to keep them in line.

If you go for the quesadilla, a side order of guacamole certainly will be in order once you've scraped up the bit that decorates the plate. Then perhaps another order just to make sure it's as good as you thought it was. Surely you won't have room for an Ibarra chocolate brownie.

For suburban branches: South Austin Grill, 801 King St., Alexandria, VA, (703) 684-8969; Austin Grill Springfield, 8430 Old Keene Mill Rd., Springfield, VA, (703) 644-3111; and Austin Grill Bethesda, 7278 Woodmont Ave., Bethesda, MD, (301) 656-1366.

B. SMITH'S
Union Station, 50 Massachusetts Ave. NE
Washington, DC
(202) 289-6188

AMERICAN   ♿

Lunch: M-F 11:30-4 **Entrees:** $12-$19
Dinner: Sun-Th 5-11, F-Sat 5-midnight **Entrees:** $12-$22
Brunch: Sat-Sun 11:30-4, $5-$22 **Dress:** Casual
Credit Cards: All major **Reservations:** Recommended
Parking: Validated, 2 hours **Metro:** Union Station
Entertainment: Jazz W-Th 8-11, Sat 8-midnight, Sun noon-4

When a restaurant is named after a New York model, the Oil of Olay girl, you expect skimpy salads and ascetic, dry-grilled fish. But that's not what you get at B. SMITH'S. The restaurant that has taken over the historic presidential waiting room at Union Station serves its bronzed salmon with butter-thickened bearnaise sauce and its salads with whole strips of bacon or plenty of Swiss cheese and Smithfield ham dressing. The menu is abundant with barbecued ribs and fried catfish, crisp onion rings and gravy-drenched mashed potatoes.

B. Smith's is a mood. The entrance has the feel of an art deco supper club, with a fan of burgundy fabric as backdrop to the maitre d's station and jazz wafting in from the lounge. The soaring, vaulted room, festooned with gilded and painted fancy work, is the match of many cathedrals. And along the side is an enclosed terrace with stone columns and wicker chairs, a hint of one of Paris' elegant squares.

The menu reads like a family album of Southern cooking, albeit with newfangled modifications. B. SMITH'S produces a full range of food, from simple to exotic, light to heavy, luscious to truly dreadful. I can't remember tasting better red beans and rice. They make me forgive the excess sugar in the corn bread that accompanies them and wish they were my full meal, not just an appetizer.

In a Southern restaurant it makes sense to save room for dessert. Both the Southern cheesecake — with cherries and nuts — and the pecan diamonds could hardly be richer, the diamonds' dough more like caramel than like cookie. And the coconut cake is about the sweetest dessert I have ever eaten — almost like fudge — but the coconut itself is fabulous, and I ate every bit to prove it. Washington might be a little embarrassed to have to import a Southern restaurant from New York. But I'll take my red beans and coconut cake wherever I can get them.

BACCHUS

1827 Jefferson Pl., NW, Washington, DC
(202) 785-0734

LEBANESE

Lunch: M-F noon-2:30 **Entrees:** $7.75-$10.50
Dinner: M-Th 6-10, F-Sat 6-10:30 **Entrees:** $12.50-$16.25
Closed: Sun **Credit Cards:** AE, MC, V
Reservations: Recommended **Dress:** Casual
Parking: Free valet at dinner **Metro:** Farragut North

U sually when I go to BACCHUS — whether the bigger, splashier Bethesda branch of this Lebanese restaurant or the cozier downtown original — I order nothing but appetizers, a tableful of *mezze*. It's a luscious evening of tasting a bit of kibbeh here and a swipe of hummus there, a smidgen of spicy, house-made sausage, a flaky, phyllo-wrapped meat or cheese triangle. And even if the hummus sometimes lacks sufficient lemon or garlic or the stuffed baby eggplant is too sour from its marinade, the food adds up to a meal of wonderful flavors. The upshot is that I'm too full to consider an entree. But at lunch, the appetizers can't be ordered alone, only with an entree. My disappointment was intensified by discovering that my favorite entree — a casserole of lamb with crisped pita and yogurt — isn't even on the lunch menu. So I followed my appetizers with kebabs.

Next time, I might just start with the kebabs and then see whether I have room for appetizers. The *lahm mechwi* — lamb shish kebab — is sensational. It's utterly lean and tender, marinated so that the meat tastes rich and nearly gamy, then grilled to a crusty finish. With it comes an irresistible pilaf, the buttery-tasting rice flecked with filaments of browned noodles and topped with crunchy almonds and pine nuts. Fish kebab is succulent, too, fragrant with lemon and olive oil and meltingly tender. It's too good to bury under its accompanying tahini dip. And chicken kebab, drizzled with a bright red ribbon of tomato sauce, is good, though no competition for the superb lamb or the fish. All this and bargain prices, too.

" . . . a meal of wonderful flavors."

For the Bethesda branch, which has an $8 set price for lunch and is open for dinner from 6 to 9:30 on Sunday: Bacchus, 7945 Norfolk Ave., Bethesda, MD, (301) 657-1722.

14

BALALAYKA

3300 M St. NW, Washington, DC
(202) 338-4544

RUSSIAN

Lunch: T-F noon-3, Sat-Sun noon-5 **Entrees:** $7
Dinner: T-F 6-10, Sat-Sun 5-10 **Entrees:** $9-$15
Closed: M **Credit Cards:** MC, V **Dress:** Casual
Reservations: Recommended F-Sat **Parking:** Street
Entertainment: F-Sat 7-11 Russian guitarist-singer

D espite all expectations, Washington still has a dearth of Russian restaurants. So I'm delighted to get cabbage borscht and herring with beets and potatoes here. The menu has all the classics: stuffed cabbage, chicken Kiev, chicken Tabaka, beef stroganoff. And it has all the little dough-wrapped specialties from various locales: Russian *pirozshki*, Ukrainian *vareniki* and *blintzi*, and Siberian *pelmeni*. But BALALAYKA operates in enough confusion that you might wonder whether some Soviet restaurant manual had been unwittingly revived.

Whatever its failings, BALALAYKA is a buoyant restaurant, dominated by a borscht-red mural depicting such important Russian figures as Solzhenitsyn, Yeltsin, Gorbachev, the owner, the chef, the guitarist and your waiter. A stuffed bear guards the service bar. Really. The herring was the hit of all my visits. A chunk of plump, deeply briny fish is served with slices of oil-slicked potato and a beet-and-onion salad. And the caviar is fresh, authentic and delicious, even served with indifferent blini. In all, the menu lists 20 appetizers, among them smoked or jellied meats, underwhelming pirozshki and several vegetable salads. There are also six soups that sound exotic and mysterious but can taste as if they've been stretched to serve too many.

"A stuffed bear guards the service bar. Really."

Entrees are unpredictable. Chicken Kozak is the surest bet, a boneless breast scattered with dill and other herbs. Chicken Tabaka — flattened and cooked so the skin is crisp and lightly seasoned with garlic and herbs — has possibilities. Lamb stew is chewy but has a rich, homey flavor that permeates its potatoes. If you must have dessert, order blini with preserved cherries and sour cream. And certainly end with tea, if only to use the filigreed metal holders for the tea glasses.

BANGKOK SIAM
307 N. Glebe Rd., Arlington, VA
(703) 524-0711

THAI   ♿

Lunch: M-F 11:30-3 **Entrees:** $6-$11
Dinner: Sun-Th 5-10, F 5-11, Sat 5-11:30 **Entrees:** $7-$11
Saturday All-Day Menu: 11:30-11, $7-$11
Credit Cards: All major **Reservations:** Recommended
Dress: Casual **Parking:** Free

This small shopping-center Thai restaurant leads you to expect little, then exceeds expectations. Faded plants hang in plastic pots, but the tables are decorated with lace cloths under glass and flowers in bud vases. Your waiter might not seem to understand your order, but he'll know the menu well enough to give you wise suggestions.

Surely he'll tell you to start with beef with lemon grass, lime juice and chili. It looks soggy and dull, but the meat is as moist as long-cooked brisket, and the herbed, tart and fragrant marinade is irresistible. This chef knows his seasonings, as you'll learn further with such other appetizers as shredded duck with lemon grass or satay with peanut sauce. He pulls his punches with the *larb*, though; this ground-chicken appetizer needs more tang.

> **"This restaurant leads you to expect little, then exceeds expectations."**

Among entrees, too, chicken dishes are the least enticing, their meat pallid and dry. Yet shrimp sautéed with fresh pepper and Thai spices is so permeated with garlic and spicy perfumes that it's worth the trip. It's hot enough to bring tears to the eyes, and its bed of fried broccoli leaves is a bonus, soaking up those scintillating juices. Look for broccoli to highlight an otherwise wan pork with garlic and pepper, too.

BANGKOK SIAM is erratic; its meat dishes lack character. But this kitchen isn't afraid of spices, and can make your tongue sizzle. Cool down afterwards with an excellent version of mango with coconut rice or yam-based custard with sticky rice.

BANGKOK ST GRILL

5872 Leesburg Pike, Falls Church, VA
(703) 379-6707

ASIAN   &

Open: Sun-Th 11:30-10, F-Sat 11:30-10:30
Entrees: $6-$8.75 **Credit Cards:** All major
Reservations: No **Dress:** Casual **Parking:** Free

This small restaurant is decorated to suggest an outdoor eating strip in Asia, its white tile floor bisected by a brick "sidewalk." The white marble tables, with their glossy, rattan-ish chairs and painted, gray wood booths, would suit a garden, and they're shaded by potted palm trees and leafy fakes with tiny lights in their branches.

Big bowls of noodles with meat, seafood or vegetable garnishes are the mainstays, meant to be spiced to individual taste at the table with vinegars, fish sauces, chilies and chopped peanuts. Appetizers are nearly superfluous. People saunter in throughout the day for a plate of noodles or a bowl of noodle soup, each a substantial meal suffused with aromatic warmth.

The soup might be curry broth with coconut milk or beef broth redolent with star anise, packed with beef, beef balls and greens. One of the most delightful noodle dishes — available with or without broth — is called Tuk Tuk Lunch Break, which looks like a tangle of ivory knitting wool, glistening with oil and permeated with sweet, golden, fried garlic. A few slices of pork rubbed with honey and five-spice powder, and a bed of green and white stir-fried bok choy, provide contrast. Both pad Thai and "drunkard's noodles," found on countless Thai noodle menus, are especially vibrant here. And the rice dishes are every bit as gutsy and full-flavored. One called the Clay Pot combines chicken, Chinese sausage, shiitakes and cashews. Another tops a mound of rice with marinated duck infused with five-spice powder, hoisin and soy sauce.

This food has the potent, straightforward spiciness you expect from street food. Its seasonings infuse the dishes with sweetness, salt, acid and fragrance. It deserves a simple finale, just fruit or warm, coconut-flavored sticky rice and sliced mango.

BeDuCi
2100 P St. NW, Washington, DC
(202) 223-3824

MEDITERRANEAN

Lunch: M-F 11:30-2:30 **Entrees:** $9-$23
Dinner: M-Th 5:30-10, F-Sat 5:30-10:30, Sun 5:30-9:30
Dinner Entrees: $10-$25 **Credit Cards:** All major
Reservations: Recommended **Dress:** Casual
Parking: Complimentary valet at dinner **Metro:** Dupont Circle

Owners Michele Miller and Jean-Claude Garrat show off the dining rooms like a couple who've just moved in to their first house. Here's the sun porch, with its slanted glass roof and walls, its brick floor, its sunny disposition even on gray days. Inside are three rooms and a bar, the main room furnished with sound-muffling carpet, dark-wood chair rails accenting white walls, and an overlay of paintings, drawings and prints.

Their restaurant serves "Mediterranean style" cooking, which means you can choose from eight or more pastas, several couscous and paella variations, even entrees from Morocco, with fanciful names and flowery descriptions. The menu at BeDuCi — short for Below Dupont Circle — is one of those something-for-everyone conglomerations. With such a long and complicated list, it's hard to find just what the chef does best. Soups aren't in the running. Grilled portobello mushroom is more satisfying (how can a portobello mushroom be bad?), and an appetizer of carpaccio, gravlax and prosciutto is a heap of good things.

The handwritten list of specials is the page to scrutinize. One day the star of the meal was a bowl of steamed mussels and clams in an herbed lime broth, one of those dishes that tempts you to use up all the bread to sop up the sauce. When in doubt, order a pasta special such as sun-dried tomato linguine with fresh artichokes and olives or squid-ink noodles topped by a flavorful tomato sauce, with shellfish and artichoke slices. Among entrees, too, specials show the most care. Vegetarians can do well with "Heather's Roasted Vegetable Brique," a stew of mushrooms, red and yellow peppers, spinach, onions and carrots wrapped in a crepe-thin layer of phyllo.

Desserts are made by Michele Miller — the likes of homey brownies with nuts and birthday-cake-style fudge frosting; sweet caramelized pineapple cobbler that is much like an upside-down cake; and dark, moist chocolate cake with raspberry jam between the layers.

18

BICE
601 Pennsylvania Ave. NW, Washington, DC
(202) 638-2423

ITALIAN

Lunch: M-F 11:30-2:30 **Entrees:** $10-$23 **Light fare:** 2:30-5
Dinner: M-Th 5:30-10:30, F-Sat 5:30-11, Sun 5:30-9:30
Dinner Entrees: $12-$26 **Closed:** July 1-Sept. 15 annually
Credit Cards: All major **Reservations:** Recommended
Dress: Casual **Parking:** Complimentary valet at dinner
Metro: Archives-Navy Memorial

What do you do when your restaurant is fizzling? Survey the competition and hire the best to bring you up to snuff. That's what BICE did. It took on Francesco Ricchi as a consultant and, sure enough, he has revived the character of this Milanese chain restaurant. It's not as glorious as it was when it opened, but BICE is again a dignified restaurant with honorable Italian cooking. The interior is handsome and clubby, the waiters know how to serve expertly, and in good weather BICE can provide one of the most comfortable outdoor cafes in town.

Ricchi's influence is apparent immediately when the bread basket arrives. Two kinds of focaccia tempt you to overindulge. And the menu offers a bewilderment of seasonal appetizers, pastas, fish and meat. Summertime's salad of red and yellow tomatoes with soft, fresh mozzarella is a classic. That and the sausage and polenta or shrimp with white beans, maybe fried calamari and zucchini or carpaccio with arugula and parmesan, would make a meal.

But there are the pastas to consider. For cool weather, there are substantial versions, with duck or game. In a lighter vein are capellini with fresh tomato or fettuccine with seafood. Green tortellini are stuffed with grainy ricotta; and cavatelli, thick as rope, might come with raw tomato, broccoli rabe and an undertone of anchovy. These are straightforward, gutsy pastas. And you can follow them with something more grand — perhaps grilled rabbit, lamb chops with artichokes and thyme juice, Angus beef or, of course, veal. Ricchi has brought his signature fish preparation: lightly crumbed and herbed, crisped and browned on the grill, so that the juices are sealed in but the delicate flavor is not upstaged. Bice retains the inevitable flaws of a multi-city chain restaurant, but it is one of the few glamorous dining spots near Judiciary Square. And it makes an espresso that could pass muster in Rome.

BILBO BAGGINS
208 Queen St., Alexandria, VA
(703) 683-0300

AMERICAN   ♿

Lunch: M-Sat 11:30-2:30 **Entrees:** $7.50-$12
Dinner: Sun-Th 5:30-10, F-Sat 5:30-10:30 **Entrees:** $15-$17
Brunch: Sun 11-2:30 **Entrees:** $8-$13
Credit Cards: All major **Reservations:** Sun-Th **Dress:** Casual
Parking: Free across street M-Th, $4 weekends

B ILBO BAGGINS has the kind of menu that leads you to order vegetarian dishes without even trying. They are plentiful, imaginative and tempting. An appetizer special one evening was a lacy potato pancake, as wide and thin as an old 78-rpm record, topped with blue cheese and floating on a light and tangy tomato sauce. It was a knockout. And among the everyday dishes, another vegetarian appetizer could be a meal in itself and was certainly worthy of a return visit. It's a tortilla pizza, the crisp, paper-thin crust exending over the edge of the plate.

For main courses, BILBO BAGGINS offers salads, pastas and sandwiches, as well as two fruit-and-cheese platters. Beyond the menu — which ranges from salmon with scallops in dill vinaigrette to beef tenderloin with sun-dried tomatoes, cream and balsamic vinegar — BILBO BAGGINS has a tempting list of wines by the glass as well as the bottle, and fresh house-made breads. (You know they're fresh because, if you stay late, any leftover loaves are likely to be pressed on you as take-home offerings.) BILBO BAGGINS is a cozy, two-story retreat of old brick and weathered wood, as relaxing as a neighborhood pub. All in all, it feels wholesome.

" . . . if you stay late, any leftover loaves will be pressed on you as take-home offerings."

BISTRO BISTRO
4021 S. 28th St., Arlington, VA
(703) 379-0300

AMERICAN   ♿

Lunch: M-Sat 11-3 **Entrees:** $8-$12
Dinner: M-Th 5-10, F-Sat 5-11, Sun. 3-10 **Entrees:** $11-$18
Brunch: Sun 10:30-3, $6.25-$11 **Credit Cards:** AE, MC, V
Reservations: Recommended **Parking:** Validated

When most restaurants advertise three kinds of burgers, they mean something like single, double and with cheese. BISTRO BISTRO, characteristically going one step further than most other casual restaurants, serves burgers of beef, turkey or lamb. Its fried calamari comes with a choice of four sauces (and it's the best seasoned, least greasy, most crunchy fried calamari you could hope to find). The oyster stew is packed with oysters (although in months-without-Rs they taste as if they've come from a jar), and its creamy broth is fragrant with pepper, Bermuda onion and Swiss chard. The other soups are sometimes even better.

In all, BISTRO BISTRO presents awfully good food at a moderate price, in a dining room where you'd feel comfortable celebrating on a Saturday night or dropping by after a hike on Sunday afternoon. The menu, creative but not outlandish, cuts a swath through salads, pizzas, pastas, meat and fish. You can find down-home meatloaf — made with veal, and its mashed potatoes studded with celery — or upscale grilled lamb, nicely marinated and fragrantly smoky, accompanied by char-edged fresh vegetables. If the chicken doesn't have enough garlic and lemon or has been overcooked, at least it comes with a commendable pile of vegetables and mashed potatoes. And while the pastas aren't luxuriously hand-made or imported from Italy, they are delicious when tossed with the likes of house-smoked scallops, spinach, herbs, shiitakes and crunchy, diced, Italian bacon in a little cream.

Brilliant? No. Satisfying? Certainly. With a list of fine draft beers and admirable wines at particularly reasonable prices, a basket of well-made breads, efficient service and a menu that suits almost any mood and delivers reliable quality, BISTRO BISTRO is indeed twice the bistro of most restaurants with the name.

Bistro Bistro also has branches at 4301 N. Fairfax Dr., Arlington, VA, (703) 522-1800, and 1181 Library St., Reston, VA, (703) 834-6300.

BISTRO FRANCAIS
3128 M St. NW, Washington, DC
(202) 338-3830

FRENCH   ♿

Lunch: Daily 11-5 **Entrees:** $8-$12
Dinner: Sun-Th 5-3 am, F-Sat 5-4 am **Entrees:** $9-$20
Credit Cards: All major **Reservations:** Recommended
Pre-Theater & Late Night: Daily 5-7; 10:30-1 am, both $18
Dress: Casual **Parking:** Valet (fee) F-Sat

BISTRO FRANCAIS has always seemed to me like the little brother among French restaurants. It's small and noisy and not quite suave enough. The tables cling to each other under a canopy of hanging plants and amid a clamor of leaded glass and mirrors. It doesn't have the smooth elegance of the big boys, but it's clearly part of the family. In fact, this is where local French chefs go to unwind after a night at their own stoves.

It looks unmistakably French, even Parisian. But its service is hesitant and hardly continental. What has kept it going strong for decades is the menu — long and interesting, catering to the onion soup and minute steak crowd along with the giblet salad and marinated tuna crowd. It's got all the traditional dishes: pâtés, melon with port, coq au vin, steak tartare and its signature rotisserie chicken with tarragon.

"This is where local French chefs go to unwind after a night at their own stoves."

And it has an extensive array of more inventive daily specials, such as an appetizer of eggplant teamed with a zesty lamb sausage and panfried cakes of salmon mousse studded with scallops. If the cooking is not brilliant, it is certainly competent.

For such ambitious French cooking, BISTRO FRANCAIS is a bargain. Few restaurants in this price range serve such good bread and vary the vegetables with each entree. The real buys, though, are the fixed-price lunch and early-bird dinners, complete with a glass of wine, soup or a truly French salad, entree and a choice of dessert from a tray of French standards. Dover sole is priced here like fillet of flounder elsewhere. And BISTRO FRANCAIS has matured well. As the sun goes down, the mirrors sparkle and the wood paneling gleams — and BISTRO FRANCAIS begins to look romantic, even quite grown up.

BISTRO 2015
Embassy Row Hotel
2015 Massachusetts Ave. NW, Washington, DC
(202) 939-4250

AMERICAN   ♿

Breakfast: M-F 6:30-10, Sat-Sun 7-10:30 **Entrees** $5-$11
Lunch: Daily 11:30-3 **Entrees:** $7.50-$13.75
Dinner: Daily 6-10 **Entrees:** $12-$21
Credit Cards: All major **Reservations**: Recommended
Dress: Casual **Parking:** Validated **Metro:** Dupont Circle
Entertainment: Pianist M-Sat at dinner

I f you're looking for an expense-account environment and serious food at pin-money prices, lunch at BISTRO 2015 in the Embassy Row Hotel is where you'll find it. Chef Jim Papovich used to cook at some of the most expensive restaurants in town (including BISTRO 2015 when it was called Lucie), but now he offers his sophisticated, inventive New American food at discount prices. You can even design your own three-course, fixed-price lunch.

Even a modestly priced lunch can include such inventive appetizers as a salad of red snapper with pine nuts, lettuce and raspberry. Soups are also luxurious: wild mushroom with pesto or lobster with red pepper. Fish entrees are elaborate and luscious, particularly rockfish with creamed and fried leeks. Vegetarians — or anyone with a large appetite — will marvel at the mound of lemon-spiked pasta surrounded by such glamorous marinated vegetables as leeks, wild mushrooms and roasted peppers.

" . . . an expense-account environment and serious food at pin-money prices."

This hotel dining room isn't exactly charming, but it is spacious, furnished with comfortable striped banquettes and tables large enough for spreading out papers. Privacy and quiet are rare assets downtown. And there's a covered terrace for dining outdoors. In summers Papovich uses the hotel's outdoor spaces for cookouts.

BISTROT LEPIC

1736 Wisconsin Ave. NW, Washington, DC
(202) 333-0111

FRENCH

Lunch: T-Sun 11:30-2:30 **Entrees:** $9-$12.25
Dinner: T-Th 5:30-10, F-Sat 5:30-10:30, Sun 5:30-9:30
Dinner Entrees: $14-$18 **Credit Cards:** All major
Reservations: Required **Dress:** Casual **Parking:** Street

Some restaurants are loved for their food, others for their service, many for their style. BISTROT LEPIC is loved for, among other things, its size and shape. This small storefront has the proportions of a typical small-town bistro in France. What's more, it has a disposition to match its sunny yellow dining room, a hostess whose enthusiasm is infectious and a reasonably priced menu that's inventive but anchored in French bistro tradition. No wonder it's full for mid-week lunch in Georgetown, where many restaurants are nearly empty at midday. BISTROT LEPIC feels good.

Its food is fine. Not wonderful, not memorable, but attractive and agreeable. I wish the crab were better picked, but I like the idea of grape leaves stuffed with crab, and I savor its lemon and ouzo mayonnaise. Grilled, marinated steelhead trout is supple and saline, its finely

"Bistrot Lepic is a charmer, not a dazzler."

diced vegetables highly perfumed with olive oil. Mussel soup with leeks and potatoes is a favorite, and appetizers include such traditional dishes as onion tart and pâté with prunes and armagnac.

Entrees also make much of bistro staples: kidneys with mustard, chicken piperade, beef with marrow and rabbit confit. Salmon is wrapped in a potato crust, its sauce sprinkled with caviar, and scallops are given an Asian touch of soy sauce and sesame oil. Liver is a favorite, though its capers, olives and sherry vinegar flavorings don't quite come together, and the lunchtime spring garden salad with seafood has a terrific tangy dressing and crisp-skinned chunks of fish, despite a slapdash quality.

In all, BISTROT LEPIC is a charmer, not a dazzler. Unsurprisingly, it's considered by many Georgetowners to be their personal secret favorite.

BLUE-N-GOLD
3100 Clarendon Blvd., Arlington, VA
(703) 908-4995

AMERICAN/CREOLE   ♿

Lunch: M-F 11:30-5   **Entrees:** $7-$16
Dinner: M-Th 5-11, F 5-midnight, Sat 3-midnight Sun 3-10
Dinner Entrees: $12-$21   **Brunch:** Sun noon-3, $3.50-$15
Credit Cards: AE, MC, V   **Reservations:** Recommended
Dress: Casual   **Parking:** Validated at lunch, free after 6
Metro: Clarendon   **Entertainment:** Nightly blues W-Th, jazz F-Sat

To start with what's most important: I'm greatly impressed by BLUE-N-GOLD'S beers. Ask your waiter for a tasting, though, since the choice is bewildering. This is a restaurant with the focus squarely on liquids. To stretch that further, the best foods I've had at BLUE-N-GOLD have been the soups. Oyster stew, for example, is delicious. The oysters themselves have that juicy metallic bite of the tastiest raw oysters, and there are lots of them, in a roasted garlic cream with celeriac, rich and suave. Salmon chowder might sound less elegant, but it is every bit as sublime, the fish soft and moist, the creamy broth slightly more delicate than the oyster stew's.

In contrast, the Voodoo chicken entree is dry, chewy and flavored with little but cayenne. The crayfish etouffe of stringy shellfish and a glossy sauce tastes of nothing more than salt and cayenne. And the hot sausages, buried under too-salty sauerkraut, are only marginally better than the cold version. Yet this is not an inept kitchen, just an erratic one. Swordfish marinated in citrus juices and bourbon comes well-browned yet sufficiently moist, and shrimp Doubloons are also carefully cooked and moist, with a nondescript, shredded-crab stuffing.

". . . a focus squarely on liquids."

For a brewpub with some sensational beers, this place has a decent kitchen. What's more, it's a great-looking dining room: Tables on two levels are lit with the most wonderful lamps, some looking like salads, others like peacock tails, even some like tongues of flame lapping at the walls. BLUE-N-GOLD'S tables are close together, and the room is crowded. But even though it's noisy, you can hear your tablemates without strain.

BOMBAY BISTRO
3570 Chain Bridge Rd., Fairfax, VA
(703) 359-5810

INDIAN   ♿

Lunch: M-F 11-2:30, Sat-Sun noon-3
Dinner: Sun-Th 5-10, F-Sat 5-10:30
Entrees: $6-$16 **Credit Cards:** All major
Reservations: Weekdays only **Dress:** Casual **Parking:** Free

You can tell a lot about a restaurant by its fish. BOMBAY BIS-TRO'S whole Maryland rockfish is marinated in yogurt, ginger, garlic and other spices. The skin is scored, and the fish is cooked over charcoal so that it is very crisp outside and deliciously blackened in spots. It's a magnificent entree. At the homier end of the menu is a vegetarian peasant dish called rava onion masala, a huge wafer-thin pancake made of lentil and rice flour folded into a square, with yellow potatoes and onions packed thickly inside. BOMBAY BISTRO serves all the curries, biryanis, tandoors and vegetarian dishes that form the common Indian repertoire. And it prepares them with such refinement that it leaves no doubt that India's is one of the world's great cuisines. Indian menus can be bewildering, but the maitre d' here doesn't let you flounder. In fact, the service is so considerate that you'd be tempted to come and sit awhile even if you weren't seeking a meal.

This is sophisticated cooking that attends to all the senses. Most important, each curry is like a painting, with its own palette of seasonings, all carefully arranged and balanced. Lamb *rogan josh* has a sauce that is thick and velvety, intricately spiced but mild, its waves of fragrance gently lapping at your taste buds. Another lamb curry, *nilgiri khorma*, is quite different. Its sauce is a dark greenish brown, thick and grainy, more complex than hot, unfolding as you savor it. These are memorable sauces. Vegetable dishes are more subtle, the spinach heightened with just a little sweetly fried onion and dotted with large, bland cubes of house-made cheese, the shredded eggplant a red-gold combination with bits of tomato and onion. And biryanis are distinctive. BOMBAY BISTRO is a warmhearted restaurant where the service is courtly, the cooking is aristocratic and the prices are proletarian.

Bombay Bistro's other location: 98 W. Montgomery Ave., Rockville, MD, (301) 762-8798.

BOMBAY CLUB
815 Connecticut Ave. NW, Washington, DC
(202) 659-3727

INDIAN   ♿

Lunch: M-F 11:30-2:30
Dinner: M-Th 6-10:30, F-Sat 6-11, Sun 5:30-9
Entrees: $7.50-$18.50   **Brunch:** Sun 11:30-2:30, buffet $16.50
Pre-Theater: Daily 6-7, $22   **Credit Cards:** All major
Reservations: Recommended   **Dress:** Jacket & tie
Parking: Complimentary at dinner   **Metro:** Farragut West
Entertainment: Pianist, dinner and Sun brunch

The foods that I crave most at the BOMBAY CLUB are not the curries but the dishes that would be right at home in an American restaurant or a French one — elegant food, albeit with the flavors and fragrances of India. They're appetizers such as crab masala, the snowy bits of crab combined with chopped tomato, ginger and herbs to form the lightest, most delicate crab salad, or scallops marinated in yogurt, broiled soft and moist, slightly caramelized and faintly scented with caraway. Mussels are infused with ginger and chopped tomato, fish fillets are red-tinged with chilies and aromatic spices. Accompanying them all is a creamy, tangy, green chutney, utterly refreshing.

For entrees, I roam among the tandoori specialties: This clay oven cooks fish wonderfully, so the salmon has a crisp edge and a luscious moistness; the trout is similarly good. And tandoori chicken is tenderized by a yogurt marinade, mildly seasoned, its flavors also sealed in by the intense fire of the clay oven. Of course, BOMBAY CLUB has the full complement of curries. You can sample them in the silvery finery of a tasting platter called a *thali*, either in a vegetarian version or one starring various meats and shrimp. The thali comes with exceptional *lacha paratha*, a whole-wheat bread composed of thin layers that curl slightly and expose countless lacy edges. If you're ordering à la carte, don't miss ordering it, or the tiny black lentils cooked overnight or the rich-tasting spiced yogurt with shredded cucumber.

Yet food is not the only attraction of the BOMBAY CLUB. This is a luxurious, comfortable dining room with the feel of a British colonial country club, waiters formally dressed and service punctuated by much bowing and scraping. Missing anything? Just a balmy evening so you can sip a Pimm's Cup at one of the sidewalk tables.

BRICKSKELLER
1523 22nd St. NW, Washington, DC
(202) 293-1885

AMERICAN

Open: M-Th 11:30 am-2 am, F 11:30 am-3 am, Sat 6-3, Sun 6-2
Entrees: $6.25-$16 **Credit Cards:** All major **Dress:** Casual
Reservations: Accepted for 6 or more **Metro:** Dupont Circle

Beer is big news these days. Some restaurants are brewing their own. Others are collecting impressive lists of microbrews. But still none can touch the BRICKSKELLER, which has almost a 40-year lead on these new beer purveyors. I don't know whether its claim to featuring the world's largest selection of beer is true, but its list of brews has climbed above 700, and the walls of this cellar are lined with their empties.

It looks like a fraternity hangout, but you don't have to be newly arrived at drinking age to enjoy the BRICKSKELLER. The service is friendly, and the food covers a range from snacks (cheese board, pizza, tempura vegetable basket or spicy wings) to full meals (buffalo steak, rum-and-lime

"Its list of brews has climbed above 700."

chicken, *kalua* pork or chicken flown in from Hawaii, or a shellfish assortment steamed in beer). There are even East European *pierogies*.

At the BRICKSKELLER, though, I turn conservative. Every time I order something adventurous, I wish I'd gotten a hamburger. The other foods are perfectly acceptable: The po' boy is stuffed with excellent fried oysters, even if the bread is flabby and the dressing is dull. The rainbow trout is fresh, and the pierogies are heart-warming. But I've learned the hard way: If anyone at the table has a burger, I'm going to want one. These burgers are terrific, whether the Brickburger with its bacon-salami-onion-cheese topping, the Down Home, combining ground beef with Italian sausage, or my favorite, the Ale Burger, seasoned with caraway and you-know-what. The fries, too, are dark and slightly sweet, clearly made from appropriately aged Idahos.

As for the beers, some people have a system. They might start with the A's, or make their way through one country or one brand. I just leaf through the book and zero in on a few new entries, then discuss the matter with my waiter. These waiters know their brews.

BRIGHTON-ON-N
Canterbury Hotel
1733 N St. NW, Washington, DC
(202) 296-0665

AMERICAN   ♿

Lunch: M-F 11:30-2:30 **Entrees:** $7-$12.50
Dinner: M-Sat 6-10:30 **Entrees:** $12.50-$24
Brunch: Sat-Sun 11-3, $12-$20 **Credit Cards:** All major
Reservations: Recommended **Dress:** Casual
Parking: Complimentary Valet F-Sat evenings
Metro: Dupont Circle, Farragut North

On the same block as two of the prettiest dining gardens in town — Tabard Inn and Iron Gate Inn — this downstairs dining room in the Canterbury Hotel has tended to be overlooked. But now that BRIGHTON-ON-N is run by Well Dunn! Catering, the menu has joined the '90s, and redecoration has brightened up the dining room with sundae colors — vanilla and nectarine. Furthermore, the service is gracious, as if the waiters were serving you in your home, helpful and enthusiastic without hovering.

"The food is witty, and even those witticisms that fall flat have left me applauding the effort."

The food is witty, and even those witticisms that fall flat have left me applauding the effort. To start, head right for the biscuits. They are so flaky they practically shatter in your hand, and they have an interesting crunch, presumably from a little cornmeal sifted into the wheat. On to appetizers, the potato-stuffed, phyllo-wrapped samosas are satisfying, but tandoori quail is the star of this course. Entrees are daunting, buried in haystacks of shredded fried vegetables and crowded with accompaniments and garnishes. Rack of lamb and seared fish fillets — they're capably cooked, but would be better with fewer ingredients robbing them of center stage. Desserts are simpler and more charming. And if there's a fruit cobbler on the menu, make sure to save room.

BUA
1635 P St. NW, Washington, DC
(202) 265-0828

THAI   ♿

Lunch: Daily 11:30-2:30 **Entrees:** $6-$7.75
Dinner: Daily 5-10:30 **Entrees:** $8-$19
Credit Cards: All major **Reservations**: Recommended
Dress: Casual **Parking:** Street **Metro:** Dupont Circle

This Dupont Circle Thai restaurant has two distinct advantages: It's so inexpensive that you can easily dine for less than $15, and on balmy days you can do so outdoors on its second-floor balcony. Even indoors, its small dining rooms are attractively decorated in a kind of hazy blue-gray that makes a meal feel like a vacation.

The cooking is standard Thai, which is to say generally good. And the extensive menu offers all the standard Thai dishes plus several variations on satays, a Thai bouillabaisse and some particularly interesting tofu dishes.

As usual, appetizers are the best bets. I love the *larb* — ground chicken spiked with lemon and chilies, to wrap in lettuce leaves — but then I always love larb. The satays may be chewy, but they are nicely seasoned. Cellophane noodles are tart and pleasant. As for entrees, chili and basil chicken has a compelling hot sauce, even if the chicken itself is without flavor. But curries can be disappointingly soupy and mild. Still, if the kitchen at BUA has its ups and downs, you can count on the service to compensate for much.

BURMA
740 6th St. NW, Washington, DC
(202) 638-1280

BURMESE   ♿

Lunch: M-F 11-3 **Dinner:** Sun-Th 6-10, F-Sat 6-11
Entrees: One menu, $6-$8 **Credit Cards:** All major
Reservations: Recommended for 5 or more **Dress:** Casual
Parking: Street **Metro:** Gallery Place-Chinatown

Chinatown has spread its wings to encompass Cantonese, Shanghai, Hunanese, Mongolian and Taiwanese cuisines. It has incorporated several Vietnamese restaurants. Yet the most exotic cooking in this enclave is at BURMA, a small, upstairs restaurant that keeps adding unusual dishes to its long menu. The bare-bones dining room looks a little more polished these days as well. And the ever-hesitant service is more communicative, though the kitchen still seems flummoxed by having to prepare for more than four people at a time.

One of the more recent dishes is also one of the best: Mango pork is lean chunks of braised meat permeated with red spice paste — a moderate hit of chili peppers included — and spiked with wedges of intense pickled mangoes that taste much like India's lemon pickle. Tamarind fish is also chili-heated, as well as tart, but fish is not BURMA'S strength, particularly

"The most exotic cooking [in Chinatown] is at Burma."

on a Monday before the week's catch is in. A third recent addition: The fried eggplant appetizer, in a light puffy batter, is meltingly soft inside and irresistible, even though it's too greasy. It's the equal of gold fingers, a favorite that translates as fried squash, and both are served with a tart, salty, wonderful dipping sauce.

BURMA serves half a dozen soups that are distillations of the restaurant's strong seasonings — chilies, lemon, tamarind, mustard plant. It has vegetarian entrees and intriguing noodle dishes. But its glory is salads, whether tofu, papaya, seafood, tea leaves, herbs, eggplant or ginger. The ones that sound the strangest taste the best. As for entrees, the curries and kebabs aren't half as interesting as such less familiar dishes as sour mustard plant, the pickliest of pickles, sauteed with bits of pork. Often, though, the main dishes are hit-or-miss. Consider them an exploration and the appetizers and salads home base.

BUSARA
2340 Wisconsin Ave. NW, Washington, DC
(202) 337-2340

THAI   ♿

Lunch: M-F 11:30-3, Sat-Sun 11:30-4 **Entrees:** $6-$8.25
Dinner: Sun-Th 5-11, F-Sat 5-midnight **Entrees:** $7.25-$15.25
Credit Cards: All Major **Reservations:** Recommended
Dress: Casual **Parking:** Valet (fee) at dinner

BUSARA has a glossy modern set of rooms with sensational furniture — plastic-coated tables in crayon colors in the dining room and, in the bar, metal tables that reflect in psychedelic hues. On a winter day it could cheer you instantly. In fall or spring, the back garden can soothe you, with its tables set around a tiny pond lush with greenery.

The menu, too, is unusual, with some mild attempts at fusing Eastern and Western cuisines. Many entrees are served Western style, with vegetables and salad greens filling out the plate. Like all Thai restaurants, though, BUSARA serves a range of mild to incendiary dishes — designated by one, two or three chili peppers on the menu.

If I'm eating with a group and willing to risk a disappointment or two, I order some of the more original and multinational dishes. If it's just myself and a friend, we play it safe with traditional Thai cooking. The old standard *larb gai* is just right at BUSARA: The minced chicken has plenty of lime and hot peppers, with lettuce leaves to fold around it. If you like dough-wrapped appetizers, the list is satisfying, from Shrimp Bikini — wrapped in spring-roll skin — to spring rolls to crab and chicken wrapped in bean-curd sheets. Then there are salads, not small appetizers as in most Thai restaurants, but large platefuls, enough for a table to share or one diner to make into a meal.

The list of entrees is immense — if you want to make it easier to navigate, just concentrate on the curries. And for contrast, a noodle dish like pad thai is mild enough to tame the curries' heat. In short, Busara combines modern sophistication with tradition, comfort with festivity and neighborly warmth with professionalism.

For this restaurant's Tysons Corner branch, where parking is free: Busara, 8142 Watson St., McLean, VA, (703) 356-2288.

32

C.F. FOLKS
1225 19th St. NW, Washington, DC
(202) 293-0162

AMERICAN/INTERNATIONAL

Lunch: M-F 11:45-2:45 **Entrees:** $4-$9.25
Closed: Sat-Sun **Credit Cards:** None; cash only
Dress: Casual **Reservations:** No
Parking: Street **Metro:** Dupont Circle

U nless you're a regular or have memorized the weekly schedule, you won't have the foggiest idea what's cooking among the half-dozen specials at C. F. FOLKS. One day they're Mexican and Southwestern, another day fish and seafood, then maybe Indian or Southeast Asian, or even American.

You can get a preview, of course, by catching a whiff of all the carry-out platters passing by as you approach this tiny restaurant, or glimpsing what's being eaten at the small sidewalk cafe as you enter the door to place your order. But whatever surprises the daily specials hold, the greatest surprise is that this is expense-account cooking at coffee shop prices. Nobody bothers with the menu — it's just made up of ordinary sandwiches. People check out the blackboard's listings instead. They could include grilled salmon with tandoori spices one day or perhaps the restaurant's superlative crab cakes another day. Linguine sometimes might be tossed with moist strips of chicken and slivered peppers, then slicked with chili oil, or it might be piled with shellfish.

"Nobody bothers with the menu . . . People check out the blackboard's listings instead."

At one lunch the range went from meat loaf with garlic mashed potatoes to steak with sauce bordelaise — both less than $10. And while you might not intend to stay for dessert after this quick-but-elegant entree, by the time you finish and catch sight of, say, the strawberry or coconut cream pies at the surrounding tables, chances are you'll probably change your mind.

C.J. FERRARI'S
14311 Baltimore Ave., Laurel, MD
(301) 725-1771

ITALIAN   &

Lunch: T-F 11:30-2:30 **Entrees:** $8.25-$10
Dinner: T-Th 5-10, F-Sat 5-11, Sun 5-10 **Entrees:** $8.50-$16.50
Closed: M **Credit Cards:** MC, V **Reservations:** Accepted M-Th
Dress: Casual **Parking:** Free

FERRARI'S white pizzas are the great culinary secret of Prince George's County. The crust is bubbly and yeasty, just as it should be, and it is topped with a pool of melting mozzarella and parmesan, enveloped in a cloud of garlic and oregano. The pizzas usually are available only at the bar and for carryout, but regular customers order a white pizza to accompany their meal in the dining room, and newcomers should prevail on the kitchen for equal rights.

The menu is surprisingly limited for an Italian restaurant, but that is probably an advantage. Seafood fans have more options than meat eaters, who have only veal or chicken; and vegetarians are limited to pasta with tomato, cheese sauce or pesto. Even so, there are tempting choices such as veal with mushroom-caper sauce, artichoke hearts and mascarpone cheese or shrimp and scallops in port wine and honey mustard sauce on seared Italian greens.

"Ferrari's white pizzas are the great culinary secret of Prince George's County."

Fried mozzarella is a fine choice to start, and it's large enough to share. Three crisp, deep-fried slabs of batter-dipped cheese and bread are accompanied by a wonderful tangy fresh tomato sauce. Keep that tomato sauce in mind for a main course too — on cappellini, ravioli or manicotti. Request your house salad with tomato-basil vinaigrette, a dressing that's as light, sharp and tangy as the marinara sauce.

Except for its heavy hand with noodle making, FERRARI'S is an endearing restaurant, and the menu is interesting even if it is short. The bread is baked in-house, and despite modest prices, FERRARI'S goes to such lengths as to make its own ice creams and serve them in a delicious cookie basket topped with a chocolate palm tree.

CAFE ATLANTICO
405 8th St. NW, Washington, DC
(202) 393-0812

LATIN AMERICAN /CARIBBEAN   ♿

Lunch: Mon-F 11:30-2:30 **Entrees:** $6-$9
Dinner: M-Th 5:30-11, F-Sat 5:30-midnight, Sun 5:30-10
Entrees: $12-$16 **Light Fare:** M-F 2:30-5:30, $4.50-$7.50
Credit Cards: All major **Dress:** Casual
Reservations: Accepted until 7:30 pm
Parket: Valet (fee) at dinner **Metro:** Archives-Navy Memorial

CAFE ATLANTICO has refined the dishes of the Caribbean and Latin America and serves them in three dining rooms stacked vertically. Mosaic tiles, long, painted panels and striped banquettes transmit hot colors from one floor to the other, and tall loft windows turn the city into framed art. The instinct for design doesn't stop there. The kitchen produces visual arts on a plate. As waiters pass by with trays for other diners, you're tempted to order the *seviche* for your living room, the passion fruit mousse for your entry hall. They'd certainly brighten your living space.

Oddly, the most beautiful dishes here are also the most luscious. The seviche is a whirlwind of juicy, briny bits of chopped fish and shellfish, tart balancing sweet, soft against crisp. Salt-cod puree — *bachalau* — has a moat of sunny, yellow, passion fruit oil. Empanadas are equally pretty, the crisply browned, sausage-stuffed half moons surrounded by concentric circles of golden and cilantro-green sauces. Only *quipes* — beef and bulgur fritters like the lightest Middle Eastern *kibbeh* — taste more beautiful than they look.

Among entrees, salmon *tamal* is wonderful, as is the dark, rich mole, thinner than the Mexican original, spooned over stewed baby chicken. Jerk chicken is skinless and boneless, neither as crusty nor as fiery as the Jamaican original. It's a bit effete. So is the *feijoada* reinvented as a mixed grill (the feijoada salad is far more interesting). The best entree, Puerto Rico's *asopao*, is close to its tradition, a pale yellow and nearly creamy shrimp and crab stew, hauntingly aromatic. The color show carries through to desserts, particularly the airy, passion fruit charlotte striped with chocolate and caramel, and the chewy, gooey, chocolate bread pudding with a cap of glazed sliced bananas. You're safe with something pale, too: the coconut tart, white on white, is sumptuous.

CAFE BERLIN
322 Massachusetts Ave. NE, Washington, DC
(202) 543-7656

GERMAN   ♿

Lunch: M-Sat 11:30-4 **Entrees:** $6-$17
Dinner: Sun-Th 4-10, F-Sat 4-11 **Entrees:** $8-$17
Credit Cards: All major **Reservations:** Recommended
Dress: Casual **Parking:** Street **Metro:** Union Station

Washington has only a couple of German restaurants, but even if there were more, CAFE BERLIN'S sweet little dining room would stand out from the crowd. You'd hardly know you were in the shadow of the Capitol at this small town house restaurant. It has such a European lilt, from the flowered tablecloths with pink underneath to the

" . . . one might be inclined to start and end with dessert."

soft accents of the staff. This is a hospitable restaurant with Old World charm. There is enough space between tables to suggest privacy and a peaceful air that encourages conversation.

The most seductive food is on the pastry display, so one might be inclined to start and end with dessert, from black forest cake to strudel. In a more conventional vein, CAFE BERLIN offers wiener schnitzel, sauerbraten and paprika-tinged stews. There are wursts, of course. And spaetzle are handmade here. Even vegetables are dressed up with the likes of dill sauce. Some dinner entrees cost three times as much as at lunch, but it's still moderately priced. And in the evening the dishes' taste is fresher and the choices are more extensive.

CAFE BETHESDA
5027 Wilson Lane, Bethesda, MD
(301) 657-3383

AMERICAN   ♿

Lunch: M-F 11:30-2   **Entrees:** $7-$14
Dinner: Daily 5-10   **Entrees:** $14-$25
Credit Cards: All major   **Reservations:** Recommended
Dress: Casual   **Parking:** Valet (fee) F-Sat

All too often in the restaurant business, one and one add up to less than one. A good restaurant expands to a second location, and neither maintains the original quality. Maybe that's happened with CAFE BETHESDA and its offspring, CAFE BETHESDA NORTH, in Rockville. At least I've found that the old CAFE BETHESDA'S food isn't quite up to past standards.

On my most recent visit the grilled chicken was a tad overcooked and its marsala sauce was unappealingly sweet and sticky. The day's special seafood salad was a big mound of boring, underdressed mixed greens with thin, tasteless strips of tuna scattered on top. But there was still much to love. The crab cakes are a vivid arrangement with a tangle of magenta-marinated red cabbage and a scattering of finely diced tomatoes and peppers on a stark white lemon cream. And the creamy crab cakes themselves are unorthodox but delicious, particularly since they are sharpened by the lemon, the cabbage and a few capers. The vegetables served with the entrees give me hope: wonderful lumpy red-skin mashed potatoes, perfectly cooked fine matchsticks of carrot, a few impeccable snow peas.

Still, the food wouldn't carry the day if CAFE BETHESDA'S service were less endearing. And on a sunny afternoon, surrounded by flower-laden window boxes and potted flowering trees under a flowered umbrella, a meal at CAFE BETHESDA is as scrumptious as a Monet, no matter what is being served.

For this restaurant's Rockville branch, which has slightly different hours and provides free parking: Cafe Bethesda North, 121 Congressional Lane, Rockville, MD, (301) 770-3185

CAFE DALAT
3143 Wilson Blvd., Arlington, VA
(703) 276-0935

VIETNAMESE

Lunch: Daily 11-2:30 **Entree:** Sun-Th $4.25-$5, Sat-Sun $7.50-$9
Dinner: Sun-Th 2:30-9:30, F-Sat 2:30-10:30 **Entrees:** $7.50-$9
Credit Cards: MC, V **Reservations:** Accepted for 8 or more
Dress: Casual **Parking:** Free **Metro:** Clarendon

All of the Vietnamese restaurants in Arlington's Little Saigon serve the standard dishes: *cha gio,* summer rolls, *pho,* grilled pork, lemon grass chicken and more. Thus, clearly the survivors are good enough to meet the competition. So how to choose? It depends on what you want to eat.

CAFE DALAT is one of the smaller restaurants, with a menu that is not as extensive as Queen Bee's down the street. Given the unadorned look of the place, you can guess that the prices are low. Most of the dishes are grilled, and that's what draws me back to CAFE DALAT: simple, lightly seasoned grilled meat or seafood. The sweet-soy marinated pork is crunchy, chewy and flavorful. Even better is the skewered seafood. The menu doesn't quite

"... heavy competition for American fast food."

explain the dish, but it's a kind of mixed-seafood mousse, formed into small balls and threaded on skewers with squares of onion and green pepper. Unlike most ground-seafood dishes, this one tastes fresh and clearly of shellfish. It's light and airy, faintly caramelized, and is meant to be wrapped with cilantro, shredded vegetables and white rice noodles in leaves of lettuce, then dipped in a golden, fruity peanut sauce. A beer and a platter of Vietnamese skewered seafood, pork, beef or chicken — that's heavy competition for American fast food.

CAFE DELUXE
3228 Wisconsin Ave. NW, Washington, DC
(202) 686-2233

AMERICAN ♿

Lunch: M-Sat 11:45-4, Sun 3-4 **Entrees:** $8-$13.50
Dinner: M-Th 4-10:30, F-Sat 4 to 11, Sun 4 to 10
Dinner Entrees: $8-$15 **Brunch:** Sun 11-3, $6-$9
Credit Cards: AE, MC, V **Reservations**: Accepted for 8 or more
Dress: Casual **Parking:** Valet (fee) at dinner Th-Sat

CAFE DELUXE looks like a French brasserie. Even better, it looks like one that's been around a while. The tile floor, chunky glassware and thick white dinner plates delivered to your table without fanfare identify this as a casual, drop-in-for-a-snack kind of restaurant. When it's crowded it has a buzz, a burbling of conversation, but even at its noisiest you can converse without strain. Maybe that's why it seems so comfortingly broken-in.

Think of this as an American diner: Would you order sea bass with lemon pepper crust in a diner? Or grilled tuna burger with pickled ginger mayo? No, you'd probably go for the bacon cheeseburger. And you'd be guessing right.

I'd also suggest another item that's in diner mode: grilled meatloaf. And the sugar snap peas are a distinct improvement on anything green you are likely to find at a diner. The menu nods to vegetarians with a grilled vegetable antipasto, a vegetable pizza and fettuccine. There's an agreeable spinach and cheese dip with terrific, crackly, thin tortilla chips for people who want to hang out without being involved in a serious meal. While the soup might not be exciting, it is house-made and meal-sized. Desserts are rich and homey, such gooey sweets as chocolate-chip cookie pie or fruit cobbler.

A micro-brewed draft beer or thick white mug of perfectly decent American coffee, sipped slowly in a calm dark booth, or a martini and a burger at the bar — those alone are good reasons to visit CAFE DELUXE.

CAFE MILANO
3251 Prospect St. NW, Washington, DC
(202) 333-6183

ITALIAN   ♿

Lunch: M-Sat 11:30-2:30 **Entrees:** $9-$21
Dinner: M-Sat 5:30-11, Sun noon-11 **Entrees:** $12-$28
Late Nite: M-Sat 11-1 am **Entrees:** $7-$15 **Dress:** Casual
Credit Cards: All major **Reservations:** Recommended
Parking: Validated at lunch, valet (fee) Th-Sat evenings

CAFE MILANO, so chic and European that you think Concorde rather than just jet set, naturally serves food so light that fashion models needn't fear hanging around for the evening. Thus, in addition to pastas (pretty snazzy ones), pizzas and a few grilled items, it also has plenty of salads, featuring such trendy greens as mache and radicchio.

My favorite one is fennel, arugula and parmesan. You'd think it'd be pretty much the same everywhere: a simple salad of fennel, arugula olive oil, lemon and Parmesan. But at CAFE MILANO it's an obvious illustration of what makes one restaurant better than another. I also like the big, chunky insalata giardino, with hunks of potatoes, tomatoes, red onions, celery and cucumber. The dressing is made with balsamic vinegar, and the garnish is fresh basil. Anitpasti also include assorted carpaccios that might qualify as salads, and the inevitable tomato and mozzarella. After that, the entrees, though light and fresh, are an anticlimax.

"Cafe Milano is more than a restaurant. As the evening grows later, it becomes a fashion show, a club, a young and trendy crowd scene."

But CAFE MILANO is more than a restaurant. As the evening grows later, it becomes a fashion show, a club, a young and trendy crowd scene — where everything sparkles, including the wine.

CAFE NEMA
1334 U St. NW, Washington, DC
(202) 667-3215

MEDITERRANEAN/SOMALIAN

Breakfast: Sat-Sun 9-11:30 **Entrees:** $4-$7
Lunch: M-F 11:30-5, Sun 11:30-5 **Entrees:** $7-$9
Dinner: Sun-Th 5-11, F-Sat 5-1 am **Entrees:** $8-11.50
Credit Cards: All major **Dress:** Casual **Reservations:** Accepted
Parking: Street **Metro:** U Street-Cardoza
Entertainment: International music F-Sat 11 pm-1 am

In some Middle Eastern countries, the real test for a bride is how well she makes her torpedo-shaped stuffed *kibbeh*. Is the meat-and-bulgur wrapper thin enough? Even enough? Light enough? Any bride who needs lessons would do well to try the kibbeh at CAFE NEMA, a small, makeshift-looking bar and restaurant down a few steps from U Street.

The owner is Somali, the chef is Egyptian, and the menu mingles Middle Eastern specialties with a few pastas and sandwiches. The Middle Eastern dishes are definitely the best, and the kibbeh is the standout. Its fine paste of beef and bulgur form the thinnest, lightest shell, and the stuffing of beef with pine nuts is spicy and fragrant. The price is a mere $2.50. The falafel and baba ghanouj are appealing, too, but the pastas don't have nearly as much character.

CAFE NEW DELHI
1041 N. Highland St., Arlington, VA
(703) 528-2511

INDIAN   ♿

Lunch: M-Sat 11:30-2:30 **Entrees:** $5.25-$7
Dinner: Daily 5-10 **Entrees:** $7-$14
Brunch: Sun 11:30-2:30, $9 buffet
Credit Cards: All major **Dress:** Casual
Reservations: Recommended on weekends
Parking: Street **Metro:** Clarendon

At CAFE NEW DELHI, you can dine under a sky of pink clouds and streaks of red, even if you're indoors. Surrounded by faux columns and photos of India's monuments, you can sip a Pimm's Cup and imagine yourself on the other side of the world.

This is a friendly, casual little restaurant, with reasonable prices. But Indian restaurants are in stiff competition with each other these days, and this one has an inconsistent kitchen.

The samosas are greaseless, and chick peas with potatoes have a lovely tart-hot coriander sauce. So why is the chicken *tikka* dry and crumbly, the spinach *pakora* dull and starchy? Butter chicken is mushy, with a vague sauce and strips of acidic peppers and some onions. Spinach dumplings are heavy, coated with a thick yellow, soggy sauce. Yet the breads are fine, and the *dal* — whole brown lentils with red beans, fairly spicy — is the most interesting version I've found.

So goes a meal, with highlights and dashed expectations. CAFE NEW DELHI is a restaurant where neighbors probably get to know its best dishes, but newcomers have to learn the hard way.

CAFE PARMA
1724 Connecticut Ave. NW, Washington, DC
(202) 462-8771

ITALIAN

Lunch: M- F 11:30-4 **Entrees:** $7-$12
Dinner: M-Th 4-11, F-Sat 4-11:30, Sun 4-10:30 **Entrees:** $8-$13
Brunch: Sat-Sun 11:30-3 **Entrees:** $10.75-$12.75
Late Nite: M-Th 10:30-1, F-Sat 10:30-2 **Entrees:** $6.25-$9.50
Credit Cards: All major **Reservations:** No
Dress: Casual **Parking:** Street **Metro:** Dupont Circle

Y ou can often see tourists examining the menus outside this small Connecticut Avenue Italian restaurant, trying to decide whether to try it. All they really need to know is displayed in the front window. In its large bay, CAFE PARMA sets up a daily antipasto buffet, and it is enough reason to venture in for a meal.

It's an exceptional deal: For a modest price ($8.95 at lunch, the last time I checked), you can eat your fill — and refill — of dozens of dishes. The best are the fresh marinated vegetables — platters of crisp green beans with onions, sliced beets, cauliflorets, shredded greens, plum tomato halves, shredded carrots or whatever else is in season. Pasta salads are pedestrian but filling, and there are several kinds of pizza, which suffer from being rolled too thick and served lukewarm. Seafood is always included, the likes of marinated squid, steamed mussels and canned anchovies. You'll find cold cuts and cheeses, the inevitable tomato-mozzarella salad (the mozzarella is better than the tomatoes) and reasonably crusty bread and bread sticks.

> **"In its large bay window, Cafe Parma sets up a daily antipasto display, and it's enough reason to venture in for a meal."**

CAFE PARMA has a long à la carte menu, too, with plenty of pizza and pasta variations, fish and seafood, and the usual Italian meat dishes. No single dish can compete, though, with the attractive display of the buffet, and nothing comes close to its value. A quiet little dining room with accommodating waiters, CAFE PARMA would be just another storefront Italian restaurant without its generous buffet.

CAFE RIVIERA
Georgetown Inn
1310 Wisconsin Ave. NW, Washington, DC
(202) 444-9600

FRENCH   ♿

Breakfast: M-F 6-10:30, Sat-Sun 7-11 **Entrees:** $7-$9.50
Lunch: Daily 11:30-2:30 **Entrees:** $7-$9.50
Dinner: Sun-Th 6-10:30, F-Sat 6-11 **Entrees:** $14-$18.50
Brunch: Sun 11:30-3:30, $20 **Credit Cards:** All major
Reservations: Recommended **Dress:** Casual
Parking: Validated valet all day

Now that Gerard Pangaud of Gerard's Place has taken over this oft-changing hotel dining room, his brand new CAFE RIVIERA looks promising. Pangaud hired as chef an old friend, Gerard Ferri, who'd just closed his one-star restaurant on the real Riviera. And after only one week Ferri was evoking the south of France in his menu and on the plate.

An appetizer tart of red snapper with basil was an airy, delicate froth in the most ethereal pastry shell. And true to Provençe, appetizers included fish soup, rabbit pâté, vegetable terrine and artichoke ragout. Artichokes showed up also among the entrees on interesting blini with a buttery version of *pistou* (France's rendition of pesto) and scallops, though Ferri needs to find better shellfish. Cod was more appealing, moist and silky, sandwiched between dense layers of eggplant gratin.

The menu is fairly short but compelling, with lamb in sweet garlic cream, chicken with hazelnut breading, sweet and sour pork confit, pasta with three preparations of duck, and either red snapper or veal stew with olives. The dessert list offers a fragile-crusted, covered tart of swiss chard (really!) with raisins and nuts that is truly delicious. There are also refreshing inventions such as citrus napoleon, minestrone of fruits, and frozen chocolate cup with three chocolates.

Even the dining room now seems pulled together, with enthusiastic and competent waiters, a fresh, sun-coast color scheme and a wine steward who knows his stuff. Speaking of which, the moderate prices on the menu are matched — even beat — by the wine prices.

CALIFORNIA GRILL
1090 Vermont Ave. NW, Washington, DC
(202) 289-2098

AMERICAN

Breakfast: M-F 6-10:30 **Lunch:** M-F 11-4 **Entrees** $2-$6.35
Closed: Sat-Sun **Credit Cards:** All major
Reservations: No **Dress:** Casual
Parking: Street **Metro:** McPherson Square

Only in America do French, Mexican and Southern California cooking add up to bargain-priced fast food. The CALIFORNIA GRILL is a self-service cafeteria and carryout where you get not just a sandwich but a meal — light or substantial, hot or cold — for well under $10.

The salads are the ubiquitous Caesar, but also a California Cobb made with chicken, avocado, eggs, two cheeses and bacon. The tostadas come with traditional fillings as well as mahi mahi. The sandwiches include BLT, egg salad, roast beef and turkey, but then there's a grilled tuna steak. And kebabs — the highlight of this menu — are well marinated, nicely charred on the grill yet moist, and they come with herbed, roasted new potatoes that could make french fries seem boring. The chicken kebab, my favorite, can compete with any you'd find at three times the price.

> **"Only in America do French, Mexican and Southern California cooking add up to bargain-priced fast food."**

It's a New Wave cafeteria, one with an emphasis on fresh vegetables and bright flavors. It's so trendy that it has an espresso bar. And the espresso bar is so trendy that it serves tapas. What will California think of next?

CAPITOL CITY BREWING COMPANY
1100 New York Ave. NW, Washington, DC
(202) 628-2222

AMERICAN   ♿

Open: Sun-Th 11 am-11 pm, F-Sat 11 am-midnight
Entrees: $7.25-$16   **Credit Cards:** All major   **Reservations:** No
Dress: Casual   **Parking:** Street   **Metro:** Metro Center

These immense, handsome brewpubs have been installed in two of the most magnificent historic buildings in the city. That's enough reason to have a look. They also feature delicious, amber-tinged brews — you can get a sampler of four if you don't have an immediate preference. With them comes a basket of soft pretzels and horseradish-mustard dip. Who needs more?

Yet there's a long menu, too, that runs the gamut from light (salad with grilled chicken breast, grilled or poached fish) to heavy (a variety of sausages, ribs, pork chops). Surely the dishes were devised to sell beer, as some of the best are hot enough to send you gasping for a cold draft. The chili has a real kick, Fireworks Shrimp is aptly named and among the sausages (which come as appetizers, salad, sandwiches or platters) there's an *andouille* with plenty of bite. Not all is spicy, though. Some dishes err on the bland side; vegetable-topped pasta with pesto, for example, can taste of little more than starch.

Habits die hard, and most people seem to stick to burgers at pubs, but then these thick, char-striped, cooked-as-ordered burgers (beef or turkey) can be worthy of the beer. They're served with thin fries, rather tasteless and chewy but so crunchy they seem as if they've been coated with flour. Fried oyster sandwich — purportedly a po' boy — is also popular, and the oysters have a pleasantly crackly cornmeal crust. Too bad they don't have a more authentic po' boy roll, though. The sleeper on this menu is the mushroom quesadilla, listed as an appetizer but certainly enough for lunch. It's rich and gooey with cheese, and comes with a brightly flavorful tomato salsa. More than Cobb salad or grilled salmon, it's a dish that seems like beer food.

The other Capitol City Brewing Company is at 2 Massachusetts Ave, NW, Washington, DC, (202) 842-2337. At this printing, two more branches were scheduled to be opened, in Arlington, VA, and Bethesda, MD.

CAPITAL GRILLE
601 Pennsylvania Ave. NW, Washington, DC
(202) 737-6200

AMERICAN/STEAKHOUSE   ♿

Lunch: M-F 11:30-3 **Entrees:** $9-$20
Dinner: Sun-Th 5-10, F-Sat 5-11 **Entrees:** $16-$29
Credit Cards: All major **Reservations:** Recommended
Dress: Jacket & tie **Metro:** Archives-Navy Memorial
Parking: Complimentary valet at dinner

THE CAPITAL GRILLE, the third branch of a Providence, R.I.-based chain, shows its dry-aged steaks not only in the raw but in the throes of molding — part of the aging process. The aging room is in full view of the street. From a distance the rows of uncut porterhouses look richly abundant. But look too closely and you'll probably order fish. Inside, the dining room has clubby dark wood and money-green window shades, hunters' prize heads on the walls and big tables set with steak knives. This is a he-man environment.

If you can overcome your introduction at the aging room window, the overriding reason for dining at the CAPITAL GRILLE is the steaks — sirloin and porterhouse. Don't look for butter-tender steaks. These have some bite and a full meaty flavor. The portions are gigantic — baked potatoes a pound each, mashed potatoes family size, and cottage fries portioned for a tableful, then piled with french-fried onions.

Light eaters will zero in on the seafood: swordfish and salmon, grilled just past rare, or large grilled shrimp on linguine. Lobsters can be steamed or broiled and generally come in giant sizes. All the seafood looks impressive, whether inch-thick fish steaks (even two inches on occasion) or the monster-sized shrimp and lobsters. And they are cooked so gently that undercooking is a far greater likelihood than overcooking. But none of the seafood has much taste; it's just nice, bland stuff. And the pasta under the shrimp is limp and soggy.

Wisdom might dictate that you start a meat-heavy meal with a salad, and there is a properly zesty Caesar. Even so, passion might direct you to the fine smoked salmon, greaseless pan-fried calamari with hot pickled peppers or baked Oysters Capital Grille, which are such spicy, grassy-spinach-topped oysters as oysters Rockefeller might aspire to be. Should you find room for dessert, you can top off your fatty escapade with — what else? — creme brulee.

CAPITOL VIEW CLUB

Hyatt Regency Hotel
400 New Jersey Ave. NW, Washington, DC
(202) 783-2582

AMERICAN   ♿

Dinner: Daily 5:30-10:30 **Entrees:** $15.75-$26
Credit Cards: All major **Reservations:** Recommended
Dress: Jacket preferred **Entertainment:** Pianist nightly
Parking: Complimentary valet **Metro:** Union Station

Except for a picnic, you couldn't have both good food and a monumental view in this city — until the CAPITOL VIEW CLUB opened. Even from the farthest table of this rooftop restaurant, you can see the drama of the illuminated Capitol dome and the charm of the Library of Congress' aged copper roof. There is little interior decoration to compete with the scene, except for etchings of the Capitol lining the entrance. Tables are spacious and well spaced; chairs and banquettes are comfortable. Table lamps shaded in black silk flicker with alcohol flames to intensify the romance of the evening.

At lunch the CAPITOL VIEW CLUB is just that — a private club. Only at dinner is the restaurant public. The menu is American (with Italian touches) and modern, original without being bizarre. A dozen appetizers, soups and salads, plus pastas available in appetizer or entree portions, give a wide range to first courses. For tourists (not to mention locals), oysters Chesapeake is the most apt — and a most delicious — beginning. Among both appetizers and entrees, the highlights are often among the specials. Salmon, halibut and sea bass, in trendy but not outrageous guises, keep company with steak, lobster and veal. Flawless rack of lamb, delicate and buttery liver, and crab cakes that are a fine advertisement for Washington — such are the possibilities, with elaborate side dishes.

The CAPITOL VIEW CLUB, atop the Hyatt Regency Hotel, makes sure you're alerted to its lavish ambitions. You're brought a hot towel when you are seated, then a relish tray — but no ordinary relish tray. The service is intensely well-meaning, though it remains obviously hotel service. And there is a price to pay for this feasting with a view, as in most hotel restaurants. But the CAPITOL VIEW CLUB succeeds far beyond our usual expectations for rooftop dining.

CARLYLE GRAND CAFE
4000 S. 28th St., Arlington, VA
(703) 931-0777

AMERICAN   ♿

Lunch: M-F 11:30-2, Sun 11:30-4:45 **Entrees:** $7-$11.65
Dinner: Sun-T 5-9, W 5-10, F-Sat 5-11 **Entrees:** $9-16.75
Brunch: Sun 10:30-2:30, $7-$15
Pre-Theater: M-Th $10 **Credit Cards:** AE, MC, V
Reservations: Recommended **Parking:** Free

This large contemporary restaurant's ground floor, with its vast bar and sea of cafe tables, is only for those who can stand near the speakers at a rock concert without earplugs. I'd certainly head for the upstairs. There the place still has all the backdrop of a party — glowing wood with matte black accents, decorative glass, immense art nouveau posters and even piped music — but it also has the comfort of upholstered booths and modulated noise. The eclectic-American menus of the two floors are not identical, but close enough. And the prices are the same.

This kitchen does well by fish. The lightly smoked grilled salmon is said to be the most popular entree. No wonder. The smoking is delicate and the salmon is cooked carefully so that the surface is nicely browned while the interior is pale pink, tender and juicy. It's topped with diced raw tomato and onion vinaigrette, which nicely cuts the sweetness of the honey-mustard cream painted in zigzags across the fish. Chicken is often a tasteless thing these days. But the chicken paillard at the CARLYLE GRAND CAFE recalls why Americans once dreamed of a chicken in every pot. Not so with the shrimp. They are large and accurately grilled but totally tasteless. Crab cakes, too, are watery and bland. Grilled pork chops are likely to be dry, saved only by basil mashed potatoes and a tart, spicy, apple chutney with appealingly firm fruit. There is plenty more to explore here, from sandwiches to steaks, and the salads look like clear winners.

When in doubt, stick with the familiar. The quesadilla weaves fragrant roasted peppers, spicy chorizo and mild cheese into a fine gooey filling for crisped tortillas, and the mound of lightly spiced onion rings served with a bottle of house-made mustardy steak sauce can deliciously serve as dinner.

CASABLANCA
1504 King St., Alexandria, VA
(703) 549-6464

MOROCCAN

Lunch: M-F 11:30-2 **Entrees:** $6-$9
Dinner: Sun-Th 5:30-11, F-Sat 5:30-11:30
Dinner Entrees: $18-$22 (5-course meal)
Credit Cards: All major **Reservations:** Recommended
Parking: Free lot **Metro:** King Street

CASABLANCA is the suburban version of downtown's Moroccan restaurant, Marrakesh, though it's a little less elaborate and somewhat less expensive. Still, the dining room is unrestrainedly ornate, with carpet-covered sofas, satin pillows and nearly private niches. And the belly dancer puts on an energetic show. Diners have a choice of fixed-price dinners, but prices can climb higher if you want to sample more than two entrees per table. In any case, the meal is plentiful and interesting, eaten with your hands from a communal platter.

You start with tomato-lentil soup and/or salads of cucumber, eggplant, potato and the like. Mild and fresh, they deserve better bread. Bastilla comes next, the luscious chicken-nut-egg pie wrapped in phyllo and dusted with powdered sugar. Entrees are chicken or lamb flavored with hot sauce, onions and chickpeas, lemon and olives or such sweet combinations as honey and almonds or prunes and sesame seeds. There is also couscous, with

" . . . the meal is plentiful and interesting, eaten with your hands from a communal platter."

or without meat. The sauces seem to be poured on the meats after cooking, since the flavors don't permeate, and the chicken with lemon and olives suffers from the bitter aftertaste of excess pith. But in the midst of all the other courses, the music and the belly dancing, the flaws take on less importance. For dessert there are mint tea and house-made cookies.

50

CASHION'S EAT PLACE
1819 Columbia Rd. NW, Washington, DC
(202) 797-1819

AMERICAN	♿

Dinner: T 5:30-10, W-Sat 5:30-11, Sun 5:30-10
Entrees: $11-$17 **Brunch:** Sun 11:30-2:30 **Entrees:** $6-$9
Closed: M **Credit Cards:** MC, V **Dress:** Casual
Reservations: Recommended **Parking:** Valet (fee)

CASHION'S serves a worldly array of dishes with an endearing hint of home cooking. It's small, flowing from indoors to out on balmy days, with a long, curved bar and walls full of sepia-toned old family photos. Everybody's friendly: the waiters, the bus-boys, the other diners. It's a casual, laid-back kind of restaurant, in the best sense — with efficient, professional service that means the diners, not the staff, can be relaxed.

The menu pays homage to vegetables; you'll never find spinach more perfectly cooked, or beets more freshly delicious. Fried green toma-toes are featured in the summer, and the season's fruits show up in tarts and gratins at dessert. I'd go back to CASHION'S if only for the crisp, buttery, golden-brown disk of potatoes Anna, an à la carte side dish that's invariably the star of the meal. As for meat and fish, CASH-ION'S seeks out king salmon and buffalo hangar steaks, pearly halibut to pan roast and rabbit to fricassee. Lamb might be spit roasted or the shank braised. And birds — guinea hen, quail or duck — are regulars.

As in most restaurants, appetizers are more exciting than entrees, even an appetizer as simple as sauteed sweetbreads with spinach. Curried mussels are the plumpest, juiciest of bivalves, in a light yellow, fra-grant cream with more of that spinach. And spinach shows up, light-ened with ricotta, in homey little ravioli. Alsatian onion tart appears among the appetizers from time to time, as do crab cakes, garlic shrimp and gumbo. Desserts are homey, often with seasonal fruits, and they can be spectacular.

The cooking is straightforward; when food is this carefully cooked and well seasoned, it needs no sauce. There's terrific,chewy, crusty bread for mopping up the juices, and the wine list shows an excellent eye at work. All this unfussy sophistication comes at prices substantially be-low those of the restaurants that are CASHION'S peers.

CHADWICK'S
5247 Wisconsin Ave. NW, Washington, DC
(202) 362-8040

AMERICAN

Lunch: M-Sat 11:30-4 **Entrees:** $7-$10
Dinner: Sun-Th 4 pm-1 midnight, F-Sat 4 pm-1 am **Entrees:** $8-$16
Brunch: Sun 10-4, $7-$9 **Reservations:** Accepted
Credit Cards: All major **Dress:** Casual
Parking: Validated discount **Metro:** Friendship Heights

Years ago, when I called the branch of CHADWICK'S in Friendship Heights to ask whether it offered a Saturday hamburger special, I was told, "We have hamburgers, and they are special." It's still true. These burgers are thick and juicy, carefully handled and cooked as rare as requested, striped with grill marks and stacked on a very good golden, chewy, sesame-seed bun with lettuce, tomato, red onion and a dill pickle. In fact, they are one of the best burgers in town, regardless of price. The fries are limp and boring, but plentiful. And the rest of the pub fare tends to be well priced, decently cooked and served with breezy good cheer.

> **"Chadwick's in Georgetown is worth remembering when you've been walking on the canal or strolling at Washington Harbour and want a quiet retreat . . ."**

CHADWICK'S in Georgetown, with its dark old wood and homey service, is worth remembering when you've been walking on the canal or strolling at Washington Harbour and want a quiet retreat from the crowds — or don't want to pay harborside prices. The other branches are appreciated by families, since children are treated like valued customers and their parents have learned to count on efficient service.

For the the Georgetown and Virginia branches, which have similar menus, hours and prices as at Friendship Heights: Chadwick's-Georgetown, 3205 K St. NW, Washington, DC, (202) 333-2565, and Chadwick's-Old Town, 203 S. Strand St., Alexandria, VA (703) 836-4442.

THE CHEESECAKE FACTORY
5345 Wisconsin Ave. NW, Washington, DC
(202) 364-0500

AMERICAN   ♿

Open: M-Th 11:30 am-11:30 pm, F-Sat 11:30 am-12:30 am,
Sun 10 am-11 pm **Entrees:** $7-$20 **Brunch:** Sun 10-2, $7-$9.50
Credit Cards: All major **Reservations:** No **Dress:** Casual
Parking: Garage, 2 hours free **Metro:** Friendship Heights

This jam-packed, family-friendly eating place could have been called the Salad Factory, but would lines have formed and crowds have waited through half the lunch or dinner hour if lettuce accounted for its fame? While small mountains of greenery sit before most everyone at lunch and many at dinner, they're largely an excuse for indulging in cheesecake: Eat all your vegetables — *then* you can have dessert.

Frankly, I prefer the vegetables. The menu lists more than a dozen salads, and each combines so many ingredients that it's hard to imagine them all fitting in one bowl. The Santa Fe salad, for example, has diced, marinated chicken with lettuce (nearly all the salads start with chicken and greens), tossed with black beans, corn, fontina cheese, olives, tomatoes and crisp tortilla strips with lime vinaigrette, cilantro pesto and spicy Asian peanut sauce. It's Santa Fe by way of Rome and Bangkok.

The concoction that most captures my fancy, though, is the Tuscan chicken salad — with the tomato-basil vinaigrette on the side. Like the other salads here, it looks like a medium-sized Alp in a bowl. The bottom layer is penne, buried under an avalanche of awfully good greens. Sweetly roasted chunks of eggplant, a few strips of roasted peppers and a lone Kalamata olive are threaded through the greens, grated cheese is sprinkled on top, and clinging to the side of the mound are three very thin and nicely charred slabs of boneless chicken breast. You've got to cut them up and distribute them throughout the greenery for best results, because on its own the chicken is dry and cindery. But when the chicken bits are mixed in, their charred flavor is an asset to the fluff of vegetables. Some salads may be short on substance and high on volume, but that must be so they can leave you feeling light, healthy — and ready for cheesecake.

CIELITO LINDO
4305 Kenilworth Ave., Bladensburg, MD
(301) 699-5787

MEXICAN   ♿

Lunch: M-F 11-3 **Entrees:** $4.75-$7
Dinner: T-Th 3-9, F 3-10, Sat 11 am-10 pm, Sun 11 am-9 pm
Dinner Entrees: $8.50-$15 **Closed:** M evening
Credit Cards: All major **Dress:** Casual
Reservations: Recommended **Parking:** Free lot

CIELITO LINDO is a real Mexican restaurant, not Tex-Mex or chain-Mex. It's a family-run, mom-and-pop kind of place that's about as close as a restaurant can get to home cooking. It's also a kind of home away from home for Mexicans yearning for familiar tastes and smells.

CIELITO LINDO has the best qualities of a mythic Mexican hole-in-the-wall without the drawbacks. It's spacious rather than cramped, spotless rather than grubby. The place is decorated with garish gold-and silver-braided sombreros, but the walls and floor are soothing pink and gray.

The menu is a long list of predictable Mexican standbys: burritos, quesadillas, enchiladas, plus a few deep-fried things such as chimichangas and flautitas. None can hold a candle to Mama's specials: Michoacan-style empanadas, big, fat, baked ovals of faintly sweet yeast bread stuffed with chicken and vegetables;

"It's a kind of home away from home for Mexicans yearning for familiar tastes."

house-made yeast rolls, perhaps stuffed with cheese; or mole, that startlingly black, grainy sauce that builds up a gradual heat in your mouth, weaving an elusive sweetness and satisfying bitterness in its wake. You can get mole with chicken, or it makes for great enchiladas. So does the tangy, modestly hot green chili sauce for the everyday enchiladas. And don't pass up the roast pork — carnitas Michoacan-style, cooked for 12 hours until the meat collapses into soft strings — or barbecued lamb. Alongside the platters come tortillas, warmly exuding the smell of cornmeal. Most of the meats are also available in soft tacos, quickly heated on the grill and a little greasy but less so than the deep-fried kind.

CITIES
2424 18th St. NW, Washington, DC
(202) 328-7194

AMERICAN/INTERNATIONAL ♿

Dinner: M-Th 6-11, F-Sat 6-11:30 **Entrees:** $12-$19.50
Closed: Sun **Reservations:** Recommended
Credit Cards: All major **Dress:** Casual
Parking: Valet (fee) W-Sat
Entertainment: Latin music, dancing Th evening

For years CITIES has been a focal point of Adams-Morgan. Half an open-to-the-street bar and also a full-blown restaurant, CITIES revamps its menu and dining room every once in a while to reflect a different urban setting. Over the years CITIES has spotlighted Paris, Los Angeles and Hong Kong, to name a few. In doing so, it has always combined the wacky (note the whimsical renditions of the cityscape) with the wonderful (note the serious cooking). The restaurant has been a meeting ground for young and old, jeans and jewels, change and tradition.

With each new theme, authentic cooking from some part of the world has been combined on the menu with some of the city's best pizzas.

" . . . a meeting ground for the young and old, jeans and jewels, change and tradition."

Signature dishes — some with a Turkish bent to reflect the ownership — also stay through the transformations. CITIES has long been known for its very good bread baked in a wood-burning oven. And its vegetarian platters are impressive enough that even carnivores have coveted them. The food is as decorative as the environment. Fronds of chives wave over the plate, salad greens are piled high and cigar-shaped pastries are poised in careful constructions. Thus, even when the cooking is erratic — where is it not? — it is continually interesting.

CITRONELLE
Latham Hotel
3000 M St. NW, Washington, DC
(202) 625-2150

AMERICAN/FRENCH   ♿

Breakfast: Daily 6:30-11 **Entrees:** $8-$12.50
Lunch: Daily 11:30-2 **Entrees:** $9.50-$17
Dinner: Sun-Th 6-10, F-Sat 5:30-10:30 **Entrees:** $24-$29
Brunch: Sun 11:30-2:30, $10-$13.50
Pre-Theater: M-F 6-6:30, Sat-Sun 5:30-6:30, $35
Credit Cards: All major **Reservations:** Recommended
Parking: Complimentary valet **Dress:** Casual

France and California meet in Georgetown, at CITRONELLE. This chain-restaurant spinoff of Los Angeles chef Michel Richard's Citrus waxes and wanes, depending on who's in the kitchen. If it's the master — Richard himself — you're in good hands. But that's rare, and the on-site chefs have been changing frequently. So stick to the basics.

Of course, basics here are much more complicated than elsewhere. They include the signature Crunchy Kataifi Shrimp — shrimp wrapped in shredded wheat pastry and deep-fried — and desserts such as a shimmering custard layered between filmy, crackly

> **"France and California meet in Georgetown, at Citronelle."**

layers of puff pastry for a napoleon that's painted with stripes of chocolate and caramel.

In any case, the restaurant is a comfortable, airy space with a laid-back California feel and a full view of the kitchen from the main dining room. The cooking's a show: layering shiitakes and puff pastry into a sky-high appetizer napoleon; poising a thin crunch of pastry atop fat, near-raw oysters and spinach for an appetizer pot pie; piling mounds of thin french fries or Maui onion rings atop the grilled chicken or the scallops. And ingredients are California-fresh — thumb-size fresh artichokes, emerald-green herbal sauces, spinach pasta as bright and flavorful as the vegetable itself. So if you happen along when a first-string chef is on the field, the food can be spectacular.

CITY LIGHTS OF CHINA
1731 Connecticut Ave. NW, Washington, DC
(202) 265-6688

CHINESE   ♿

Lunch: M-Thu 11:30-3 **Entrees:** $6-$10
Dinner: M-Th 3-10:30, F 3-11, Sat noon-11, Sun noon-10:30
Dinner Entrees: $7-$12 **Credit Cards:** All major
Reservations: Recommended **Dress:** Casual
Parking: Validated evenings **Metro:** Dupont Circle

A s Chinatown shrinks, CITY LIGHTS OF CHINA keeps growing. It's now tripled its original size, and depends on little more than pale green walls and mirrors to set the mood. The entrance crowds up, the service bogs down, but the cooking doesn't falter. It's bright, and it's crunchy where it should be and tender where it counts — and the flavors hit all the right buttons.

Over the years I've built a list of favorite dishes — eggplant with garlic, stir-fried spinach, crispy fried beef with its caramelized glaze and red-pepper heat, and pungent, slippery little chili-hot dumplings. The star of the show, however, is the Peking duck, as much for the dining room's performance as the kitchen's. The skin is as glossy as lacquer and nearly devoid of fat. The meat is moist and not overdone, and it's always available freshly cooked, even at lunch. The carving is a dance of considerable grace.

"The star of the show is the Peking duck, as much for the dining room's performance as the kitchen's."

CITY LIGHTS OF CHINA has a broad menu, yet the kitchen can handle the range with competence. Its sauces aren't greasy, its vegetables are never overcooked, and its portions are so large that you are likely to leave with the makings of tomorrow's lunch. On the down side, the service is more efficient than attentive; it's not a place that cossets its diners. But if there are shortcomings in the service, there are none in the quality of ingredients. It's the food that counts here.

CLYDE'S OF CHEVY CHASE
76 Wisconsin Circle, Chevy Chase, MD
(301) 951-9600

AMERICAN	&#9855;

Lunch: M-Sat 11-4:30 **Entrees:** $6-$12
Dinner: Sun-M 4:30-11, T-Th 4:30-midnight, F-Sat 4:30-12:30 am
Dinner Entrees: $7-$19 **Credit Cards:** All major
Reservations: Recommended **Dress:** Casual
Parking: Validated **Metro:** Friendship Heights

It's the Orient Express. It's the Indy 500. It's the Air and Space Museum. It's CLYDE'S OF CHEVY CHASE. Surely this is the largest Washington restaurant investment since Red Sage, an extravaganza complete with a model train circling overhead and a reproduction of an Orient Express parlor car as your booth. These aren't second-rate imitations but luxurious replicas, with glove-soft leathers and inlaid woods.

Downstairs the menu is more casual and pizzas are available, as is a gigantic bar. Upstairs isn't exactly formal, but the dining room is conversation-friendly — bustling but not noisy. The menu offers every indulgence. Vegetarians are wooed with curry, couscous and a melange of lentils, brown rice and pasta. Meat eaters will find rotisserie duck and chicken as

"It's the Orient Express. It's the Indy 500. It's the Air and Space Museum."

well as steaks in three sizes, while seafood fanciers can have their rockfish wild, their mahi mahi with tropical fruits and their shellfish Thai-style. Most of the menu reads better than it tastes, and you'd be safest ordering one of the justly famous CLYDE'S hamburgers. Another hint: The kitchen copes better with fish than with meat.

It's all probably a plan to allow room for dessert. You can leave happy if you finish your meal with the chocolate bread pudding, warm and sufficiently bittersweet, with ice cream and whipped cream melting over it. And cappuccino custard mousse cake is adorable, constructed as a coffee cup with a cookie handle.

58

CLYDE'S OF GEORGETOWN
3236 M St. NW, Washington, DC
(202) 333-9180

AMERICAN

Lunch: M-F 11:30-4, Sat 10-4 **Entrees:** $5.50-$11
Dinner: M-Th 4:30-10:30, F-Sat 4:30-11:30, Sun 4:30-10
Dinner Entrees: $5.50-$16 **Pre-Theater:** M-F 4-6, 20% discount
Late Nite: F-Sat 11:30-1 am, Sun 10-2 am, $7-$13
Brunch: Sun 9-4, $6-$14 **Credit Cards:** All major **Dress:** Casual
Reservations: Recommended **Parking:** Receipt for validation

Who would have expected Georgetown's first big-time saloon would become known for its produce? CLYDE'S has been reinventing itself. The atrium now has a 16th-century stone chimney piece, and large vintage model planes hang from the glass ceiling. The Victorian omelette room has been converted to a cherry-paneled tavern with oil paintings of sporting life over the booths.

Burgers are still featured — beef or turkey. And CLYDE'S chili is, too — though that is also available in cans from your neighborhood fancy food shop. Yet the mainstays are not beef but those contemporary, light, protein hits, chicken and salmon, appearing as appetizers, salads, sandwiches and entrees with an abundance of local vegetables to accompany them.

> **"The menu changes daily . . . But sometimes I wonder if the chef changes from minute to minute."**

The menu changes daily, giving the chef a chance to react to the market. But sometimes I wonder whether the chef changes from minute to minute. Rarely have I found such wide swings in a restaurant's food. The service is at least as erratic. CLYDE'S still makes a fine burger, and it has mastered rotisserie chicken. If I had to bet blindly, though, I'd put my money on appetizers: Chicken tenderloin strips sauteed with aromatic vegetables. A succulent eggplant terrine. Or the hidden gem of the menu, rings of tender white squid served in a hot iron skillet with sliced green olives, chunks of Roma tomatoes and tangles of well caramelized onion. It puts even good fried squid to shame. CLYDE'S has a nifty draft-beer list, as one would expect, and a wine list that's value-conscious. It even boasts of serving filtered water in its pitchers.

COCO LOCO
810 7th St. NW, Washington, DC
(202) 289-2626

BRAZILIAN/MEXICAN

Lunch: T-F 11:30-2:30 **Entrees:** $10-$20
Dinner: M-Th 5:30-10, F-Sat 5:30-11 **Entrees:** $16-$27
Closed: Sun **Dress:** Casual **Credit Cards:** All major
Reservations: Recommended **Parking:** Valet (fee) evenings
Metro: Gallery Place **Entertainment:** Dancers 11 pm Sat

A small bite or a pig-out — that's the range at COCO LOCO, where now you can now have it all. No longer must you choose between *churrascaria* (the Brazilian rotisserie feast) and tapas at COCO LOCO; this colorful, hip Brazilian-Mexican restaurant has blended its two parts so your table can mix and match.

Choosing the churrascaria is bound to leave you groaning. First you fill a plate from the vast cold buffet: salads of red beans, black beans, white beans, corn and all kinds of vegetables, plus the inevitable pasta salads. Then you try to resist overeating from the bowl of soft, fragrant coconut rice and the wedges of crisp, oven-roasted potato. At the same time, waiters roam the floor with skewers of meats: heavily herbed chicken sausage, chorizo that develops a slow burn as you eat it, intensely moist — and deliciously greasy — chicken thighs, juicy and rare beef round with enough flavor to justify its chewiness, mild and fatty pork ribs and turkey wrapped in bacon, which doesn't manage to keep it dry or make it tasty. Individually, the meats are flawed, but together their munificence compensates.

But that's not the best of COCO LOCO. The long list of Mexican tapas — some large enough and priced high enough to be considered a meal — offers great originality and painful excess of choices. Even the obvious — quesadillas, chiles rellenos — are here re-created grandly. Wild mushroom quesadilla is a puffed, fried, golden brown triangle rather than the usual floppy pale tortilla. Its two sauces, one hot and one creamy mild, are elegant. Shrimp is served atop a round of black, squid-ink rice and a fluff of fried parsley. Homely zucchini becomes a spongy, sweetened custard halfway between entree and dessert. From a simple salad to a mini-paella, sausage to lobster, the tapas would take a month to fully investigate, and it would be a delicious month.

COEUR DE LION
Henley Park Hotel
926 Massachusetts Ave. NW, Washington, DC
(202) 414-0500

AMERICAN

Breakfast: Daily 7-11 **Entrees:** $2.50-$9
Lunch: Daily 11-2:30 **Entrees:** $10-$16
Dinner: Daily 6-10 **Entrees:** $12-$26 **Tea:** Daily 4-6, $6.50-$11.50
Brunch: Sat 11-2:30, $8.75; Sun 11:30-2:30, $19.95
Credit Cards: All major **Reservations:** Recommended
Dress: Jacket **Parking:** Validated Valet **Metro:** Metro Center
Entertainment: Jazz/dancing F-Sat evenings

COEUR DE LION, in the Henley Park Hotel, is so civilized, so English. The dining rooms are small and hushed. In one, tall windows with tiny panes of pale yellow stained glass impart a medieval look. In another, floor-length paisley tablecloths, old brick and artwork — tapestries and oils — anchor the room firmly in tradition, despite the modern atrium ceiling and mirrored walls. These dining rooms are intimate, personal and totally comfortable. The service, too, skirts the usual pitfalls of hotels. It seems both English and American, formal and friendly, intently professional yet jovial and enthusiastic, service meant to be noticed.

The menu reflects the modern American trend of mingling tastes and cuisines: soy sauce glazes and Mediterranean olive purees, accents of tropical papaya and Scandinavian dill, sesame noodles from Asia and goat cheese ravioli from Europe, not to mention Maryland Eastern Shore crab cakes. The recipes are adventurous and the prices immodest. This is no workaday hotel kitchen.

It's also not always consistent. Rely on those crab cakes, crisp-edged and buttery, constructed of lump crab and just enough creamy, well-seasoned binder. This kitchen does well with low-fat "alternative selections," too. Among the devil-may-care dishes, the best bets are those that include something plainly grilled or poached. The key is simple: COEUR DE LION has a way with light dishes. Save your extravagance for dessert. The list is a glossary of cream in all its forms: sour cream and cream cheese in the cheesecake, heavy cream in the creme brulee, not to mention ice creams. Light and heavy, competent and clumsy — this hotel kitchen, like most of them, is erratic. Yet, after the candlelight, the medieval art and the solicitous service, do you care?

COPPI'S
1414 U St. NW, Washington, DC
(202) 319-7773

ITALIAN   ♿

Dinner: M-Th 5-midnight, F-Sat 5-1am, Sun 5-11 pm
Entrees: $7-$11.50 **Credit Cards:** All major
Reservations: No **Dress:** Casual **Metro:** U Street-Cardoza
Parking: Free after 8 at Reeves Center

Something's always just opening at the New U, which is one reason the neighborhood reminds me of Adams-Morgan a decade or two ago. The difference is that Adams-Morgan's restaurants have tended to be ethnic, while U Street's are more trendy and pseudo-ethnic. Most have been disappointments. Thus I return to COPPI'S, even though it is too noisy and neglectful of its customers when it's crowded. Moreover, the prices are higher than this spare pizza parlor warrants, and a few of the dishes are perennial disappointments.

What I like are the pizzas and calzones, with their chewy, slightly grainy dough blistered from the wood-burning oven. The fillings and toppings use high-quality ingredients (pancetta, Westphalian ham, portobello mushrooms, fresh vegetables and imported cheeses), generously applied. Combinations are well chosen — I particularly like the ham, basil, mozzarella, diced tomato and portobello, and the Nutella dessert calzone. And the list of antipasti is unique, especially the mustardy salads of cauliflower with salami or jicama and pancetta.

COPPI'S has added some interesting dishes from Liguria, all of them cooked in the wood-burning oven. Smoked risotto is the star here, reeking of garlic and stringy with melted cheese. Skip the bland shrimp, and investigate something more seasonal. And hope for a quiet evening or opt for carryout. COPPI'S also has a larger location on Connecticut Avenue in Cleveland Park. Unlike the original, it has two ovens, so it can handle a larger menu that includes fresh pastas and fish entrees.

For the Cleveland Park branch, which also has added an $8.50-$10 brunch on Saturday and Sunday: Coppi's Vigorelli, 3421 Connecticut Ave. NW, Washington, DC, (202) 244-6437.

COTTONWOOD CAFE
4844 Cordell Ave., Bethesda, MD
(301) 656-4844

AMERICAN/SOUTHWESTERN   ♿

Lunch: M-Sat 11:30-2:30 **Entrees:** $6-$8
Siesta menu: 2:30-5:30 $4-$7.25
Dinner: Sun-Th 5:30-10, F-Sat 5:30-11 **Entrees:** $12.65-$21
Credit Cards: All major **Reservations:** Recommended
Dress: Casual **Parking:** Valet (fee) at dinner

The Southwestern feeding frenzy cooled down and left us with a few of the best chili-spiked restaurants, which by now are considered old favorites. COTTONWOOD CAFE has remained not just because of its consistently good food, but because it is one of our most comfortable Southwestern restaurants.

It's Tex-Mex for grownups. The booths are well cushioned, the sound level is conducive to conversation, and the appointments are handsome and lively without approaching garish. Even more important, the service is watchful but not intrusive. The great secret of COTTONWOOD CAFE is that lunch prices are as little as half the dinner prices. True, the portions are smaller, and lunch doesn't offer such luxuries as shrimp-and-pinon pancakes, achiote duck or tenderloin with green chili corn pudding. But at mid-day you can still find greaseless incendiary "snake bites" (shrimp-and-cheese-stuffed fried jalapenos); fine Aztec chicken broth with avocado, cheese and grilled chicken; the enchiladas and tacos; fragrant and creamy chicken-and-shrimp Kachina pasta and several imaginative chicken and smoked turkey sandwiches. COTTONWOOD CAFE'S food is more refined — and expensive — than its neighbor, Rio Grande Cafe. But its serenity is worth the money.

> **"The great secret of Cottonwood Cafe is that lunch prices are as little as half the dinner prices."**

CRISP & JUICY
4540 Lee Highway, Arlington, VA
(703) 243-4222

LATIN AMERICAN/ROTISSERIE CHICKEN

Open: M-Sat 11-10, Sun. 11-9 **Entrees:** $4.15-$8.35
Credit Cards: No; cash only **Reservations:** No
Dress: Casual **Parking:** Free

Y ou can take the name of this rotisserie-chicken carryout at face value, and the chicken is so aromatic you probably could close your eyes and find CRISP & JUICY from a block away. This is food that cries to be taken to the nearest picnic table for a succulent, messy feast.

The menu lists a few sandwiches, and maybe they're good. But why bother to try them when the alternative is the most wonderful rotisserie-cooked chicken? It's not only marinated, but it has been rubbed with spices under the skin so the flavor permeates the bird. It turns over a wood fire inside a bright orange cooker, and the finished meat — the white **"You can take the name of this rotisserie-chicken carryout at face value."** as well as the dark — is tender and juicy, not to mention impeccably crisp-skinned. With the chicken you get a choice of a clear, tart and peppery cilantro-spiced dipping sauce, a thick, yolk-yellow mustard sauce or a creamy, pink garlic sauce that tastes like France's aioli with a punch.

One of these birds probably could serve three people, but they are so good you'll probably not want to share between more than two. To fill in the meal, C & J sells tangy coleslaw, fragrant black beans with rice, an interesting potato salad and fried yucca, crunchy and greaseless. And before you leave with your dinner, consider tomorrow's lunch; the chicken is also sensational cold.

For the two Maryland branches of Crisp & Juicy: 1331G Rockville Pike, Rockville, MD, (301) 251-8833, and Leisure World Plaza, 3800 International Dr., Silver Spring, MD, (301) 598-3333.

DEAN & DELUCA CAFE
3276 M St. NW, Washington, DC
(202) 342-2500

AMERICAN   ♿

Open: Sun-Th 9 am-8 pm, F-Sat 9 am-9 pm
Entrees: $4-$7.25   **Credit Cards:** AE, MC, V
Dress: Casual   **Reservations:** No   **Parking:** Street

It's not the food that's imported from New York to Washington's DEAN & DELUCA CAFES. It's the style. These self-service cafes use Washington breads — baguettes, focaccia, onion rolls — for sandwiches, and the same produce as everyone else. But those grilled chicken or eggplant slices on baguettes with tomatoes, arugula, mozzarella or whatever have a flair that compensates for the too-chewy bread or the skimpy portion of chicken.

The salads look bright, taste lively and have clever little touches: dried cranberries in the wild rice, blue cheese in the pasta, a generous sprinkling of raspberries atop the mixed fresh fruit. To drink, there are chic bottled waters, all the current espresso variations and sometimes fresh lemonade made to order. And to finish, the counter is spread with pastries from one end to the other.

"It's not the food that's imported from New York . . . It's the style."

DEAN & DELUCA CAFES let the underpinnings of the room show and the food serve as decoration. They are stylish little interludes, places for a quick light meal (though the line is slow, so the quick part is sometimes more in the eating than in the serving). They're a prelude to the theater downtown or a reward for shopping in Georgetown. A sweet indulgence.

Dean & Deluca Cafes has two other branches, also in the District of Columbia: 1299 Pennsylvania Ave. NW, (202) 628-8155, and 1919 Pennsylvania Ave. NW, (202) 296-4327.

DELRAY GARDEN AND GRILL
4918 Delray Ave., Bethesda, MD
(301) 986-0606

VIETNAMESE   ♿

Lunch: M-F 11:30-2:30 **Entrees:** $6-$10.50
Dinner: Daily 5-10 **Entrees:** $7-$13.75
Credit Cards: AE, MC, V **Dress:** Casual
Reservations: Recommended on weekends
Parking: Complimentary valet F-Sat **Metro:** Bethesda

A little off Bethesda's beaten track, DELRAY GARDEN AND GRILL is a friendly, family-run Vietnamese restaurant that clearly has taken over from a chicken place. The walls are edged with chicken motifs, and they're covered with chicken art. There's even a chicken Whistler's Mother. And the copper pots, farm implements and ladderback chairs suggest America far more than Vietnam. DELRAY looks like a living, breathing Hallmark card.

With one exception: Inside the entrance is a grill, where shrimp on sugar cane is sizzling away. Like the decor, the service couldn't be sweeter. One evening the hostess was carrying a couple's baby around so they could eat in peace.

The two best dishes I've found on DELRAY'S menu are beef wrapped in grape leaves, grilled to a smoky finish on that open grill, and a casserole of chicken in a golden curry sauce, grainy with coconut milk and more flavorful than chili-hot. Other entrees cry out for seasoning, whether lemon-grass grilled beef or spicy grilled chicken. The *cha gio* — rice-paper spring rolls— are small and meaty here. The cold imperial rolls, on the other hand, are surprisingly short on meat and shrimp. And stir-fried dishes slip into soupiness.

Unlike most Vietnamese restaurants, DELRAY pays attention to desserts. Fried bananas could use a crisper batter, but they are worth ordering for their delicious tart puree of mango, which tastes like tropical applesauce. On second thought, I'd be glad to have just a bowl of the mango puree.

DUANGRAT'S

5878 Leesburg Pike, Falls Church, VA
(703) 820-5775

THAI

Lunch: M-F 11:30-2:30, Sat-Sun 11:30-3 **Entrees:** $7-21
Dinner: M-Th 5-10:30, F 5-11, Sat 3-11, Sun 3-10:30
Dinner Entrees: $10-$21 **Credit Cards:** All major
Reservations: Recommended **Dress:** Casual **Parking:** Free
Entertainment: Thai classical dancing Sat evenings Jan-April

The oldest of the countless glamorous Thai restaurants here, DUANGRAT'S has been busy opening its third extension, BANGKOK ST GRILL, down the block. Even so, it can still compete with the newer, more flamboyant Thai places.

The dining room is spacious and pastel-pretty, and the waitresses wear silk gowns in sherbet colors. The menu is long, divided between old-familiar and exotic-new dishes such as cod with pickled mangoes and cashews in chili-lime dressing, assorted fish fillets with stir-fried vegetables in sweet-and-sour lychee fruit sauce, appetizers of salmon and potatoes fried in a purse-shaped shell, or crab and shrimp with coconut and cilantro in rice paper.

"The menu is long, divided between old-familiar and exotic-new dishes."

It's hard to miss with this kitchen. I'm enthusiastic about the new things I try — meltingly soft plantains in a tempura batter, chicken bhram in its mellow, spiced peanut sauce with crisp fried shallots. And the old favorites are often done with special flair here; the crab-and-pork-stuffed fried chicken wings are the most succulent I know, and shrimp (or pork or beef) with crisp garlic and white pepper has that crunchy, chewy, fried-garlic texture and hauntingly delicate flavor that I haven't found elsewhere in years.

A few dishes slip, particularly the weak and vapid mustard-greens soup, and the heat and acid could be turned up in the seafood-lime salads. Yet all's well with dessert. The Thai sweet I adore, sticky rice with mango, is here accompanied by cubes of smooth amaretto custard, and the rice itself, simmered with faintly sweet coconut milk, glossy and chewy, is beyond wonderful.

DUBLINER
Phoenix Park Hotel
520 N. Capitol St. NW, Washington, DC
(202) 737-3773

IRISH/AMERICAN

Breakfast: Daily 7:30-10 am **Entrees:** $3.25-$8
Lunch: Daily 11-3 **Entrees:** $6-$12
Dinner: Daily 3-11 **Entrees:** $8-$15
Late Night: M-Sat 11-1, Sun 11-midnight, $4-$8
Brunch: Sun 11-3, $3.75-$12 **Credit Cards:** All major
Reservations: Accepted for 6 or more **Dress:** Casual
Parking: Street **Metro:** Union Station
Entertainment: Irish music M-Sat 9 pm-1 am, Sun 7:30-midnight

The place has an aura. That means the wood paneling has grown glossy and brown through the years, the dark wood tables are worn so that your elbows almost feel cradled, and the etched and stained-glass windows look as if they should have cracks (which they do). THE DUBLINER is an old Irish pub, casual and easygoing, with food that's easy to define: mediocre. This is a restaurant for the I-don't-need-a-power-lunch crowd.

The Auld Dubliner Amber Ale is a big draw. While the low prices and highly appealing atmosphere are components for a winning formula, there has to be more reason for lines to form at lunch. It's gotta be the beer. The barley mushroom soup tastes like an experiment in suspending grains in a salt solution, and the lamb is chewy enough to serve as your exercise for the day. The vegetables are tasteless, and the coffee is worse.

> **"The Dubliner is an old Irish pub . . . with food that's easy to define: mediocre."**

What to order? Burgers and grilled chicken sandwiches are probably the safest bets. Look for a cold plate special of roast duck salad with arborio rice atop a Caesar salad and surrounded by fresh fruit. It's a sleeper, utterly delicious.

ELLIS ISLAND
3908 12th St. NE, Washington, DC
(202) 832-6117

AMERICAN/IRISH   ♿

Open: M-Sat 11:30 am-11 pm, Sun 11:30-10 **Entrees:** $9-$16
Brunch: Sun 11:30-3 **Entrees:** $6-$8
Credit Cards: All major **Reservations:** Recommended
Dress: Casual **Parking:** Free lot **Metro:** Brookland-CUA

I rish pubs aren't what they used to be. They're more ambitious, and this one's better. ELLIS ISLAND RESTAURANT & PUB, a spinoff of Capitol Hill's Irish Times, brings to the Catholic University area a restaurant priced low enough for students and nice enough for them to show off to their parents. Where else can you find Keats' poetry and a three-cheese pizza on the same menu?

The place has a scrubbed, blond-wood look, with seating at the bar, tables or booths (or in a small, bricked rear courtyard if the weather is nice). The beer list features local Wild Goose brews on tap. And the menu is small but cuts a wide swath. You can order anything from a basket of fresh-cut french fries to a proper dinner of, say, a lightly smoked and grilled fillet of salmon with rice and buttery fresh spinach. The current pub favorite, fried calamari, is one of the kitchen's glories, tender under its crunchy cornmeal coating. The pizza crust, too, has a cornmeal graininess, plus an agreeable addition of sliced plum tomatoes. It's not great pizza, but it has an honest, handmade quality. The menu also features ribs and burgers, pastas and a grilled vegetable salad.

"Where else can you find Keats' poetry and a three-cheese pizza on the same menu?"

For such a small menu, desserts take up a lot of space. And given such choices as strawberry shortcake, coffeecake, chocolate sour cream cake and lemon poppy-seed cake (not to mention daily specials, perhaps apple pie or sweet potato pie), you might be tempted to skip right to the end.

ENRIQUETA'S
2811 M St. NW, Washington, DC
(202) 338-7772

MEXICAN   ♿

Lunch: M-Sat 11:30-2:30 **Entrees:** $6.50-$12.50
Dinner: Sun-Th 5-10, F-Sat 5-11 **Entrees:** $9-$12.50
Credit Cards: AE, MC, V **Reservations:** Accepted for 5 or more
Dress: Casual **Parking:** Street

While other Mexican restaurants in town were serving just tacos and enchiladas, this colorful Georgetown spot was introducing Washington to real Mexican food. For years it's been a Georgetown landmark with its pastel banners of paper lace and hand-painted chairs in primary colors. Space is tight and tables are close, but this is meant to be a sociable place.

The menu is still long and interesting, with regional dishes new to Washington. But the cooking has lost its luster. An appetizer of mussels is generous — a bargain — but the tangy herbed sauce has evolved into something mild and tomatoey. A squeeze of lemon is needed to bring it to life.

"Enriqueta's is no longer a marvel; it's a place to find an unusual menu and good value at lunch."

Tacos and enchiladas are certainly available, and so are *chiles rellenos*. But they're not just the standard red-sauce stuff. The stuffed peppers, with their fruit-meat filling, have long been a signature dish. And the menu lists several fish dishes that show the varied styles of Mexico's regions. Yet the glory of ENRIQUETA'S, its dark and intricate mole sauce, is nowadays too sweet and thick, not nearly as mysterious as it once was. The cooking can be careless. ENRIQUETA'S is no longer a marvel; it's a place to find an unusual menu and good value at lunch.

EYE STREET CAFE
1915 I St. NW, Washington, DC
(202) 457-0773

AMERICAN/MEDITERRANEAN

Lunch: M-F 11-3 **Entrees:** $5-$17
Dinner: M-Th 5-9, F-Sat 5-10 **Entrees:** $6-$18 **Closed:** Sun
Credit Cards: All major **Reservations:** Recommended
Dress: Casual **Parking:** Street **Metro:** Farragut West

E YE STREET CAFE has been growing up. This small restaurant started as a Middle Eastern cafe with pizza, open for lunch and weekday dinners. Then it broadened its dinner menu. Now the entrees go well beyond pizza and *shish taouk*.

The pizzas are excellent, baked in a wood-burning oven and topped with an international repertoire of ingredients ranging from thyme paste with sesame, onion, feta and tomato to caramelized onions with black olives and anchovies. And the breads, similarly wood-baked, have all the flavor and elasticity one could hope to find. Okay, so the cooking can be erratic, the breads underbaked, the sauces undependable. It's a work in progress.

Beyond the rotisserie and kebab cookery, hummus and *dolmas*, EYE STREET CAFE now serves eclectic American creations such as spice-rubbed grilled shrimp on white beans with pancetta or warm spinach

" . . . one of those restaurants that often turns first-timers into avowed regulars."

salad with feta and prosciutto as satisfying appetizers, and contemporary fish dishes like seared near-raw tuna with balsamic vinegar sauce.

When you hit it right, the seasonings are tantalizing, the cooking is careful right down to every haricot vert. And given the warm-hearted staff and the moderate prices, EYE STREET CAFE is one of those restaurants that often turns first-timers into avowed regulars.

FELIX

2406 18th St. NW, Washington, DC

(202) 483-3549

AMERICAN

Dinner: T-Th 5:30-10, F-Sa 5-10:30 **Entrees:** $12-$18
Brunch: Sun 11-2:30 **Entrees:** $6.25-$8.75
Pre-Theater: T-Sun 5:30-7:30, $18 **Closed:** M
Credit Cards: All major **Reservations:** Recommended
Dress: Casual **Parking:** Valet (fee) weekends
Entertainment: Dancing Th-Sat 11 pm-2:30 am

Bright lights, big city and giant martinis — FELIX strikes a mid-point between Manhattan and Miami's South Beach. Chef Richard Poye characterizes his style as influenced by American, French and Asian "but not a fusion of these cuisines."

For such a small and reasonably priced menu, FELIX is studded with glamorous possibilities: peppered foie gras, quail, bison or Muscovy duck breast. The chef makes his own pasta — the likes of saffron-poppy seed linguine. FELIX also offers homelier ingredients, from chicken (organic) to pork chops (double thick) to a vegetarian entree of quinoa and eggplant folded into a ruffled turnover.

Cured or smoked salmon on a potato pancake is a familiar appetizer that never grows tiresome. Here the pancake is lacy and crisp, the salmon house-cured and succulent; it's wonderful. Seafood ravioli, all too often dreary, is delicious in Poye's hands. Among the salads are trout and cress with spiced pecans, arugula with beets and quince and a Thai-spiced chicken with noodles that is barely spicy but makes a light and refreshing first course or entree.

Among the entrees, Poye times the charred peppered tuna "sashimi" perfectly. Lamb shank osso bucco is meltingly tender and richly browned, topped with chunks of braised root vegetables. The entree that exceeds expectations is the tender, juicy pork chop, moistened with a slightly creamy pan sauce excited by bits of bacon, olives and oregano. Poye ekes unexpected flavor from spaghetti squash, tames the cloying quality of beets and mellows bitter kale. Even if one dish or another doesn't quite work, nobody's going to go hungry at FELIX. Not with the possibility of a moist, custardy chocolate and cherry bread pudding with mint anglaise for dessert. Or layered mango and coconut parfait, a creamy ooze with plenty of ripe fruit and shredded coconut.

FIO'S
Woodner Apartments
3636 16th St. NW, Washington, DC
(202) 667-3040

ITALIAN   ᕫ

Dinner: T-Sun 5-10:45 **Entrees:** $5.50-$13 **Closed:** M
Credit Cards: All major **Reservations:** Accepted for 7 or more
Dress: Casual **Parking:** Free garage

This has to be the most hidden restaurant in Washington. With no sign on the street, it's tucked way back from the Woodner's vast apartment-building lobby. And this odd restaurant has room to waste, which it does with a jukebox in the empty lounge and various furnishings that look dropped off on their way to the attic.

So the decor is slapdash. That fits. The service is as homey as if you'd dropped in on friends unexpectedly, and the wine list is priced hardly above soft drinks. The menu seems far too long for a restaurant that's often near-empty, and it is. So the specials are the dishes to order. Further advice: Concentrate on the appetizers. The list of specials is fascinating. Who else serves chick peas with chestnuts? And when this chef makes fettuccine with smoked salmon and cream sauce, the sauce is light, the pasta is thin and supple and the smoked salmon is luscious, slightly crusty but not cooked so long that it turns strong.

> **"This has to be the most hidden restaurant in Washington."**

With entrees, though, the highlight is often the side dish — the peppers and mushrooms. Swordfish might be beautifully complemented by lemon, capers, wine and sauteed onions, but the fish is overcooked. Lamb shank is meltingly tender but needs seasoning. Saltimbocca tastes of ham and cheese but not of veal. Yet the prices are so stunningly low that it seems churlish to complain. And if you're still hungry afterwards, all the better. It would be a shame to not have room for blackberry granita.

FOOD FACTORY
4221 N. Fairfax Dr., Arlington, VA
(703) 527-2279

PAKISTANI

Open: M-F 11am-10 pm, Sat-Sun noon-10
Entrees: $5-$6.50 **Credit Cards:** No; cash only
Reservations: No **Dress:** Casual
Parking: Free lot **Metro:** Ballston

The Washington area is now thickly studded with kebab places, and much of the credit is surely due to the FOOD FACTORY. Not only was it among the first, it's still among the best, cheapest and most atmospheric.

Entered from an alley and sharing its space with an ethnic grocery, the FOOD FACTORY is self-service and strictly basic. You choose your kebab from the refrigerator case of raw, skewered meats or your curry dish from the steam table. You order at the counter and wait at a long bare table for your kebab to be charcoal-grilled. You pick up

"It's still among the best, cheapest and most atmospheric" of kebab restaurants.

your plastic plate of food on a red plastic tray. And you fill yourself on well under $10.

The kebabs aren't quite as dazzling as they used to be, but they are still generous. Lamb's the best, vinegary from its marinade, though it's likely to be chewy. Chicken, rubbed with red spices, has lately tended to be dry. Kebabs are better than they sound, though, once you've spread them with the garlicky yogurt dressing and wrapped them in the house-made flat bread. The accompanying lettuce and tomato salad is tawdry, but you can end your meal on a grace note of house-made Afghan ice cream.

FRATELLI
5820 Landover Rd., Cheverly, MD
(301) 209-9006

ITALIAN

Lunch: M-Sat 11-4 **Entrees:** $6-$11
Dinner: M-Th 4-10, F-Sat 4-11, Sun 4-9 **Entrees:** $9-$13
Brunch: Sun11-3, $12 **Credit Cards:** AE, MC, V
Reservations: Recommended on weekends
Dress: Casual **Parking:** Free lot

C heverly has traded in an old Howard Johnson's in favor of an ambitious Italian restaurant. What's even better, the prices are still at HoJo's level.

FRATELLI is decorated with brick and faux columns, its spaciousness is emphasized by mirrors, and its tables are set with burgundy napkins and a couple of carnations. Its staff seems so happy to be here that the maitre d' is likely to sing as he comes to table, and the server turns the bread description into a ballad. Okay, so the cooking's not great. But no staff tries harder. And where else can you find a hot anti-pasto plate of crab-stuffed mushrooms, fried cala-

"Where else can you find a hot antipasto plate of crab-stuffed mushrooms, fried calamari, clams casino, grilled shrimp and steamed mussels for anywhere around $6?"

mari, clams casino, grilled shrimp and steamed mussels for anywhere around $6? FRATELLI serves enormous, cheesy pizzas, though their toppings could use some zip and the crust doesn't taste house-made.

The tomato sauce is light and pleasant, so the pastas are good bets. Watch out for overcooked fish and oversalted sauces, press the waiter to tell you what's freshest, and look forward to homey, supersweet, hand-made cannoli for dessert.

FULL KEE
509 H St. NW, Washington, DC
(202) 371-2233

CHINESE

Lunch: M-F 11-3 **Entrees:** $4.25-$5.75
Dinner: M-Th 3-1 am, F 3-3 am, Sat 11 am-3 am, Sun 11 am-1 am
Dinner Entrees: $8-$15 **Credit Cards:** No; cash only
Reservations: Accepted for 6 or more **Dress:** Casual
Parking: Street **Metro:** Gallery Place-Chinatown

Washington's Chinatown has plenty of excellent cooking, but its inconsistency is maddening. Some of the restaurants have good dishes and bad dishes. Others have good days and bad days. The chefs play musical stoves, so the restaurants even have good and bad months or seasons. As a result, I'm at a loss to wholeheartedly recommend one restaurant.

But for the combination of Chinese atmosphere, interesting menu and good value, I find FULL KEE always satisfies. In part, I favor it for its open kitchen, because it's fun to watch the cooks wrapping dumplings and scooping noodles from the giant cauldrons in the front window. And for a comforting lunch you can't beat the Hong Kong-style shrimp dumpling soup, a big bowl of broth (fairly wan)

> **" . . . it's where some of the city's top European and American chefs come to eat after work."**

filled with bobbing dumplings of whole shrimp and shreds of mysterious vegetables.

While that's enough reason to remember FULL KEE, there is also a long menu of standard Cantonese stir-fried dishes, bright and glistening, generously portioned. And there is one I haven't seen elsewhere, a combination of shrimp, scallops and squid fried in a light crunch of flour coating and seasoned with peppered salt and bits of green chilies. Other restaurants serve similar fried squid or shrimp, but this combination makes nibbling irresistible while you wait for your dumplings to be simmered to order.

Late at night, FULL KEE can make for interesting sightseeing, since it's where some of the city's top European and American chefs come to eat after work. They're likely to order the whole steamed fish. That's an impressive recommendation for any restaurant.

GABRIEL
Radisson Barcelo Hotel
2121 P St. NW, Washington, DC
(202) 956-6690

SPANISH/LATIN AMERICAN/MEDITERRANEAN   ♿

Breakfast: M-F 6:30-11, Sat 7-11, Sun 7-10:30   **Entrees:** $7-$9.25
Lunch: M-F 11:30-2:30   **Entrees:** $5.50-$10
Dinner: M-Th 6-10, F-Sat 6-10:30, Sun 6-9:30   **Entrees:** $7.50-$22
Brunch: Sun, 11-3, buffet $16.75   **Credit Cards:** All major
Reservations: Recommended   **Dress:** Casual
Parking: Complimentary valet   **Metro:** Dupont Circle

Greggory Hill is a chef who loves abundance. He produces plates crammed with accompaniments, garnishes and salsas, and he fills every possible time slot at Gabriel with interesting treats. Sundays there's a grand and satisfying brunch buffet, during weekend happy hours a bargain-priced tapas buffet, and weekdays a modestly priced lunch buffet. The emphasis is Latin, from a luxurious paella to tangy chorizo slices, though the buffets might also include black-bean cassoulet, couscous and very American wood-grilled vegetables.

In case you don't like buffets, Gabriel has à la carte menus at lunch and dinner, and a tapas list at any hour, which includes curried spinach with crispy fried mozzarella, as well as empanadas and grilled quail stuffed with blood sausage.

Nevertheless, it's the à la carte menu that shows the breadth of Hill's skills — he gives everything a twist. He turns rustic Salvadoran *pu-pusas* into an elegant starter, with barely cooked, slightly caramelized sea scallops as the filling, Tacos are done with rabbit and black beans and tamales with sweet potatoes and green onions, accompanied by chili-rubbed grilled shrimp — both delicious appetizers. With an entree of seared salmon, the bonus is a wrapper of serrano ham, which forms a crisp crust and steams the interior with a subtle smokiness. The deeply crusted, house-made bread adds pleasure to them all.

Hill often tends to add one sauce too many, a disruptive slosh of black beans or a distracting extra flavor to every dish. But such charming excess is easy to forgive in the flurry of good things to eat.

GALAXY
155 Hillwood Ave., Falls Church, VA
(703) 534-5450

VIETNAMESE   ♪

Lunch: Daily 11:30-3 **Dinner:** Daily 5-11
Closed: T **Entrees:** $5-$25 **Credit Cards:** All major
Reservations: Recommended **Dress:** Casual
Parking: Free **Entertainment:** Dancing F-Sun evenings

They say the best Chinese restaurants are those where Chinese dine. What about a Vietnamese restaurant where not only Vietnamese are dining but a Vietnamese wedding party takes up half the room, men at other tables sing Vietnamese songs about San Francisco, and several Vietnamese couples spend a long evening nibbling and sipping snifters of brandy with soda?

With its huge crystal light fixture reflected in glass tabletops, GALAXY looks half cafe and half nightclub. Even if it didn't serve food, it would serve as a fascinating introduction to Vietnam. Our waitress offered up tales of her Vietnamese childhood along with our dinner.

As for the food, there's one dish to remember: appetizer No. 15, an addictive mixture of chopped baby clams with shredded pork, peanuts, onions, hot peppers, mint and ginger. It's piled on a red cabbage leaf and comes with two plate-sized, puffy crackers studded with black seeds. It's served warm and seasoned hot; with a wedge of lime to squeeze over it before you scoop up bits of the clam mix with pieces of the puffy cracker. The appetizer list also includes the usual rice paper-wrapped spring rolls — *cha gio* — and three other kinds of pork rolls served cold. And there are greasy but pleasant rice cakes, small custardy hemispheres with bits of shrimp and scallion — appetizer No. 5.

I'd fill up on appetizers here. Entrees suffer by comparison. Scallops are topped with a thick red sauce shot with cilantro, lemon grass, chilies and garlic, but it is too sweet and the scallops are chewy. Jumbo shrimp are expensive and, for the price, the salt-cooked version is disappointing. Yet the menu is long, with plenty of seafood and noodle dishes. In light of the party atmosphere, the most appropriate might be the steam boats, seafood entrees you cook at the table. Add a bottle of brandy, and you, too, might be inspired to sing about San Francisco.

GALILEO
1110 21st St. NW, Washington, DC
(202) 293-7191

ITALIAN

Lunch: M-F 11:30-2 **Entrees:** $11-$19
Dinner: M-Th 5:30-10, F-Sat 5:30-10:30, Sun 5-10
Dinner Entrees: $17-$30 **Credit Cards:** All major
Reservations: Recommended **Dress:** Casual
Parking: Complimentary valet at dinner **Metro:** Foggy Bottom

For well over a decade GALILEO has set the standard for Italian restaurants in Washington. Even while chef Roberto Donna has been racing around town opening new restaurants — I Matti, Il Radicchio, Pesce, Arucola — he keeps updating the menu of his spacious, dignified flagship (often inflating the prices as well). No simple asparagus salad here: The freshest of asparagus is moistened with black truffle vinaigrette and parmesan or with a fried egg to stir as an enrichment into an aromatic dressing. Donna's grilled portobello mushroom was the inspiration for dozens of others around town, yet none matches his. And the season's most dewy produce appears in a creamy risotto, atop handmade bow tie pasta or in fragile stuffed pasta. When GALILEO is doing its best, no restaurant does better. That's what brings me back despite its frustrating inconsistencies.

In season, foie gras and game weigh in, and the breads have been so improved as to tempt you to overindulge. Overall, though, even the main courses have been lightened these days. Locally grown greens are mounded atop a small, crisp-edged risotto cake to accompany silken sea bass. Smoky grilled radicchio or spring onions, and sheer sauces of balsamic vinegar, heighten the flavors of simple sauteed or roasted fish or meat. No cream, no butter, not even a noticeable amount of olive oil weighs down this cooking.

But whatever restraint is exercised in the main course is let loose in desserts. Not that they are heavy — far from it. But they are as elaborate and fanciful as the savory courses are simple and serious. Above all, they are new. Sure, there's a classic tirami su. But there is also a crisp version, layered with fragile sheets of pastry, nuzzled by a transparent fan of caramelized sugar, a fillip of whipped cream, a scooplet of fabulous ice cream and a crosshatching of caramel sauce. The sludgy-cannoli era is over.

GENEROUS GEORGE
3006 Duke St., Alexandria, VA
(703) 370-4303

ITALIAN   &

Summer Hours: Sun-Th 11-11, F-Sat 11-midnight
Winter Hours: Closed one hour earlier each day
Lunch Entrees: $6-$11 **Dinner Entrees**: $6-$14
Pre-Theater: M-F 3-6, $2-$3 off select entrees **Dress:** Casual
Credit Cards: DIS, MC, V **Reservations:** No **Parking:** Free lot

G ENEROUS GEORGE is a high-volume, much-loved pizza fun house strewn with '50s kitsch where everything is turned into a pizza. Even the pastas are served on a pizza crust. This restaurant knows what it's about, because the pizza crust is its strongest suit. It's puffy and crispy, yeasty and chewy, a dreamboat pizza crust. And if you are looking to enjoy it at rock-bottom prices, go at lunch on a weekday. That's when personal-size pizzas are available.

I like the combo with everything — fennel-spiked sausage, pepperoni, black olives, Canadian bacon, peppers, Genoa salami, quartered fresh mushrooms, slices of fresh tomato (and, I confess, anchovies). It's like an open-face pizza sandwich, so thick are the fillings. And it's enough for 1 1/2 people. So I'd bring a couple of friends, **"A much-loved pizza fun house strewn with '50s kitsch where everything is turned into a pizza."** order two combos and three bathtub-sized iced teas. I'd skip the pastas and the salad, which is overpriced for iceberg lettuce and bottled dressing. Maybe the regular pizza is as good a bargain or better, but the personal pizza serves more crust per portion, and that's the point of this pizza, after all.

For the two other Virginia branches of Generous George, which have mostly similar hours, menus and prices: 7031 Little River Turnpike, Annandale, VA, (703) 941-9600, and 6131 Backlick Rd., Springfield, VA, (703) 451-7111.

GEORGIA BROWN'S
950 15th St. NW, Washington, DC
(202) 393-4499

AMERICAN/SOUTHERN

Open: M-Th 11:30-11, F 11:30-midnight, Sat 5:30-midnight, Sun
11:30-11 **Entrees:** $11-$19 **Brunch:** Sun 11:30-3, $22
Dress: Casual **Credit Cards:** All major
Reservations: Recommended
Parking: Evening valet (fee) **Metro:** McPherson Square
Entertainment: Gospel or jazz group for Sun brunch

GEORGIA BROWN'S is a belle of the modern South. Grits and black-eyed peas appear as pan-fried cakes with a garnish of chopped tomato. The limas bite back rather than melt on the tongue, and the rice pudding has been crossbred with creme brulee. Collards were at first cooked so lightly that they crunched, but under pressure GEORGIA BROWN'S began to serve two options, so traditionalists could also enjoy them soft and sodden — the Southern way. The kitchen is inventing an upscale, nearly Northern repertoire of dishes. To its

" . . . an unprecedented mix of races, ages and salary levels in a luxurious downtown restaurant."

credit, it relies on fine ingredients — fresh shrimp with their heads on. But some of the Southern character has been lost in the shuffle. You might not even notice it's Southern, but just find GEORGIA BROWN'S a handsomely decorated, spacious and quiet upscale restaurant.

Something's clicking here, even if it's not the food — which improves if you make serious use of the peppered vinegar on the table. GEORGIA BROWN'S is a crossroads at lunchtime, an unprecedented mix of races, ages and salary levels in a luxurious downtown restaurant. It's the Florida Avenue Grill crowd with Gold Cards.

GERARD'S PLACE
915 15th St. NW, Washington, DC
(202) 737-4445

FRENCH

Lunch: M-F 11:30-2:30 **Entrees:** $13.50-$19
Dinner: M-Th 5:30-10, F-Sat 5:30-10:30 **Entrees:** $16.50-$32.50
Closed: Sun **Reservations:** Recommended
Credit Cards: All major **Dress:** Casual
Parking: Valet (fee) at dinner F-Sat **Metro:** McPherson Square

Behind a modest facade on McPherson Square, this is one of Washington's hidden glories. A small restaurant decorated mostly with sophisticated use of color, GERARD'S has a menu with no more than a dozen entrees, just over a dozen appetizers and a five-course tasting menu at dinner (with a vegetarian option). Even the descriptions of the dishes sound modest: an appetizer of sauteed scallops with a parsley mousse, an entree of vegetable ragout with spices.

But there is nothing modest about chef Gerard Pangaud's talent. Those scallops are so succulent and their fluffy and buttery parsley puree so vibrant that conversation stops as people react to their first bite. The vegetable ragout has an amazing quality: Each vegetable — asparagus, turnips, lentils, mushrooms and more

" . . . one of Washington's hidden glories."

— retains its firmness and flavor as if it has been cooked briefly and intact, yet all meld as if they had been simmered together with their pungent spices for days. It's a dish to convert the meat lover. On the other hand, roasted rack of veal is coddled with slow and careful cooking and garnished with a jewel of salsify-wrapped vegetables. Salmon, too, is cooked slowly so that its flesh barely gels, a beautiful texture. Then there are three different preparations of foie gras, as well as lobster in ravioli or poached with a flowery ginger-lime-sauternes sauce. And, keeping pace with the savories' quality, there are light and fragrant desserts, from a blood-orange soup to a lemon crepe soufflé, plus a sweet hint of the tropics in the fragile, crisp napoleon of pineapple, mango, coconut and caramel.

GERARD'S has dignity but no stuffiness, a honed menu that is as fascinating as many vastly larger. It's the kind of restaurant every gastronome hopes to have on a list of the little-known treasures of Paris.

GERMAINE'S
2400 Wisconsin Ave. NW, Washington, DC
(202) 965-1185

ASIAN/VIETNAMESE

Lunch: M-F 11:30-2:30 **Entrees:** $6-$11
Dinner: M-Th 5:30-10, F-Sat 5:30-11, Sun 5:30-10
Dinner Entrees: $7-$20 **Credit Cards:** All major
Reservation: Recommended
Dress: Casual **Parking:** Valet (fee) at dinner

When a restaurant plays to full houses year after year, you know there's good reason. At GERMAINE'S, which was Washington's first luxurious Southeast Asian restaurant when it opened decades ago, the reasons for its steady popularity include satays and Asian entrees grilled over an open hearth, and an emphasis on seasonal ingredients in a full range of Asian dishes, both classical and creative.

Now there's more. Chef-owner Germaine Swanson revisited her native Vietnam in recent years, and she brought back the inspiration for new dishes. She's added calamari sauteed with leeks and tomato, crisp whole fish with ginger and lime sauce, grilled fish buried under fresh dill on thin rice noodles, meats sautéed with lemon grass and onion and lunch specials of noodles and noodle soups. Not only has she revamped the menu, but she's redecorated the large, comfortable dining rooms so that they are as light and as colorful as her food.

" . . . it would be hard to choose wrong here."

GERMAINE'S modern cooking is not fusion food. It is rooted in tradition. But where other Vietnamese restaurants use beef jerky in their fiery, shredded, papaya salad, she uses crunchy, highly seasoned shreds of fresh beef. Her mango salad with sweet, juicy little shrimp is lusciously tropical. Her pine cone fish is among the most endearing fried fish imaginable. And no other curry in town is as succulent as her delicate and refined lamb curry.

The menu is dizzyingly long and varied, but given the top-quality seafood, the lean and tender meats, the abundance of fresh herbs and the charcoal grill, it would be hard to choose wrong here.

GOLDONI
1113 23rd St. NW, Washington, DC
(202) 293-1511

ITALIAN

Lunch: M-F 11:30-2 **Entrees:** $11-$19
Dinner: M-Th 5:30-10, F-Sat 5-10:30, Sun 5-10
Dinner Entrees: $15-$26 **Credit Cards:** All major
Reservations: Recommended **Dress:** Casual
Parking: Validated lot **Metro:** Foggy Bottom

When a chef breaks out on his own to open his first restaurant, often he's timid at first, or maybe too ambitious and experimental. In either case, I frequently wish I could wait a year to give him a review. Thus it's been with GOLDONI, where chef Fabrizio Aielli has come out from under the wing of Galileo's Roberto Donna. My most recent meal at GOLDONI, however, was a triumph, the work of an experienced chef comfortable in his surroundings and showing the range of his talent.

A layered appetizer of potato, eggplant and fontina cheese with a chunky light sauce of dried tomatoes and a garnish of fried basil leaves blended into it was a distillation of a Mediterranean garden on a plate. The pasta, fat stuffed tortelli with a heady black filling of portobello mushrooms and ricotta, was su-

> **"My most recent meal at Goldoni was a triumph."**

perb: delicate in texture, straightforward and powerful as the best of Italian cooking. A veal entree — tenderloin rolled with asparagus, frittata and prosciutto, poised on a glossy brown rosemary sauce with a garnish of asparagus and spinach — was far more elaborate. It was also astonishingly good. Then there was Aielli's signature: fish grilled whole until the skin is slightly charred and the flesh is steamy white, served with soft polenta and sautéed mushrooms. Nothing simpler, nothing more delicious.

For dessert, who could eat more than a little sorbet? But with such choices as herbed lemon or blackberry with pepper and red wine, one certainly wouldn't want to miss out. Cooking isn't all at GOLDONI. The food is enhanced by a dignified serving staff and a soaring, skylit, white dining room — modern and spare, yet lush with murals that hint of the Renaissance.

GREENWOOD
1990 K St. NW, Washington, DC
(202) 833-6572

AMERICAN/SEAFOOD   ♿

Lunch: M-F noon-3 **Entrees:** $9-$14
Dinner: M-Th 6-9, F-Sat 6-10 **Entrees:** $13-$18
Closed: Sun **Credit Cards:** All major
Reservations: Recommended **Dress:** Casual
Parking: Street **Metro:** Farragut West

GREENWOOD is tucked away at the top of the escalator in a K Street mini-mall, a hard site to love. At night the mall is deserted, but at lunchtime the scene is more lively. Chef Carole Greenwood has added heartwarming touches — stacks of cookbooks, each topped with an apple, and racks of newspapers. She's had rustic murals of giant fruits in Caribbean colors painted to cover the walls.

The menu is limited to seafood and vegetarian dishes — five or six appetizers, six or seven entrees. Greenwood has plucked flavors from the Middle East, Europe and Asia. Baklava is savory and vegetarian — with eggplant, potato, walnuts and a wild mushroom glaze. Thailand's pad thai is made with lobster, Vietnam's pho with mussels.

Greenwood's signature appetizer is a trio of dips — spicy lentil, Mediterranean carrot and beet-caraway — set on a plate of Belgian endive, baguette slices and purple olives. Among entrees, I've loved the cobb salad with its bright red tomatoes, good blue cheese, delicious smoky, crunchy strips of shiitake "bacon" and perfect asparagus. Another delicious, almost-meaty dish is the tuna burger, plain fare made glorious with coarsely chopped fish grilled as rare and juicy as a tuna steak. It's served with a tiny mound of delicious tomato salad, a whole head of oozy, soft, roasted garlic, fine tartar sauce and vinegary mango relish to spread on the bun, and a mountain of truly wonderful french fries. Seared tuna steak is a more glamorous and equally excellent variation.

Other dishes can be stodgy: a too-cute crab cobbler or misguided pad thai, heavy lentil dishes or underseasoned pastas. Salads and sandwiches are the creations most likely to live up to expectations. And desserts show Greenwood at her best, paying attention to the seasons with sweets featuring sweet potatoes, apples, pears, cranberries — whatever is best in the market.

THE GRILL FROM IPANEMA
1858 Columbia Rd. NW, Washington, DC
(202) 986-0757

BRAZILIAN   ♿

Dinner: M-Th 5-11, F 5-midnight, Sat 4-midnight, Sun 4-10
Dinner Entrees: $9-$16   **Brunch:** Sat-Sun noon-4, $12
Credit Cards: All major   **Reservations:** Recommended
Dress: Casual   **Parking:** Street   **Metro:** Dupont Circle

The name alone should be enough to make the restaurant, but THE GRILL FROM IPANEMA has a lot more going for it. This Brazilian restaurant sizzles, from its incendiary spiced shrimp to its pulsating late-night music.

If you're looking for an Adams-Morgan scene, hit the GRILL after 11 p.m. If you're looking for good Brazilian food in a quieter mode, go earlier. No matter the hour, though, the restaurant is witty and chic, with gauzy, man-made palm leaves waving from matte black tree trunks and tropical colors undulating across the dining room.

The *caipirinhas* — extra-strength clear liquor barely diluted with fresh limes — make you feel young and beautiful and on vacation. The menu offers plenty to choose from among the seafood stews with palm oil and coconut milk, the marinated grilled fish, the steaks well seasoned and seared, and chicken imbued

"This Brazilian restaurant sizzles, from its incendiary spiced sprimp to its pulsating late-night music."

with garlic and pepper. But there is one standout here. It's *feijoada*, the black bean stew filled with a mysterious conglomeration of sausages and pork parts, to be spooned over rice and complemented with orange wedges, shredded collards and grainy farofa. It's only served Wednesdays, Saturdays and Sundays; on the off days you'll have to make do with the elegant black bean soup. But that's like watching Black Orpheus on a small screen — or Dona Flor with only one husband.

HAAD THAI
1100 New York Ave. NW, Washington, DC
(Entrance on 11th Street)
(202) 682-1111

THAI   ♿

Lunch: M-F 11:30-2:30 **Entrees:** $6-$8
Dinner: M-F 5-10:30, Sat noon-10:30, Sun 5-10:30
Dinner Entrees: $7-$14 **Credit Cards:** All major
Reservations: Recommended **Dress:** Casual
Parking: Street **Metro:** Metro Center

Thai restaurants are no longer considered exotic. They've become our everyday restaurants, much as Chinese restaurants used to be. And the Washington area has so many terrific Thai restaurants that I probably could include a couple dozen among my favorites. So why single out HAAD THAI? Many Thai restaurants have food this good. And if there is one near you, you may want to substitute it for this.

What HAAD THAI has going for it is a downtown location — most Thai restaurants are in the suburbs, and few restaurants this good are within a short walk of the D.C. Convention

The dishes "remind you how delicious standard Thai food can be."

Center. But that's not all. It also has an imaginatively decorated dining room, circled by a pink and black mural of the Thai coast. The service is solicitous, too.

None of which would be important if the food weren't good. It is fairly simple — no lavish ingredients, just standard shrimp, scallops, beef, pork, chicken breast that's a little dry and vegetables that don't go much beyond carrots and snow peas. Yet it is seasoned with care, in light-textured sauces with plenty of fragrance and flavor. It shows refinement and delicacy. The hot dishes are boldly peppered but not macho-searing. The sweet sauces are a little too much so, but still compelling. These aren't dishes that teach you about the breadth and heights of Thai cooking; they merely remind you how delicious standard Thai food can be.

HEE BEEN
6231 Little River Turnpike, Alexandria, VA
(703) 941-3737

KOREAN/JAPANESE

Lunch: M-F 11:30-2:30 **Entrees:** $7-$8
Dinner: M-Th 2:30-11, F 2:30-11:30, Sat 11-11:30, Sun 11-10
Dinner Entrees: $10-$18 **Credit Cards:** All major
Reservations: Accepted **Dress:** Casual **Parking:** Free lot

Most restaurants become less ethnic over time, accommodating to American tastes and ways. HEE BEEN is the opposite. Its waitresses — dressed in gauzy silk, embroidered gowns — are these days less likely to speak enough English to explain the food, and much of the menu is not translated. Thus you have to guess whether the noodles are cold or hot, thick or thin, and whether you will get your barbecued short ribs already cooked or have the fun of cooking them yourselves.

That difficulty is balanced by the fact that HEE BEEN offers gracious service, bargain prices and a long list of intriguing Korean and Japanese dishes. If you don't know much about Korean food, you can make a memorable meal of just the barbecues. Short ribs are marinated in sweetened soy and garlic, cut off the bone and snipped into small tender squares. There's thinly sliced beef bulgogi, and pork either mild or spicy. Chicken, squid, fish, tongue, shrimp — many things are barbecued here. They come with a cup of miso soup and about 10 little dishes of condiments: *kim chee*, marinated bean sprouts, sesame spinach, and such. You also get leaves of lettuce and a sweet, thick bean sauce to spread on the lettuce before you wrap your meat and condiments into it. The meal ends with orange slices and a cup of cold, cinnamon-flavored buckwheat tea with three pine nuts afloat in it. Beyond barbecues, you can venture into *bibim baps* — rice bowls topped with meat and vegetables or even raw fish for you to toss together — or julienned raw beef with slivered pears, sesame and hot-sweet seasonings. You can explore the soup-stews, the vinegary and spicy, thin and wiry buckwheat noodle dishes, even that old standby, sushi.

The restaurant fills up early, often with families. Observe their tables for lessons in what to order and how to deal with the components of these complex and fascinating meals.

88

HIBISCUS CAFE
3401 K St. NW, Washington, DC
(202) 965-7170

CARIBBEAN

Dinner: T-Th 6-11, F-Sat 6-midnight **Entrees:** $11.50-$27.50
Closed: Sun-M **Credit Cards:** All major **Dress:** Casual
Reservations: Recommended **Parking:** Street

Even after years, diners at HIBISCUS CAFE tell owner Jimmie Banks how they miss Fish, Wings & Tings, his now-closed Adams-Morgan restaurant. Me, too. It was more convenient than HIBISCUS, bargain-priced and open for lunch. Now fans have to seek chef Sharon Banks' cooking in a far corner of Georgetown. It's still the best Caribbean food in town, though, and the parking is easy.

More important, the two-level dining room, with neon art and electric colors, is every bit as much fun as the old space. And Sharon's larder has moved upscale to quail, rack of lamb, filet mignon and lobster (served with shrimp in a spicy coconut butter sauce). Her menu is as vibrant as ever, composed of adventurous adaptations of Jamaican classics with her own personal touch. Caribbean creole sauces are teamed with seafood and modern tricolor pasta or with blackened fish. Jerk seasonings are employed not just on chicken wings but on grilled quail and chicken salad with mango vinaigrette. Curry spices flavor sauteed vegetables or shrimp. Scotch bonnet peppers are a regular, but this is not food that sears the mouth: It's so refined that you can taste the salmon under its gingered black beans and mango vinaigrette, and the smoked lamb chops are delicate in their midnight-dark sauce.

"I'd be happy to spend an evening just nibbling from an appetizer platter."

I'd be happy to spend an evening just nibbling from an appetizer platter: the Jamaican bread called *bake*, lightened and stuffed with slices of shark, accompanied by pineapple chutney (fabulous), whole head-on fresh shrimp marinated with scotch bonnet peppers (easily among the best shrimp in town), seafood fritters that are an uptown version of Caribbean conch fritters (terrific), fire-eating jerk buffalo wings, crisp fried calamari and delicate rock shrimp tempura with a scotch bonnet dipping sauce. This is a meal (and a bargain). The only problem is, you'll probably need to make another trip for dessert.

HITCHING POST

200 Upshur St. NW, Washington
(202) 726-1511

AMERICAN/SEAFOOD

Open: T-Sat noon-midnight **Closed:** Sun-M
Entrees: $3.75-$20 **Credit Cards:** No; cash only
Reservations: Accepted **Dress:** Casual

There's no sign in front of this big old house with its glassed-in porch. So the only indication that it's a restaurant might be the steady stream of customers from the Old Soldiers Home across the street. Inside, the focus is on the TV and bar. Everyone seems to know everyone else.

The menu is small: fried seafood, crab cakes in season, gumbo, beans with ham hocks and sandwiches. You'd never guess that the fried seafood was going to be remarkable, yet in important ways it is. The shrimp and scallops themselves are nothing

> **"This is a cozy, homey place that takes its time and can't be rushed."**

special — the usual frozen stuff. But they're coated with a terrific, light, greaseless batter and have been fried so quickly that they are utterly juicy. And while the gumbo is in need of seasoning, it's packed generously with seafood.

The vegetables are so delicious that you might make a meal of them. The macaroni and cheese is actually pasta shells, clinging to each other in a great cheesy ooze. Home fries are crisp and brown at the edges, soft and moist where they aren't crisp, and veined with caramelized onions. They're sensational. Greens have that essential, basic cooked-greens taste with no bitterness. And if you get the eggy, pickle-spiked potato salad the day it's made, it's memorable.

This is a cozy, homey place that takes its time and can't be rushed. Everything is prepared to order. And there's the TV to keep you entertained while it is.

HOUSTON'S
1065 Wisconsin Ave. NW, Washington, DC
(202) 338-7760

AMERICAN/SOUTHWESTERN   ♿

Open: M-Th 5-11, F 5-midnight, Sat 12-midnight, Sun 12-11
Entrees: $7-$25   **Credit Cards:** All major
Reservations: No   **Dress:** Casual   **Parking:** Street

There must be a huge shredder assigned its own quarters in the rear of HOUSTON'S so it can, without deafening anybody, just churn out endless julienned vegetables for countless salads.

Salads are big sellers here. And HOUSTON'S serves big salads, the kind that without a doubt make a meal. There's a Chef Salad — called the Sunbelt — with bacon, chicken and croutons added to the usual ham and cheese. There's the Club Salad, with fried chicken, bacon, egg and avocado instead of the usual turkey, bacon and ham. And there's a Caesar salad made with no egg. The most popular salad is said to be the grilled chicken salad. I can understand why. It's a big bowl piled with a mountain of ice-cold shredded greens — iceberg, romaine, red cabbage and spinach — and plentiful strips of chicken, with julienned carrots and tortilla strips for crunch. It's no doubt one of the most user-friendly salads you'll encounter: Everything is bite-sized and well tossed, so with a single stab of the fork you can get a cross section of tastes and textures.

"There must be a huge shredder assigned its own quarters in the rear of Houston's . . ."

And this being HOUSTON'S, the salads and other dishes are presented by cheerful and thoughtful servers, in a clubby wood-and-leather dining room. HOUSTON'S is easy to like. Of course, that's its problem. It gets too crowded and noisy, and no chicken salad, bowl of chili or even a top-notch burger is worth a long wait. That's why I like HOUSTON'S in the middle of the afternoon for a late lunch, when this high-quality chain restaurant is nearly mine alone to enjoy.

For the two other branches of Houston's: 7715 Woodmont Ave., Bethesda, MD, (301) 656-9755, and 12256 Rockville Pike, Rockville, MD, (301) 468-3535

HUNAN CHINATOWN
624 H St. NW, Washington, DC
(202) 783-5858

CHINESE

Lunch: Daily 11-3 **Entrees:** $7.50-$15
Dinner: Sun-Th 3-10, F-Sat 3-11 **Entrees:** $9-$25
Credit Cards: All major **Dress:** Casual
Reservations: Recommended for 6 or more
Parking: Street **Metro:** Gallery Place-Chinatown

We do not usually think of Chinatown as a place to go for a quiet meal in a soothing dining room. HUNAN CHINATOWN contradicts that preconception. It's decorated in shades of brown, from the tan quarry tile floor to the softly lit monochromatic artwork. The chairs are well upholstered, the service is **" . . . shows its stuff with tea-smoked duck."** dignified, and lest it sound cramped or dull, one wall of beveled mirrors expands the space and adds glitter.

Its menu is routine for a Hunan restaurant, but its food is certainly above average. Chicken is moist, sauces and dressings are clean and spicy, vinegary and sweet in proper balance. Dumplings are fine here. And as City Lights of China is the place to go in the city for Peking duck, HUNAN CHINATOWN shows its stuff with tea-smoked duck.

I MATTI
2436 18th St. NW, Washington, DC
(202) 462- 8844

ITALIAN

Lunch: M-Sat noon-2:30 **Dinner:** Sun-Th 5:30-10, F-Sat 5:30-10:30
Entrees: $10-$17 **Light Fare:** M-Sat 2:30-3, $4-$9
Late Nite: F-Sat 10:30-11, $6-$10 **Credit Cards:** All major
Reservations: Recommended **Dress:** Casual
Parking: Valet (fee) dinner T-Sat

It has taken me a long time to warm up to I MATTI. I've gradually been drawn back to it for the uniqueness of its menu, and once there I've appreciated the casual, nicely worn look of the place, no longer as self-consciously chic as it once was. This is a moderately priced Italian restaurant that strives far more than most.

Like most Italian restaurants, I MATTI has more dishes than one can

> **"It's the kind of food we imagine our Italian counterparts eating every day, and we envy them."**

hope to explore: antipasti, polentas with various cheeses or sausage, pizzas ranging from basic to cauliflower puree with smoked prosciutto and mozzarella, green salads with the likes of portobello mushrooms or beets and goat cheese, creative pastas and homey entrees. That's just the standing menu; the list of daily specials can run to two dozen.

I'd be glad to make a meal of soft polenta, maybe with buckwheat or raw egg yolk and cheese, but an appetizer or side dish will do. The pastas sound intriguing: ravioli with turkey and chestnuts, pumpkin tortelloni with salted ricotta. Wiry, chewy, handmade spaghetti is satisfying, with thick, meaty slices of portobello mushrooms and whole cloves of garlic.

Entrees have a twist — the shrimp cooked on a hot stone at the table with a garlic and orange sauce, the chicken stewed with rabbit sausage and chunks of mushroom as a kind of glamorous cacciatore. This is not cooking to pique one's aesthetic sense; it is sensible cooking of fine flavor and straightforward quality. It's the kind of food we imagine our Italian counterparts eating every day, and we envy them.

I RICCHI

1220 19th St. NW, Washington, DC
(202) 835-0459

ITALIAN

Lunch: M-Fri 11:30-2 **Entrees:** $13-$26.50
Dinner: M-F 5:30-10, Sat 5:30-10:30 **Entrees:** $15-$28.50
Closed: Sun **Credit Cards:** All major **Dress:** Casual
Reservations: Recommended **Parking:** Complimentary at dinner

I RICCHI watchers take readings on this Tuscan restaurant and complain that the tomato- or herb-topped focaccia is spongy these days (it is). They say that the place has gone downhill (it hasn't) and that the prices are outrageous (some are). And I, too, waver, grousing that the specials and such extras as coffee steeply escalate the bills.

Even so, I find both the food and the dining room satisfying and refreshing. The room has that simple, Tuscan, earth-toned dignity. And I love the down-to-earth pastas such as **"Everybody here seems to order seafood, and no wonder."** tortelloni stuffed with ricotta and spinach in just a wash of sage butter, or spaghettini in a thick, coarse and wonderful tomato sauce with mushrooms and lightly cooked shrimp.

As for entrees, everybody here seems to order seafood, and no wonder. It's cooked on a wood-burning grill. The fish is lightly crumbed and bursting with juices, perhaps topped with a bit of herbed tomato puree or with lemon and herbs. Shrimp grilled with lemon and fresh herbs, skewered with peppers and onions, is an invigorating light lunch. And while the accompaniments hardly vary — crusty fried polenta and some vegetables such as undercooked green beans on every dish — I can't resist that polenta. For dessert, a little sorbet or just that overpriced but properly thick espresso leaves me feeling deliciously virtuous.

IL RADICCHIO
1509 17th St. NW, Washington, DC
(202) 986-2627

ITALIAN   ♿

Open: M-Th 11:30 am-11, F-Sat 11:30-midnight, Sun 5-11
Entrees: $5.50-$14.50 **Credit Cards:** All major
Dress: Casual **Reservations:** No **Parking:** Street

I like the formula here: an endless bowl of spaghetti with the sauce or sauces of your choice bought à la carte from a long list, nicely wood-baked pizzas with a wide variety of toppings, a few sandwiches and specials from the rotisserie. I like the prices: modest. I like the environment: sweet colors and whimsical murals of barnyard animals and outsize vegetables. And now that the lines have abated and reason can reign, I like the service: breezy and efficient.

IL RADICCHIO is Roberto Donna's restaurant chain, and so far it's spread to Georgetown and Rosslyn. Nobody would compare it with his Galileo or I Matti.

" . . . this is Italian almost-fast food."

The chairs are flimsy, the floors are bare. The tomato sauces are likely to run thin, the rotisserie lamb (Thursday's special) is dreary, and the pasta is neither homemade nor exotically shaped — it's just plain old spaghetti. The point is that this is Italian almost-fast food — quick, easy and cheap, yet still authentic and good. For less than $10 you can eat admirable, yeasty, puffy pizza with respectable ingredients, or have as much pasta as you can eat, topped with seasonal sauces containing fresh herbs, in-the-shell seafood and reliably virginal olive oil.

For the two other branches of Il Radicchio: 1211 Wisconsin Ave. NW, Washington, DC, (202) 337-2627, and 1801 Clarendon Blvd,, Arlington, VA (703) 276-2627.

IL RITROVO
4838 Rugby Ave., Bethesda, MD
(301) 986-1447

MEDITERRANEAN   ♿

Lunch: M-F 11:30-2:30 **Entrees:** $6.75-$16
Dinner: M-Th 5:30-11, F-Sun 5:30-1 am **Entrees:** $8-$19
Credit Cards: All major **Dress:** Casual
Reservations: Recommended **Parking:** Free

The service is what makes this attractive, starkly white Mediterranean restaurant stand out from the crowd. Intelligent, gracious, efficient, helpful — the waitress can make the food taste all the better. And the food, which ranges the entire Mediterranean, is often fine.

Pretty salads piled into a pastry bowl, smoked salmon in a lime dressing, crusty spiced lamb sausage, sauteed portobello mushrooms or fried calamari are good beginnings. And if I had the choice, I'd go right from appetizers to dessert. The entrees include pastas, risotto, sometimes paella, and seafood poached, grilled or stewed. Moroccan scaloppini of lamb with mint is agreeable if unexciting. Salmon is in

"If I had the choice, I'd go right from appetizers to dessert."

danger of being left on the grill far too long. Vegetables have been cooked nearly to a paste, and couscous has been dry and bland, while paella has been excessively damp.

Yet it's worth sticking around for crepes suzette, a simple version but deliciously nostalgic. Or for a light ending, sometimes there's a whole peeled navel orange topped with syrup and preserved orange peel. Not glamorous enough? You can have it flamed.

INN AT LITTLE WASHINGTON
Middle and Main Streets
Washington, VA
(540) 675-3800

AMERICAN

Dinner: M-W-Th-F 6-9, Sat 5:30-9:30, Sun 4-9 **Fixed-Price:** $78-$98 **Closed:** T (except October, May) **Credit Cards:** MC,V **Reservations:** Required **Dress:** Jacket & tie

R are is the restaurant worth driving longer than an hour and spending more than $100 a person, but this one is. Even fewer acclaimed chefs stay close by their stoves in these days of chef-as-celebrity, but Patrick O'Connell does.

The INN is modeled on an English country house, every corner touched with beauty (don't miss the flowers in the restroom stalls). The service is a ballet, with no detail overlooked. Dinner is fixed-price, starting with a demitasse of memorable soup and perhaps a couple of canapes, then four courses and tiny after-dinner sweets. Appetizers are the problem: The seasonally changing menu contains so many daz-zling creations that in spring alone one might want to order the sea-food risotto, the quail with homemade blackberry vinegar, the tuna tartare and certainly the napoleon of lobster and potato crisps with caviar. But then there's also the lamb carpaccio, the luscious salmon five ways, the two versions of foie gras (one with ham and black cur-rants, the other cold, with pears and riesling jelly). And if either the *boudin blanc* with sauerkraut or the *vitello tonnato* is on the menu, I wouldn't dream of missing it.

While entrees are not necessarily the stars, the array is sumptuous. Seafood is abundant, typically lobster with grapefruit, native rockfish, or a tuna steak topped with foie gras. Red meat makes a strong show-ing with a magnificent tenderloin, rack of lamb in various guises, venison or veal. Then there's the unexpected vegetarian show stopper, what the menu bills as a "portobello mushroom pretending to be a filet mignon."

Desserts walk a tightrope between country-homey and urbane, with plenty of seasonal fruits represented in between the half-dozen choco-late selections. But the choice is made easy: You can sample seven desserts on one plate, or just settle for an after-dinner drink — and then wish to start this great show all over again.

JALEO
420 7th St. NW, Washington, DC
(202) 628-7949

SPANISH

Open: Sun-M 11:30-10 pm, T-Th11:30-11:30, F-Sat 11:30-midnight
Lunch Entrees: $7.50-$10 **Dinner Entrees**: $10.50-$15
Credit Cards: All major **Reservations:** Recommended
Dress: Casual **Parking:** Valet (fee) at dinner
Metro: Archives-Navy Memorial, Gallery Place-Chinatown
Entertainment: Flamenco dancers W evenings

Has JALEO slipped a notch? Could be. Its paella was soupy and chewy when I last tried it. But the waiter treated us as if this were our own private restaurant, and who would come here for anything but tapas, anyway? The tapas list is long and the prices are reasonable. How much can you complain about these complicated tidbits when most cost less than $5 and two could serve as lunch?

I'll never try enough JALEO tapas to render comprehensive judgment, particularly since I can't resist ordering some repeatedly. *Pinchitos* are a row of tiny, succulent, grilled chorizos on a bed of mashed potatoes enriched with olive oil and garlic. Potatoes are a sub-specialty: fried potatoes slathered with spicy tomato sauce and the garlic mayonnaise called *alioli,* cold potato salad, room-temperature Spanish omelet with onions and potatoes. Alioli also shows up on fried calamari and on bay scallops.

> **"I'll never try enough Jaleo tapas . . . since I can't resist ordering some repeatedly."**

Chicken is not to be missed when it's grilled and topped with green olives and capers. JALEO offers choices of cold and hot sausages, an array of Spanish cheeses, salads luxurious with beef or crab and bacon or refreshingly simple with endive, apples, almonds and cheese. Even so, I could suggest improvements; the mushroom tart is heavy and dry, though its hazelnut crust is utterly refined.

The attraction here is variety. You can order traditional favorites (shrimp with garlic) or recent inventions (duck with fresh plums); light dishes (tomato-cucumber salad with avocado) or heavy (lamb chop on garlic). Or you can sit in the shadow of painted flamenco dancers while you sip sangria, listen to flamenco music and slowly work your way through a plate of olives and *manchego* cheese.

JAPAN INN
1715 Wisconsin Ave. NW
Washington, DC
(202) 337-3400

JAPANESE

Lunch: M-F noon-2 **Entrees:** $8-$12
Dinner: M-Th 6-10, F-Sat 6-10:30, Sun 5:30-9:30
Dinner Entrees: $16-$36 **Credit Cards:** All major
Reservations: Recommended **Dress:** Casual **Parking:** Free lot

After a team of Japanese craftsmen built the vast, two-story JAPAN INN and filled it with subtly beautiful woodwork, the restaurant was fashionable for years. Then, as more — and more intimate — Japanese restaurants opened, attention shifted. There are other restaurants where you can find better sushi or more extensive menus. There are places where the food is more reasonably priced.

"There is no Japanese restaurant that offers greater comfort." And there are places with a greater sense of connection between the kitchen and the diner. There is no Japanese restaurant, though, that offers greater comfort. From the large parking lot to the sumptuous entry hall, from the greeting (and the goodbye) by half a dozen staff members to the choice of dining areas (regular, Japanese-style, sushi bar and table-top grilling), this restaurant exudes luxury. Even the main dining room is actually several small rooms that offer a feeling of privacy.

And the food is fine. You can order a sampling of five appetizers — the chef's whims — or choose something à la carte, notably the luscious, seared-yet-nearly-raw, thin-sliced yellowtail or the tangy salads. Entrees — in the regular dining room — include teriyakis, sushi and sashimi assortments, tempura (it's soggy and greasy, so move on) and cooked-at-the-table entrees such as *shabu shabu* and *yosenabe*. Unfortunately, these participatory dishes must be ordered for two, though a diner not sharing can come close enough to them with a bowl of *udon* noodles packed with seafood, vegetables and a barely poached egg floating in the fragrant broth.

JAPAN INN is no longer thrilling. But, as the preponderance of native Japanese dining there suggests, it is authentic and satisfying.

JIN GA
1250 24th St. NW, Washington, DC
(202) 785-0720

KOREAN   ♿

Lunch: Daily 11:30-2:30 **Entrees:** $8.95
Dinner: Daily 2:30-10:30 **Entrees:** $10-$15
Credit Cards : All major **Reservations:** Recommended
Dress: Casual **Parking:** Street **Metro:** Foggy Bottom

Formerly a Japanese restaurant priced sky-high, this Korean restaurant inherited beautiful furnishings, added more and staffed the dining room with waitresses in ethereal embroidered silk gowns. They don't necessarily understand the fine points of English, but they are gracious and try hard.

This restaurant has the only under-$10 soup-and-entree lunch in town that comes with a curved banquette and oversized table in a hushed and handsome dining room. Lunch specials are served on lacquered trays with chopsticks, but forks are available.

The cooking is very good, and even if you are doing it yourself on a tabletop grill, the waitresses guide you toward delicious results. The mainstays are *kalbi* (beef ribs) and *bulgogi* (thinly sliced beef), both of which arrive raw for you to grill (or already sizzling on metal platters at lunch). The menu goes on to grilled fish or fish stews, noodle soups and rice tossed with meat and vegetables. Most important, meals are accompanied by a tableful of condiments,

> **"This is a meal to nibble slowly, tasting a bit of this and a smidgen of that."**

including explosively peppery *kim chee*, lightly vinegared cucumbers and bean sprouts, tiny dried fish, and various peppered and vinegared vegetables.

This is a meal to nibble slowly, tasting a bit of this and a smidgen of that. The process is relaxing and sociable. The meal ends with a shallow cup of refreshingly cold, sweet, cinnamon-scented buckwheat tea with pine nuts floating in it. Dessert is superfluous.

JOCKEY CLUB
Ritz Carlton Hotel
2100 Massachusetts Ave. NW
Washington, DC
(202) 659-8000

FRENCH/AMERICAN

Breakfast: M-F 6:30-11, Sat-Sun 7-11:30 **Entrees:** $4.50-$14.50
Lunch: Daily noon-2:30 **Entrees:** $11.50-$23
Dinner: Daily 6-10:30 **Entrees:** $24.50-$30
Credit Cards: All major **Reservations:** Recommended
Dress: Jacket & tie **Parking:** Complimentary valet
Metro: Dupont Circle

In the JOCKEY CLUB'S 30-plus years here, the more it has changed, the more it has stayed the same. The hunt-club knick-knacks and horsy artwork are unwavering. The homey red-and-white tablecloths are still dressed with a single red rose. The yellow glass lanterns continue to throw a warm light against the cave-dark wood. This is the look of relaxed money, the restaurant version of silk cravats and tweed. Not that anyone would wear tweed at the JOCKEY CLUB. No, it's definitely dark suits. And handed-down pearls for the wives, gold lame blouses for the girlfriends. The waiters, too, are among the most formal in town.

The management wouldn't dare do away with the Traditional Baked French Onion Soup, the Caesar salad or the crab cakes that became famous three decades ago. "Our traditional *Pommes Souffles* are available," boasts the menu, and it invites you "to order any of our JOCKEY CLUB tableside specialties."

The grand-hotel standby, Dover sole, is the real thing here. Another mainstay is rack of lamb. The list of entrees continues with gently up-

" . . . the restaurant version of silk cravats and tweed." dated luxuries: lobster with beurre blanc, beef with *perigourdine* sauce and foie gras; steak with roasted garlic puree. At lunch there are also a couple of pastas, plus several salads that are warm or cold edible still lifes. All this comes at a hefty price, just as you'd expect in a grand hotel dining room where you can order the finest *pommes souffles* — potato chips puffed into balloons — outside of New Orleans, and where there's an entire cart of dessert choices, plus endearing little petits fours, with your coffee. Year after year.

KINKEAD'S

2000 Pennsylvania Ave. NW
Washington, DC
(202) 296-7700

AMERICAN/SEAFOOD

Lunch: M-Sat 11:30-2:30 **Entrees:** $9.50-$16
Dinner: Sun-Th 5:30-10, F-Sat 5:30-10:30 **Entrees:** $18-$22
Brunch: Sun 11:30-2:30, $22 **Credit Cards:** All major
Reservations: Recommended **Entertainment:** Jazz at dinner
Dress: Casual **Parking:** Complimentary valet after 5

With most seafood restaurants, the best you can hope is that they will stock high-quality fish and simply treat it kindly. KINKEAD'S takes a breathtaking leap to another plane. Mussels take on a new personality in a heady lemony broth with slices of garlic and chunks of chorizo. Grilled squid, my favorite appetizer here, shows its most tender moments under a light coating of crumbs and herbs, skewered and grilled and bedded down with creamy polenta. Grouper grows tiresome elsewhere, but at KINKEAD'S it's at its most silky, encouraged into liveliness with a crunchy cornmeal crust, a subtle tomatillo vinaigrette and a crisp-edged potato-poblano hash. Hardly ever would I order seafood ravioli after the countless bland, pasty versions I've tasted. But at

> **"Kinkead's takes a breathtaking leap to another plane."**

KINKEAD'S it's a star, the pasta filmy and the seafood filling haunting with shellfish flavors. What's more, teaming it with eggplant and fennel was inspired.

Did I say grilled squid is my favorite appetizer? So is KINKEAD'S seafood chowder. And its fried soft-shell clams with fried lemons. Not to mention its tuna *carpaccio* with shaved fennel salad. And did I call this a seafood restaurant? That's not to demean its meat dishes, which are far more ambitious than the usual seafood restaurant's nod to steak and chicken. Furthermore, the wine list shows a depth of wisdom, and the desserts are both homey and seasonal. Even the bread is excellent. The sprawling upstairs dining room at KINKEAD'S offers nooks and crannies, as well as a full view of the open kitchen. Its downstairs lounge invites diners who don't want to commit to a whole formal meal, and there's piano music to boot.

KOSHER EXPRESS
5065 Nicholson Lane, Rockville, MD
(301) 770-1919

MEDITERRANEAN KOSHER

Lunch: Sun-F 11-2 **Dinner:** M-Th 5-8
Closed: F evening, Sat **Entrees:** $4-$6.50
Credit Cards: None; cash or check
Reservations: No **Dress:** Casual
Parking: Free **Metro:** White Flint

K osher restaurants in this country took a great leap forward with the popularity of Middle Eastern food. Once vegetarian diets became prevalent and such dishes as hummus became familiar, restaurants no longer had to adjust American or European recipes to make them kosher. They could just serve Israeli food and swim right in the mainstream. Thus, as the old rye bread ad insisted, you don't have to be Jewish to love KOSHER EXPRESS.

Express it is. Most dishes are ready to heat in a display case. You order at the counter, pick a soft drink from the cooler and wait to take your food — in foam plastic plates and carryout boxes — to your table. The best deal is a sampler with your choice of five salads, a couple of pieces of falafel and a couple of rounds of pita. The salads range from Moroccan carrots to several eggplant concoctions, tabooli or hummus. And a side table has a fascinating array of condiments — including pickled lemons — to dress up your falafel sandwich.

"As the old rye bread ad insisted, you don't have to be Jewish to love Kosher Express."

KOSHER EXPRESS also serves hot dishes: fish fillet, some pastas and a vegetable couscous that's generous but badly in need of hot sauce or other seasoning. There are heavy but savory stuffed pizzas, and doughy *bourek*, those large pastries filled with eggplant, zucchini and the like. If you're looking for traditional, Eastern European sort of kosher cooking, there are potato knishes with real old-fashioned handmade dough. At the end of the meal, you'll appreciate the carryout boxes that have served as your plates. You're likely to have plenty of leftovers, and they're already packed to take home.

LA BERGERIE
218 N. Lee St., Alexandria, VA
(703) 683-1007

FRENCH   ♿

Lunch: M-Sat 11:30-2:30 **Entrees:** $11-$14
Dinner: M-Sat 6-10:30 **Entrees:** $15-$24
Closed: Sun **Credit Cards:** All major
Reservations: Recommended on weekends
Dress: Casual **Parking:** Validated discount

What a civilized restaurant. One has the sense that it has been here forever and that it will be here forever more, neither changing nor falling behind the times. The dining room is a calm space, traditional but not stuffy, festive but not flashy. The tables are arranged for privacy, and the chairs are designed for comfort. The brick walls are softened by paisley draperies and tapestries, and crystal chandeliers provide flattering light. Most important, the waiters operate as a team, familiar with their work and their customers.

The menu celebrates French traditions in such dishes as *garbure* — a soup of vegetables and white beans — along with a long list of fish in classic sauces, a real coq au vin and a few Basque specialties, including an almond-filled pastry among the sparkling, perfect tarts. The preparation is sure-handed and professional without being showy, though it carries on that traditional French failing of oversalted broth. The vegetables are particularly nice — diced potatoes sauteed with mushrooms, perhaps, and a mix of buttery fresh cauliflower, broccoli and carrots. Simple and just right. This is not newsworthy food, or food to draw raves; rather, it's consistently agreeable, year after year.

"This is not newsworthy food, or food to draw raves; rather, it's consistently agreeable, year after year."

LA CHAUMIERE
2813 M St. NW, Washington, DC
(202) 338-1784

FRENCH ♿

Lunch: M-F 11:30-2:30 **Entrees:** $9-$14
Dinner: M-Sat 5:30-10:30 **Entrees:** $14-$18
Closed: Sun **Credit Cards:** All major
Reservations: Recommended **Dress:** Casual
Parking: Validated for 2 hours at Four Seasons, evenings

This Georgetown French restaurant, two decades old, is best enjoyed on a wintry day when you crave coziness. Ask for a table near the stone fireplace; since it is in the center of the room, your request should be easy to accommodate. And order something richly old-fashioned.

On Wednesday that could be couscous, on Thursday cassoulet. And every day it could be snails with garlic butter or puffy, airy *quenelles de brochet* in dark, lobster-enriched sauce. There's a sort of bouillabaisse, though sharper and more peppery than is traditional. Some days you'll find delicate *boudin blanc*; other days the special might be dark blood sausage. Here's a menu that regularly features tripe or rabbit or brains, and often serves dishes that require braising or stewing, the long cooking methods that have been upstaged by grilling.

"Ask for a table near the stone fireplace . . . And order something richly old-fashioned."

That said, it must be added that the food can be lackluster, sometimes stodgy and less exciting than it sounds. This is a restaurant whose creative energy has settled into a cozy somnambulance. Still, LA CHAUMIERE has always been known for a wine list that's intelligently chosen and fairly priced; even the wines by the glass are high-quality bargains. The service is thoughtful and the dining room is comforting, especially in sight of the blazing fire.

LA COLLINE
400 N. Capitol St. NW, Washington, DC
(202) 737-0400

FRENCH   ♿

Breakfast: M-F 7-10   **Entrees:** $5-$8.75
Lunch: M-F. 11:30-3   **Entrees:** $8.75-$16.25
Dinner: M-Sat 6-10   **Entrees:** $18.75-$21
Closed: Sun   **Credit Cards:** All major   **Dress:** Casual
Parking: Free garage after 5   **Metro:** Union Station

The more chefs come and go in this city, the more we ought to appreciate those with staying power. And Robert Greault at LA COLLINE, above all, deserves tribute. His LA COLLINE is a last bastion of such French classics as *quenelles de brochette Nantua* and *tripes a la mode de Caen* (updated with fresh morels in season). But he hasn't rested on his laurels after all these years. His menu is also modern enough to encompass current trends. He smokes his own salmon and trout, he stuffs ravioli with lobster and shiitake mushrooms and he dresses his tortellini with smoked portobellos and sundried tomatoes; he flavors his chicken salad with Asian peanut dressing in a Francophile bon bon chicken and his shrimp comes with Thai curry sauce. Knowing there isn't much you can do to improve on simply sauteed soft-shell crabs with a squeeze of lemon, he doesn't do much, just sprinkles them with an inspired mixture of pistachios, pecans and walnuts. If you're looking for richness, head right for the terrine of fresh foie gras, the real thing, at a mere $8.75 for buttery luxury. Or remind yourself of the heartiness of authentic onion soup under a blanket of cheese.

If you prefer something light, salmon is delicately cooked and subtly dressed with a julienne of leeks and a light moistening of vermouth sauce. That will leave room for a dessert from the irresistible array on the rolling cart. Key lime pie? It's as tart as you could wish. Lattice-crust apple pie? There's no flakier puff pastry, no more tangy and fragrant apple filling than LA COLLINE'S.

As befits Capitol Hill, LA COLLINE is quiet and discreet, its high-backed leather booths allowing privacy and its quietly dignified environment endowing every conversation with a sense of importance. No wonder it has staying power.

LA FERME
7101 Brookville Rd., Chevy Chase, MD
(301) 986-5255

FRENCH   ♿

Lunch: T-F noon-2 **Entrees:** $5.75-$10.75
Dinner: T-Sat 6-10, Sun 5-9 **Entrees:** $15.75-$20.75
Closed: M **Reservations:** Recommended
Credit Cards: All major **Dress:** Casual
Parking: Free lot **Entertainment:** Evening pianist

When you want to get out of town but not too far, LA FERME fills the bill. Even though it's on the edge of the city, it's a spacious, slightly countrified, comfortable and dignified dining room with a vine-covered terrace, in a quiet spot along Chevy Chase's pretty Brookville Road. And it's immensely popular for leisurely suburban lunches. The service is polished and the food is sedately French. Here's a place to take a visiting aunt or to have a family reunion. It has something for everyone, plenty of panache, and moderate prices for its level of luxury.

You can count on LA FERME for gently grilled, absolutely fresh fish —say, swordfish or Dover sole. Along with the expected meat offerings, it also lists venison and cha-

"Here's a place to take a visiting aunt or to have a family reunion."

teaubriand. Its veal is sauced with calvados and mushroom cream, its duck with cider and turnips, its liver with port wine and truffles. And the plates are garnished with a colorful bouquet of vegetables — though they are sometimes less luscious than picturesque. LA FERME serves the classics — onion soup, lobster bisque, even a refined variation of bouillabaisse. And it ventures tentatively into new tastes, creating a deliciously rich lunchtime pasta with duck confit and a touch of Southwestern chili heat.

Even so, there are no bold breakthroughs here. This is nice food, considerately served, reliable if not dazzling. No wonder LA FERME has thrived through the decades.

LA FOURCHETTE
2429 18th St. NW, Washington, DC
(202) 332-3077

FRENCH

Lunch: M-F 11:30-4 **Entrees:** $7-$21
Dinner: M-Th 4-10:30, F-Sat 4-11, Sun 4-10 **Entrees:** $9-$21
Credit Cards: All major **Dress:** Casual
Reservations: Recommended on weekends **Parking:** Street

When spring comes, I think of sitting at a sidewalk table and eating garlicky, anise-scented bouillabaisse. When winter threatens, I think of a warm, old-brick dining room and a steaming tureen of bouillabaisse. In either case, I think of LA FOURCHETTE, a small nugget of France in Adams-Morgan

LA FOURCHETTE looks like a Parisian cafe of old, a cafe with its own cafe — in mural form — wrapping around the walls. Its tables have no cloths, its chairs have no cushions, but it has an air of tradition and comfort. Most important, its menu lists such nearly forgotten French classics as veal tongue with mustard cream, sweetbreads with mushrooms, crepes with seafood or with chicken in cream sauce, and that immense

" . . . a small nugget of France in Adams Morgan."

and satisfying bouillabaisse. On my last visit, the menu listed four versions of mussels: vinaigrette, provençal, mariniere and simmered in basil cream with gnocchi and zucchini.

LA FOURCHETTE serves such appetizers as a serious onion soup, a deliciously fragile crab and spinach flan with old-fashioned lobster sauce, pâtés and snails and garlic sausage with potatoes in vinaigrette. Among the entrees there are humble omelets and grand Dover sole. Prices are modest — Dover sole at trout prices, *entrecôte bercy* at hamburger prices. And the cooking is endearingly authentic and sometimes wonderful. Where else can you find on one dessert tray such traditional choices as floating island, filled crepes or tart tatin? As for me, I can't resist the extravagant restraint of the orange sections in Grand Marnier with caramelized orange peel.

LA MICHE
7905 Norfolk Ave., Bethesda, MD
(301) 986-0707

FRENCH   ♿

Lunch: T-F 11:30-2 **Entrees:** $9.50-$13
Dinner: M-Sat 6-9:45, Sun 5:30-8:45 **Entrees:** $17-$23
Closed: Sun in August **Reservations:** Recommended
Credit Cards: All major **Metro:** Bethesda
Parking: Valet (fee) for lunch and dinner

While countless French restaurants have come and gone, LA MICHE has stayed for almost two decades, a restaurant that evokes the French countryside with its baskets hanging from the ceiling and cozy provincial furniture. The menu is long, the list of daily specials is longer, and over the years the style has been adjusted to today's lighter tastes. No longer does puff pastry dominate the appetizer list, though it prettily garnishes many dishes.

Yet lightness isn't carried very far. The appetizer list features creamy, eggy mousses and flans made of spinach or foie gras, and sauces are plentiful. LA MICHE remains distinctly old-fashioned.

In many cases that's to its advantage. If you want to find a traditional lobster bisque, with the intense flavor that can only be extracted from the shells, this is the place to find it. And if you like your spinach enveloped in creamy custard and enriched with butter sauce, the spinach flan here will leave you

"La Miche often pleases but seldom excites."

dreaming of more. Along with today's simple grilled fish, LA MICHE still prepares yesteryear's coq au vin (unfortunately, it exhibits yesteryear's habit of overcooking the chicken). Seldom does lamb taste so distinctly and wonderfully like lamb as when LA MICHE serves its long, thin tenderloins infused with garlic and poised on a bed of pale green flageolets. And where else nowadays could you find a plate of canapes available among the appetizers?

The menu is sumptuous. But the cooking isn't always so. LA MICHE often pleases but seldom excites. It attempts so much but carries the cooking out as if in a rush. When I order next time I'm there, maybe I'll just ask: What does the chef really feel like cooking tonight?

LA TOMATE
1701 Connecticut Ave. NW, Washington, DC
(202) 667-5505

ITALIAN   ♿

Lunch: Daily 11:30-4 **Entrees:** $11-$12
Dinner: M-Th. 4-10:30, F-Sat 4-11, Sun 4-10
Dinner entrees: $11-$20 **Credit Cards:** All major
Reservations: Recommended **Dress:** Casual
Parking: Street **Metro:** Dupont Circle

In spring, tulips bloom in front of this glass-walled, wedge-shaped restaurant. It becomes the most visible dining spot on Connecticut Avenue. Inside, flowered vinyl tablecloths suggest spring even in winter. Vinyl? Yes, but dressed up with cloth napkins. LA TOMATE is light, bright and lively. It has all the activity and bustle of a trattoria, with tables so small and close that you'll have no trouble seeing a preview of your possibilities on your neighbors' plates, but it's not so noisy you'd have trouble conversing. If you seek a little less noise, ask for a table upstairs. Service is quick and unobtrusive.

The menu is Italian despite the restaurant's French name, and the dishes are largely familiar standards. Regulars praise the chicken-vegetable soup and the pastas. But zucchini croquettes are so heavy as to threaten to gum up the conversation. Tomato sauces and spinach dishes are good bets. Seek also the simple dishes such as butterflied trout,

> **" . . . a basic, modestly priced trattoria despite a few gastronomic pretensions."**

smoked on the premises, with lemon and herbs. Vegetables are stodgy, and anything fancy is risky. This is a basic, modestly priced trattoria despite a few gastronomic pretensions.

LADDA
4201 Connecticut Ave. NW, Washington, DC
(202) 686-9999

THAI   ♿

Lunch: M-F 11:30-2:30 **Entrees:** $6-$8
Dinner: M-F 4:30-10:30, Sat-Sun noon-10:30
Dinner entrees: $8-$13 **Credit card**s: All major
Reservations: Recommended for 6 or more
Dress: Casual **Parking:** Street **Metro:** UDC-Van Ness

Thai cooks, using hot chilies and cold lettuce, have perfected the marriage of fire and ice in their appetizer salads of beef, seafood or chicken. The best introduction to Thai salad art is *larb*, finely chopped chicken tossed with onions, scallions, hot green chilies and cilantro and dressed with lemon or lime juice. It's served with leaves of iceberg lettuce, and the idea is to spoon some of the larb onto a lettuce leaf, wrap it up into something approximating the shape of an egg roll and eat it by hand. Chances are it will be a mess, but a most delectable mess. At LADDA, the chicken is warm, cooked fresh so that the chopped bits are juicy. The onion and scallion taste almost sweet against the lemon and chilies, and the lettuce mutes the heat and the acid. This deceptively plain little plate of food creates high drama when it comes to taste.

LADDA also serves the usual charcoal-grilled beef salad, mixed seafood in a lime-chili marinade and cold shrimp with lots of onions on a bed of dark green lettuce in a ketchup-red chili and lemon-grass dressing. The shrimp salad appetizer is only

"Chances are [the larb] will be a mess, but a most delectable mess."

on the dinner menu, and while you can order it at lunch, I'd wait for dinner. It's the dinner chef who has mastered this aromatic, tart-hot dressing. When this shrimp salad is dressed right, it's sweet, sour, hot and cold. Beyond appetizers, the standout dish at this glossy little Thai restaurant is chicken-coconut soup, fiery and fragrant, the coconut milk adding the image of sweetness with the actuality.

LAFAYETTE
Hay-Adams Hotel
800 16th St. NW, Washington, DC
(202) 638-2570

AMERICAN

Breakfast: M-F 6:30-11, Sat-Sun 7-11 **Entrees:** $11-$14
Lunch: M-Sat 11:30-2 **Entrees:** $14-$25.75
Afternoon Tea: Daily 3-4:30, $15 **Brunch:** Sun 11:30-2, $35
Pre-Theater: Daily 5:30-6:30, $30 & $40 **Credit Cards:** All major
Reservations: Recommended **Dress:** Jacket recommended
Parking: Complimentary valet at dinner **Metro:** Farragut North
Entertainment: Pianist evenings and Sun brunch

Under a crystal-chandelier sky, enclosed by vanilla walls and dressed in floor-length tablecloths and gold brocade, the LA-FAYETTE dining room, through its soaring windows, keeps a close eye on the White House just across Lafayette Square.

The menu is loaded with "Health Smart Selections." They're also taste-bud smart. Spaghetti squash usually tastes like melon rinds run through a shredder. But chef Martin Saylor coaxes the best out of this winter vegetable. Lobster and pearl couscous is the most luxurious of the health-conscious choices; Saylor proves that once in a while somebody can embellish plain lobster and make you glad he did. Among the more devil-may-care dishes is smoked trout hash, an irresistible appetizer with its subtly smoky and vinaigrette-sharpened diced potatoes, carrots and shards of trout under a top hat of foie gras and fried quail egg. An appetizer that could serve as an entree is the phyllo tart piled with a buttery frenzy of dark, woodsy mushrooms. More extravagant entrees include such delicious constructions as thick veal medallions on arti-choke puree, draped with a puffy brown parmesan soufflé, or filet mi-gnon under a beret of mushroom-stuffed ravioli.

And if you're not the least concerned with restraint, there's afternoon tea. Choose among 10 teas, properly brewed and poured into your cup through a silver strainer by an attentive and dignified waiter. Thought-fully nibble very British and totally unseasoned, crustless sandwiches. Scrape every driblet of thick cream onto an impossibly light and rich scone, and wonder where such fragrant strawberries were grown. Try every offering on the trolley of tiny pastries and cookies; then have one more lemon tartlet, because you will hardly ever find another so wonderfully sour and lemony.

L'AUBERGE CHEZ FRANCOIS
332 Springvale Rd., Great Falls, VA
(703) 759-3800

FRENCH

Dinner: T-Sat 5:30-9:30, Sun 1:30-8 **Full Dinner:** $29.75-$38.50
Closed: M **Reservations:** Inside, needed 4 weeks in advance
Credit Cards: All major **Dress:** Jacket & tie **Parking:** Free

Elsewhere, people are talking about a resurgence of French restaurants. In Great Falls, French has long prevailed. In its more than two decades, L'AUBERGE CHEZ FRANCOIS has hardly ever had empty tables, certainly not on weekends. That has less to do with food than with a sense of celebration and generosity. The dining room looks like a Gallicized setting for "The Sound of Music," with waitresses in dirndls and waiters in red vests. The menu is enormous, and the fixed-price dinners include garlic bread, herbed cottage cheese, a generous salad, a tart palate-cleansing sorbet and after-dinner cookies — all in addition to the usual appetizer, entree and dessert. Portions are abundant, prices are moderate and service is more than considerate.

Even more, the food is good. Sometimes it's wonderful, other times merely pleasant. Anything with sauerkraut — the choucroute with duck, pork and foie gras or the smoked fish version as an appetizer — benefits from the chef's lifelong understanding of Alsatian cooking. And if nobody will share the restaurant's signature salmon *en croûte* with you, a lone diner can sample its cousin, salmon with fish mousse. Remember that Alsatians are experts at foie gras and duck confit, and order accordingly. With this long list of traditional and modern dishes, light fish and richly sauced steaks, classics from bouillabaisse to cassoulet to kidneys with mustard, choosing is difficult. Desserts are no easier. How can one pass up the fresh-plum tart? The lime tart? The intensely chocolate creations or the towering souffles?

On my latest visit the soft-shell crab was flabby and not worth its surcharge, the squab was overcooked and the meringue-like *kugelhopf* was too sweet. But in such a big, busy restaurant, unevenness is no surprise. And the flaws are easily forgiven; after starting a meal with raspberry-flavored champagne in CHEZ FRANCOIS' garden, even an ordinary meal can seem ambrosial.

L'AUBERGE PROVENCAL
Route 2 Box 203, White Post, VA
1-800-638-1702, (540) 837-1375

FRENCH   ♿

Dinner: W-Sat 6-10:30, Sun 5-9 **Fixed-Price:** $57
Closed: M-T **Credit Cards**: All major **Dress:** Jacket required
Reservations: Recommended **Parking:** Free

This small inn looks like just what I would hope to find at the end of a drive in the country. The public rooms are divided into charming spaces, from a cozy lounge with sofas for lingering before or after dinner to French provincial dining rooms with large windows overlooking a peaceful field. It also has a gift shop, in case the French provincial pottery proves irresistible.

Yet this is no casual drop-by-for-a-bite country eatery. It serves grand and expensive fixed-price dinners of five courses, including a palate-cleansing sorbet before the entree. The presentations are dramatic and architectural, with pastry ladders and waving branches of herbs. Seafood is whipped into

> **" . . . just what I would hope to find at the end of a drive in the country."**

mousses, perhaps with nuggets of oyster hidden inside. Sweetbreads might be moistened with port sauce and sprinkled with capers in sharp contrast. Much of the cooking, though, seems to have the flavor refined right out of it. I preferred L'AUBERGE PROVENCAL'S cooking in its earlier, more robust mode.

In general, appetizers, soups and salads outshine the entrees, and dessert is the highlight. If you consider it worth a long ride and a $150-a-couple tab for a bucolic Old World setting and masterly service, you'll at least be rewarded in the end with a truly fine creme brulee.

114

LAURIOL PLAZA
1801 18th St. NW, Washington, DC
(202) 387-0035

MEXICAN/SPANISH

Open: M-Th 11:30-11, F-Sat 11:30-midnight, Sun. 3-11
Entrees: $6-$16 **Brunch:** Sun 11-3, $5-$9
Credit Cards: All major **Dress:** Casual **Parking:** Validated
Reservations: Recommended M-Th; accepted until 7 pm F-Sat

Success definitely has spoiled LAURIOL PLAZA, but I still love to sit outside in the L-shaped sidewalk cafe. Its site remains one of the most lively urban corners in the city. And the ultra-thin, crisp chips with a tart margarita or pisco sour are enough to warrant an evening of people watching.

The once-Spanish menu has gone Tex-Mex, with fajitas upstaging the Spanish dishes. Those fajitas are actually very good. Amend that: The fajita meat is excellent, smoky and rare. But the guacamole is bland, the *pico de gallo* more so. And the formerly wonderful chile relleno, as well as ordinary tacos, haven't the zest they once had.

What does that leave? *Masitas de puerco* are still pungent, the chunks of tender meat permeated with bitter orange. And I retain hope for the other Spanish dishes. While most of the crowd tucks into enchiladas, tacos and fajitas, I'm more interested in duck with tart orange sauce or garlicky chicken. As long as the weather allows, all of us would rather line up for an outdoor table than dine indoors here.

LAVANDOU

3321 Connecticut Ave. NW, Washington, DC
(202) 966-3002

FRENCH

Lunch: M-F 11:30-2:30 **Entrees:** $9.50-$13
Dinner: Sun-Th 5-10, F-Sat 5-11 **Entrees:** $13-$17
Pre-Theater: Daily 5-6:30, $15
Credit Cards: All major **Reservations:** Recommended
Dress: Casual **Parking:** Free **Metro:** Cleveland Park

This Provençal restaurant is so small you might have to squeeze past diners to reach your table, and when it is crowded, the close quarters and low ceiling turn it into an oven. So why is it continually popular? Its Cleveland Park neighbors love its countrified French look, its menu of little-known Provençal dishes and its gentle prices. Regulars find the service friendly. And those who know their way around the menu find some very appealing food.

Newcomers, on the other hand, have to put up with erratic service — sometimes the waiters are jolly, but it can be difficult to flag them when you need a drink, a fork or the check. And the cooking is no more consistent than the service. An appetizer of chickpea crepe is topped with zesty, well-dressed crab meat and capers, while an entree of lentil pancake with grilled sweetbreads tastes as if the sweetbreads had been boiled rather than grilled, then served without seasoning.

> **"Your second visit is likely to be better than your first."**

The choices are adventurous, with fish dishes such as grilled tuna in a feisty, aged vinegar sauce on a bed of white-bean puree, or bouillabaisse of cod, and old-fashioned meat preparations such as daube of beef, lamb stew with artichokes and bacon-wrapped pork tenderloin cooked in Provençe's bandol wine. So LAVANDOU can be worth the inconveniences, and your second visit is likely to be better than the first.

LE CAPRICE
2348 Wisconsin Ave. NW
Washington, DC
(202) 337-3394

FRENCH

Lunch: M-F 11:45-2 **Entrees:** $8-$9.50
Dinner: M-Th 6-10, F-Sat 6-10:30, Sun 6-9:30 **Entrees:** $16.50-$22
Credit Cards: All major **Reservations:** Recommended
Parking: Valet (fee) after 6 pm

It's one of the smallest spots in town for fine dining, yet its kitchen boasts two chefs, both young Alsatians. LE CAPRICE is a tiny gem, polished brighter than ever. Alsace suggests foie gras. And here it is superb, satiny and buttery, served with toasted brioche. That region's frog legs are boned and wrapped in puff pastry, though the best part of this appetizer is the salad with creamy dressing and a fluff of fresh dill. Onion tarts are famous in Alsace, and LE CAPRICE'S version with Roquefort is deliciously caramelized, oozing and earthy. Surely a rich, meaty choucroute will appear in winter, and the Alsatian wines here are tempting — not least for their modest prices. These regional specialties are endearing, all the more so for being served in two dining rooms as romantic as a chocolate box or on the sidewalk terrace.

The rest of the long menu, though, is inconsistent and often over-reaching — particularly the elaborate entrees such as lobster and shiitake ravioli, tuna with Provençal vegetables, duck with cassis vinegar sauce or tournedo perched on a lacy potato pancake with layers of eggplant, tomato and zucchini alongside. Yet disappointments fade in light of the desserts. In this city smothered with chocolate desserts, LE CAPRICE'S three-chocolate terrine is still a standout. A souffléd raspberry tart is flowing and creamy in its flaky crust, and a plate of assorted miniature desserts — with whipped cream pipings to keep the sauces from overlapping — is like a display of edible fireworks — a dazzler.

> **" . . . a tiny gem, polished brighter than ever."**

Mondays are couscous nights, and at lunch the buffet is as fresh and appealing as a picnic. The everyday menu has seasonal, fixed-priced dinners and à la carte listings. So whatever the day, whatever the hour, a meal at LE CAPRICE is always an event.

LE GAULOIS
1106 King St., Alexandria, VA
(703) 739-9494

FRENCH   &

Open: M-Th 11:30-10:30 pm, F-Sat 11:30-11 pm
Closed: Sun **Entrees:** $5.75-$19.50
Credit Cards: All major **Reservations:** Recommended
Dress: Casual **Parking:** Free after 6

Once a cozy French restaurant downtown, LE GAULOIS is large and anonymous in Alexandria, with lots of wood, plenty of bustle and no particular charm. It hardly matters, though, for its menu is well loved.

Those who know their way around start with a modestly priced and well-chosen wine from France or Virginia, and pick their dinner not from the printed menu but from the long, typed list of specials. There might be six seasonal soups in addition to the three regulars. Appetizers are likely to include such seldom encountered and very French dishes as brains in vinaigrette. Entrees follow in seasons, and in winter tend to be rich and homey concoctions such as bouillabaisse, cassoulet or puff pastry filled with seafood and perhaps sweetbreads in a creamy, aromatic wine sauce. In summer, a myriad of meat and seafood salads appear, though richness is not totally left behind: Amidst the updated composed salads you'll also find rich and nostalgic dishes such as airy, creamy quenelles. Desserts are home-style French classics.

Perfect? No. I've had tired pâtés and pastries. And LE GAULOIS is too busy a place for the welcome to exhibit much warmth. Still, it is efficient, and often enough the real welcome is in the cooking.

118

LE LION D'OR
1150 Connecticut Ave. NW, Washington, DC
(202) 296-7972

FRENCH

Dinner: M-Sat 6-10 Entrees: $20-$32
Closed: Sun Reservations: Required
Credit Cards: All major Dress: Jacket & tie
Parking: Validated garage Metro: Farragut North

Chef Jean-Pierre Goyenvalle is the keeper of the flame. He's the last chef from Washington's heyday of French restaurants who is still serving elegance in all its facets: tableside carving, pastry wrappers and monumental soufflés. His menu is long enough to anticipate every taste, and if he doesn't always dazzle us with creativity, he satisfies us with impeccable details. And, if you choose carefully, he can suit today's taste for lightness and simplicity. There is, for example, a whole fish baked in a pastry crust so the flavors and juices are sealed in. It is spare perfection even before you spoon on a bit of beurre blanc. More sumptuous are roasted pigeon, tender and gamy, moistened with a light touch of brown sauce and surrounded with sauteed wild mushrooms, and such seasonal game dishes as guinea hen in a lightened variation on coq au vin, or pheasant — served with a croustade of magnificently seasoned liver.

LE LION D'OR offers a daunting list of daily specials, appetizers of lobster or crab, entrees of fish, meat and game, and perfectly cooked, simply prepared vegetables. On the menu is foie gras in half a dozen guises: wrapped in ravioli, tossed with the finest handmade noodles or artichokes, or even with lobster and haricots verts, not to mention as a terrine. And don't miss the tiny corn pancakes topped with oysters, caviar and beurre blanc. As entrees, meat and fowl tend to be more satisfying than most of the fish dishes, and old-fashioned dishes more successful than modern. For dessert there's a rolling cart of highly professional pastries. But that's not the end. In remembrance of another era, coffee is accompanied by an assortment of butter cookies, a tray of sugared nuts and chocolates, even tiny pastries and eclairs if you hit it right. Prices are high, except for some stunning bargains among the older wines. What makes the tab worthwhile is the sumptuousness of the dining room and service, the tableside carving, boning and flaming. Safe from the winds of trends, dinner at LE LION D'OR is solid in its tradition.

LE REFUGE
127 N. Washington St., Alexandria, VA
(703)548-4661

FRENCH

Lunch: M-Sat 11:30-2:30 **Entrees:** $7-$14
Dinner: M-Sat. 5:30-10 **Entrees:** $14-$20
Pre-Theater: T-Th 5:30-7, $16 **Closed:** Sun
Credit Cards: All major **Dress:** Casual
Reservations: Recommended **Parking:** Street

I'm not sure how LE REFUGE does it. It crams in so many tables that neighbors become intimates, and the walls are decorated with empty cheese boxes and wine bottles. Yet it's still one of the most charming French restaurants in town. Despite the come-on of unopened wine bottles on the tables whining for you to buy them, and the waiters' tired-looking open-collar shirts, LE REFUGE looks Parisian. Its pink tablecloths and vases of small flowers brighten the scene a bit, but mostly it's the friendly bustle that does the job.

The regular menu is a 1950s American version of a French restaurant: beef Wellington, salmon in puff pastry, onion soup, pâté, bouillabaisse and chicken in mustard cream. The specials, though, are more modern. And the list of options is long, though the quality of the cooking varies so much from dish to dish that it is hard to recommend a strategy for ordering. One oddity works in your favor: LE REFUGE is one of the rare restaurants whose entrees are the best dishes. So you might as well order some sure bet such as a salad to start, and concentrate on the second course. While the leg of lamb is cut so thin you suspect a machine did the job, it is well infused with garlic and moistened with a nice brown sauce. What solidifies the perennial appeal of LE REFUGE, though, are the vegetables. A whole array surrounds the entree: a rosette of whipped sweet potatoes, a fan of zucchini and tomato slices, florets of butter-drenched broccoli and satisfying, old-fashioned potatoes lyonnaise all on one plate.

For dessert, you can forget the '90s with ice cream-stuffed profiteroles or a wedge from a giant fruit tart. Don't plan on lingering for the evening, though. You'll probably be shamed into relinquishing your place to the waiting diners looking hungrily at your table.

LE RIVAGE
1000 Water St. SW, Washington, DC.
(202) 488-8111

FRENCH

Lunch: M-F 11:30-2:30 **Entrees:** $10-$15
Dinner: M-Th 5:30-10:30, F-Sat 5:30-11, Sun 5-9
Dinner Entrees: $13-$22 **Pre-Theater:** Daily 5:30-6:30, $17
Credit Cards: All major **Reservations:** Recommended
Dress: Casual **Parking:** Valet (fee) **Metro:** L'Enfant Plaza

Waterfront restaurants are largely big-business, tour-bus dining factories, but right next door to the typical Phillips Flagship is a French restaurant so nice it wouldn't even need a water view to recommend it. LE RIVAGE is Gallic to the core, spacious and comfortable without being particularly beautiful. That's fine, since its decor is the Potomac, right out the window. It has a large deck overlooking the water, the boat dock and the Maine Avenue seafood market. And it has a menu filled with appealing French food, much of it seafood.

While most waterfront seafood restaurants simply defrost, heat and serve the likes of Alaskan crab legs or frozen, breaded seafood dinners, LE RIVAGE goes so far as to smoke its own salmon. Its fish is not only fresh, but it's prepared with obvious care. Its crab bisque is a spicy, earthy, house-made broth that's just a variation on the classic lobster bisque, and there's also a Riviera-style fish chowder.

The standing menu lists the typically French mussels in white wine, lobster in beurre blanc, gratin of seafood and meat dishes from duck breast with cassis to beef stew with mushrooms. The most interesting items on the menu, however, are the daily specials. That's where you'll find the fresh catch — the usual farmed salmon fillets, to be sure, but offered in a modern French manner with seasonings like lemon grass or sometimes blackened with Cajun spices. The vegetable accompaniments are bright and firm (and there's a Provençal vegetable stew for vegetarians), the salads are tangy and crisp, and LE RIVAGE makes all its desserts, from the sorbets to the tarts of seasonal fruits. You can sample the full range of desserts on a whimsical mock palette with nearly a dozen little dishes arranged along the rim, enough for two or even more. Just the thing for after the theater at Arena down the street.

LE VIEUX LOGIS
7925 Old Georgetown Rd., Bethesda, MD
(301) 652-6816

FRENCH   ♿

Dinner: Sun 5-9, M-Th 5:30-9:30, F-Sat 5:30-10
Entrees: $15-$24 **Credit Cards:** All major
Reservations: Recommended **Dress:** Casual
Parking: Complimentary valet **Metro:** Bethesda

The half-timbered building that houses LE VIEUX LOGIS is so bedecked with window boxes and trellises, so overflowing with flowers, that it seems like the cusp of Wonderland. Inside, the French farmhouse fantasy is reinforced by the restaurant's wooden shutters, copper cauldrons and whitewashed walls. LE VIEUX LOGIS is an old-fashioned French restaurant with new fashions on its menu.

While LE VIEUX LOGIS serves such clichés as lobster bisque and onion soup, they're fresh from this kitchen rather than reconstituted or poured from cans. Chef Trent Conry even gives them a twist: asparagus with the lobster, port wine in the onion soup. The daily special soups are predictable, and any kid with a blender could make a gazpacho to equal Conry's. But the mushroom soup manages to be intensely flavorful and creamy yet light. The clue to appreciating this kitchen is to seek the straightforward dishes. They're not as plain as they might sound, and they outshine the fussier preparations. Among appetizers, for example, the marinated Danish herring is a revelation. The appetizer medley of wild mushrooms is equally luscious, though not as rare.

Most entrees are better than the appetizers. A whole Cornish hen is quartered and grilled until the skin is nearly midnight-dark and flaky-crisp; its flavor is heightened by undercurrents of ginger, citrus and mild, beige-green Ligurian olives. Lamb is almost as seductively simple. Fruit-and-meat is a theme here: apples and mushrooms with veal, raspberry sauce and bacon with liver. Fish entrees head in the other direction: red-wine and shallot sauce with salmon, mustard flavoring plaice, lemon and thyme on shrimp and citrus sauce on honest-to-goodness Dover sole. The supporting elements — bread, wine list, desserts — are pedestrian. You can find a decent bottle to drink, and if blueberry bread pudding is on the dessert cart, you're in luck. But the emphasis is on solid cooking with a bit of flair, and on good-natured, bustling service.

LEBANESE TAVERNA
2641 Connecticut Ave. NW, Washington, DC
(202) 265-8681

LEBANESE   ♿

Lunch: M-F 11:30-2:30, Sat 11:30-3 **Entrees:** $7.75-$13.50
Dinner: M-Th 5:30-10:30, F-Sat 5:30-11, Sun 5-10
Dinner Entrees: $9.75-$15.50 **Credit Cards:** All major
Reservations: Accepted 5:30-6:30 **Dress:** Casual
Parking: Free lot **Metro:** Woodley Park-Zoo

The walls are the color of sand, and arches that suggest a court-yard. Potted trees hint of gardens, etchings and photos of old Lebanon establish the cultural setting, and the open kitchen is as lively as an open-air market. On a weekend evening the hubbub is loud, the mood exuberant. So if you are looking for quiet, you'll need to find another time or place.

A Lebanese dinner is at its best a group activity, because with a table-ful of people you can order a proper *mezze* — an array of appetizers that can be a prelude to dinner or dinner itself — mostly served in charming, handmade pottery bowls. The menu lists almost two dozen appetizer possibilities. I'd focus on pastry-wrapped cheese or spinach pies. The meat choices are also special — tiny spicy sausages called *maanek*, milder beef patties called *sujok*, the raw lamb and cracked wheat paste called *kibbeh nayeh*, or the oval cooked *kibbeh*, its thin, even, beef-wheat shell stuffed with ground lamb and nuts.

Note the wood-burning oven that produces LEBANESE TAVERNA'S breads. A falafel sandwich is wrapped in a house-made pita, and a huge, paper-thin, pale bread comes wrapped around the *kafta mechwi* and the rotisserie chicken. That chicken is the best main dish I've tried, its skin crisp and fairly tingling with spices. Chicken is also handled with respect in a kebab, *shish taouk*, lemony from its mari-nade. I'd choose chicken over lamb and beef here. Peppered red snap-per is succulent in its soft, walnut-lemon sauce, and shrimp kebabs offer large shrimp, smoky from the grill, yet still juicy. In all, the food tastes better in a conglomeration of dishes than dish by dish. The combinations enhance each — mild, spicy, tart, crisp, oozing, hot, cold — by their contrasts. And they add up to a festive meal.

For the Virginia branch of Lebanese Taverna: 5900 Washington Blvd., Arlington, VA, (703) 241-8681.

LEDO
2420 University Blvd E., Adelphi, MD
(301) 422-8622

ITALIAN

Open: M-Th 9 am-11 pm, F-Sat. 9 am-midnight, Sun. 9 am-10 pm
Entrees: $6-$12 **Pre-Theater:** Daily 4-6, 10% off
Credit Cards: MC, V **Reservations:** Accepted for 8 or more
Dress: Casual **Parking:** Free lot

After decades of going to LEDO, I finally ventured beyond the pizza, fried ravioli and eggplant parmesan, since the waitress recommended the fried chicken. Actually, the chicken was crisp and juicy, very good stuff. And there are probably other good things on the vast Italian and American menu. But I can't see any reason to tear myself away from the pizza (even though LEDO'S pizza is now sold everywhere from our Virginia suburbs to Ocean City). This is square pizza, its dough a cross between pie crust and bread, and the thick tomato sauce is rather sweet but also nicely spicy. The toppings are plentiful, the favorite being bacon.

> **"I can't see any reason to tear myself away from the pizza."**

It's a tradition to start with fried ravioli, which are a kind of glorified convenience food in that they taste like canned ravioli breaded and deep-fried. Mainly they are a vehicle for eating that thick and aromatic tomato sauce by the bowlful. And then you go on to pizza.

LEDO is always busy, inevitably crowded and noisy, more a dining hall than a dining room. Considering the circumstances, the service is terrific. After doing duty at LEDO, those waitresses could meet any task with aplomb. At breakneck speed they serve, clear, bring you another beer just as you're emptying your last bottle and wrap your leftover pizza even before you've made a move to go. LEDO is an institution. Every institution should feed us so well.

LEGAL SEA FOODS
2020 K St. NW, Washington, DC
(202) 496-1111

AMERICAN/SEAFOOD

Lunch: M-F 11-4, Sat-Sun noon-4 **Entrees:** $7-$17
Dinner: M-Th 4-10:30, F-Sat 4-11, Sun 4-10 **Entrees:** $12-$28
Credit Cards: All major **Reservations:** Recommended
Dress: Casual **Parking:** Valet (fee) evenings **Metro:** Farragut West

LEGAL SEA FOODS, in its nearly half a century, has grown from a small grocery into a chain of 10 Boston-area restaurants, five retail markets, a mail-order operation and two Washington restaurants. These restaurants have hundreds of seats. Their menus list well over three dozen entrees. LEGAL SEA FOODS is such a vast operation now that every seafood item — even the Maryland crab, they say — must be sent to its New England processing plant for inspection before it arrives on your plate.

Actually, that's its strength. I'm afraid to eat raw oysters most places, but I feel safe at LEGAL. I have no hesitation here to order my tuna rare or my clams on the half shell. LEGAL'S policy is to inspect all its shellfish for bacteria. It buys fish directly at the docks, demands the last-day catch and monitors its temperature every 30 seconds along the way to the restaurant. That's the secret to appreciating LEGAL SEA FOODS: Its buying and handling are brilliant; its cooking is institutional.

Order a piece of fish — scrod or swordfish if you're a nostalgic New Englander, bluefish or haddock if you are a real fish lover, tuna if you prefer swimming in the mainstream, salmon or char if you like mild, pink, farm-raised fish. Have your fish grilled, or if you want to be a little bolder, order your fish Cajun style; it's also grilled, but rubbed with teasingly spicy yet barely hot Cajun seasonings. Of course LEGAL serves wonderful lobsters, pearly and tender, appropriately steamed or — a bow to the South — baked and stuffed with crab. A more modest option is a lobster salad roll, the traditional, flat-sided hot dog roll buttered and toasted, packed with an extraordinary amount of succulent lobster in a minimum of mayonnaise. Don't forget the fabulous fried onion "strings" and the terrific fried soft-shell clams. In general, keep your order simple, and think New England.

Legal Sea Foods also has a branch at 2001 International Dr., McLean, VA, (703) 827-8900.

LES HALLES
1201 Pennsylvania Ave. NW, Washington, DC
(202) 347-6848

FRENCH/STEAKHOUSE   ♿

Lunch: Daily 11:30-4   **Entrees:** $11.75-$20
Dinner: Daily 4-midnight   **Entrees:** $13.25-$22.50
Credit Cards: All major   **Reservations:** Recommended
Dress: Casual   **Parking:** Valet (fee) at dinner
Metro: Metro Center, Federal Triangle

A slab of steak, a pile of fries and thou. In an odd way, LES HALLES is a most romantic restaurant. It's big, it's public and it's a beefy kind of place, but it's also charmingly French, with an old-fashioned pâté-and-cassoulet menu and pleasantly anonymous service. It has the comfortable, unhurried, tie-loosened feel of a brasserie. Most important in good weather, it has a spacious sidewalk cafe, partly covered by an awning.

I go to LES HALLES for an *onglet* — a tender but fibrous and exceptionally flavorful, boneless, hangar steak — cooked rare (which really means rare here) — and for greaseless, crisp fries. I start with the *petatou de chevre*, a small construction of diced portobellos and potatoes, served warm under a mantle of goat cheese, accompanied by a mountain of green salad. Or I might

"A slab of steak, a pile of fries and thou."

have the *frisee aux lardons*, a chicory salad with chunks of bacon and Roquefort-smeared toast. The pâté is gutsy and the *rillettes* powerful. Or you can get salmon tartare, classic onion soup or snails to start. Entrees include the brasserie regulars: blood sausage, mussels in white wine, tartar steak and a cassoulet so rich and meaty that it could have seen you through past blizzards and the ones to come. There's fish, of course, but I think of this as a meat haven. Crisp, unctuous duck *confit*, rotisserie lamb — they're LES HALLES fare. The mainstay, though, is steaks: sirloin, skirt, the bargain-priced "steak, frites, salade," or that unbeatable hangar steak.

LESPINASSE
Sheraton-Carlton Hotel
923 16th St. NW, Washington, DC
(202) 879-6900

FRENCH ♿

Breakfast: M-F 7-10, Sat-Sun 7-11:30 **Entrees:** $6-$21
Lunch: M-F noon-2 **Entrees:** $22-$27
Dinner: M-Sat 6-10 **Entrees:** $26-$39
Tea: Daily 3-5, $19 **Closed:** Sun **Dress:** Jacket required
Credit cards: All major **Reservations:** Recommended
Parking: Complimentary valet at dinner **Metro:** Farragut North

W hat's a world capital without a $105 fixed-price dinner? No sooner did Jean-Louis Palladin move out of Washington than LESPINASSE moved in with prices to take our breath away. But it's only a branch of New York's glorious restaurant in the St. Regis Hotel. And that's the crucial point. Gray Kunz, an extraordinary chef, has installed his sous chef, Troy Dupuy, in Washington, and promises to visit often. The style is Kunz's — French-American and slightly Asian, boldly adventurous yet with flavors as clear as a bell — but this is cooking "in the school of" rather than directly by the master. Thus, while Dupuy has yet to prove himself, we are expected to pay Kunz-worthy prices.

The first menu is small and brilliant, à la carte as well as fixed-price, with starters such as foie gras and figs in a dark, ruby-tinted port sauce as potent as a jolt of electricity. Shellfish as an appetizer and lobster as an entree are swimmingly fresh and taste more so for floating in Eastern-perfumed, nearly briny broths. Luxuries such as caviar, truffles and wild mushrooms keep company on this menu with humble cod, earthy salsify, chickpeas and whole grains that perform as equals to the more haute ingredients. The potential is exciting, but in the startup days there have been the kinds of missteps one doesn't tolerate in a $20 appetizer or $30-plus entree.

The dining room is palatial, with sun-yellow walls highlighting the magnificent ornate ceiling. Several dining room staff are from Jean-Louis, and the city has seen no smoother service than theirs. Sommelier Vincent Feraud has a well deserved national reputation. And there is one unheralded surprise: Pastry chef Jill Rose is creating elaborate fantasies in sugar, fruit and chocolate that are not only light on the tongue but are so gorgeous that you'll be tempted to photograph them before you eat them.

LEVI'S BBQ

1233 Brentwood Rd. NE, Washington, DC

(202) 635-3991

AMERICAN/SOUTHERN/BARBECUE

Open: M-Sat 11 am-10 pm **Closed:** Sun
Entrees: $4-$13.50 **Credit Cards:** MC, V
Reservations: No **Dress:** Casual
Parking: Free lot **Metro:** Rhode Island Avenue

Until Levi and Gloria Durham set out to solve the problem, the only way to get real, eastern North Carolina barbecue in Washington was via Federal Express. Now you can enjoy it here at three LEVI'S locations where pork is smoked on-site for 12 hours, overnight, so it's fresh for the lunchtime rush. Piled on a sesame-seed roll with a big dollop of coleslaw, LEVI'S barbecue is the kind of irresistible sandwich that makes you want to turn the car around and go back for another as soon as you're done.

Levi's serves more than barbecue. And it serves more varieties of barbecue than North Carolina chopped pork. The main locations are full-service, soul-food cafeterias. North Carolinians would shake their heads, but the steam table features pork ribs and beef ribs thickly slathered with tomatoey sauce that would be more familiar in Texas or Kansas than in the Carolinas. The steam table is also likely to be piled with such down-home necessities as baked or barbecued chicken, meatloaf, smothered pork chops, beef liver, Salisbury steak, pig's feet, chitterlings or fried seafood (whole fish, fillets, scallops, shrimp, oysters, crab cakes). And vegetables: greens fragrant with vinegar, potato salad enlivened with pickles and celery seeds, yams, butter beans, long-stewed cabbage and string beans. Unfortunately, the potatoes taste like instant and the hush puppies are heavy. The sleeper is the pork chop sandwich. The chop is half an inch thick and batter-fried; though it's reminiscent of chicken-fried steak, it's far more juicy and incomparably more delicious.

These are big, bustling cafeterias that concentrate on carryout but have plenty of sit-down space. And eating-in has one major advantage: It's a short trip for that second sandwich.

For the two Maryland branches of Levi's BBQ: 6201 Livingston Rd., Oxon Hill, MD, (301) 567-0050, and 5310 Indian Head Highway, Oxon Hill, MD, (301) 567-1700.

LOUISIANA CAFE
713 8th St. SE, Washington, DC
(202) 543-5400

AMERICAN/CREOLE ♿

Lunch: T-F 11:30-4 **Entrees:** $6-$11
Dinner: T-Th 5:30-10, F 5-midnight, Sat 6-midnight
Dinner Entrees: $15-$20 **Brunch:** Sun 11:30-4, $28
Closed: M **Credit Cards:** All major **Reservations:** Recommended
Dress: Casual **Parking:** Street **Metro:** Eastern Market
Entertainment: Jazz F-Sat nights and for Sun brunch

Chef James Shivers has that Cajun palate. He can make a roux as black as midnight without its tasting burned. His holy trinity of green onions, celery and bell peppers blends into sauces as a medley rather than a disconnected group of solos. His sauces are both hot and mellow, so intricate that they tease you into sopping up every last trace. You could miss all that, though, and never know that you'd simply had the bad luck to order the losers on the menu. Some dishes are as dreary as the others are tantalizing. And no matter what your luck, you have to come prepared to wait.

With two layers of tablecloths and waiters in black tie and formal pleated shirts, LOUISIANA CAFE is more glamorous than one might expect from its name. Even so, the mood is more friendly than formal, and the management exudes a gracious warmth.

Dishes to seek are hearty, homey stewed things. Red beans and rice is crowded with shredded meat and sausage in a thick brew of herbs and hot spices. Creole gumbo is a knockout, a dark, earthy broth that's peppery but also much more. It's packed with crab in the shell, shrimp and sausage. It's a mystery how a chef who serves soggy, gray, blackened steak smothered with big hunks of celery in thick, pasty tomato sauce, or jambalaya that tastes like Spanish rice gone wrong, can whip up such a great gumbo and a crayfish *etouffe* of such character. The crayfish themselves are not a standout, but they become regal in their creamy, Tabasco-spiked sauce, fragrant with minced onions and peppers. It's one of those magical Louisiana classics. For dessert, the classic is house-made sweet potato cake with nutted cream cheese frosting. And, like any good New Orleans kitchen, LOUISIANA CAFE gets its coffee right.

LUIGINO
1100 New York Ave. NW
Washington, DC
(202) 371-0595

ITALIAN

Lunch: M-F 11:30-2:30 **Entrees:** $8.25-$14.50
Dinner: M-Th 5:30-10:30, F-Sat 5:30-11:30, Sun 5-10
Entrees: $12.50-$22.50 **Pre-Theater:** Daily 5:30-7, $18.50
Credit Cards: All major **Reservations:** Recommended
Dress: Casual **Parking:** Street **Metro:** Metro Center

Washington once had hardly any good Italian restaurants. Now it has wonderful ones of all sorts: expensive and inexpensive, traditional and modern, Milanese and Tuscan. LUIGINO, a handsome, contemporary, art deco revival dining room in an authentic art-deco ex-bus station, is an Italian restaurant with a long menu of dishes that might be at home in France as much as Italy.

It's a restaurant full of energy, with flames crackling in the wood-burning stove and cooks working at full tilt in an open kitchen. Cheerful waiters in brightly patterned vests serve with considerable zest. And in addition to the printed menu, there's a two-page list of daily specials and a wine list that has an endearing Italian selection at prices that make you breathe a sigh of relief.

It's not a restaurant, however, where I would concentrate on the pasta. The menu is heavy on ravioli, and those ravioli have a stolid thickness and meager filling. The dishes that tempt me are the light and adventurous ones. An appetizer of frittata wedges — thin omelets of onion and artichoke — is piled on shredded arugula with a tomato salad that's even delicious out of season. And salmon breaks away from boring, repetitious, grilled fillets to be served here in crisp-edged, sauteed chunks, with

" . . . dishes that might be at home in France as much as Italy."

other chunks of carrots offering a teasingly close contrast of color and texture, on a pool of dark green spinach sauce so vivid it takes your breath away. Even the everyday menu explores more than the usual veal and chicken: goat stew, duck in garlic sauce, and, instead of the usual sausage, one made from chicken. Or you can order grilled fish, the usual and unusual pizzas, even the inevitable veal Milanese and *tirami su*.

LUNA GRILL & DINER
1301 Connecticut Ave. NW, Washington, DC
(202) 835-2280

AMERICAN   ♿

Breakfast: All day, 7:30 on, $2-$6
Lunch and Dinner: M-Th 11:30 -10, F-Sat 11:30-11
Entrees: $5-$12 **Brunch:** Sat-Sun 10-3, $3-$8
Early Bird: M-Sat 4:30-7, $10 **Credit Cards:** All major
Reservations: No **Dress:** Casual
Parking: Street **Metro:** Dupont Circle

Newcomers will discover at LUNA GRILL & DINER the whimsy of painted sunbursts and lunar ceramics, the prices of a small-town luncheonette and the homey good cooking of a diner where the kitchen has learned modern lessons about cutting the fat.

You won't find balsamic vinegar on this menu. It's a diner. Think plain food: meatloaf, turkey and stuffing, breakfast all day. You can find a grilled cheese sandwich or chicken salad three ways: as a side dish, a salad or a sandwich. The pastas don't stretch beyond vegetarian lasagna, stuffed shells and spaghetti with the usual half a dozen sauces, none of them memorable. Order something brown and meaty, preferably with potatoes. The burger here is thick and crusty brown, juicy because it's been lightly handled in the forming, and if you ask for it rare you'll get it rare.

Normally, I don't order a steak sandwich at a diner outside of Philadelphia, but LUNA has taught me a lesson. Its steak sandwich isn't the thin-shaved, Philadelphia style but something better. This is an actual steak, more than a quarter-inch thick. Blow an extra dollar on darkly caramelized fried onions and fat slices of mushroom, and any of this steak's flaws will be well hidden. The meatloaf is also succulent, and you can get a chicken breast roasted or grilled.

Unlike most diners, LUNA serves grilled vegetables so aromatic and oil-glossed that they'd satisfy as a meal by themselves. Still, what's a diner meal without potatoes? The french fries here are soft, thick and greaseless — just wonderful. Fried sweet potatoes are plump and moist, with crunchy charred edges. But who could pass up the mashed potatoes, so rough and lumpy, with a crater of gravy? On my first visit to LUNA GRILL, the woman at the next table ordered a bowl of mashed potatoes for dessert. She was a woman who knows what's what. I bet she had the fries as an appetizer.

MAINE AVENUE WHARF

1100 Maine Ave. SW, Washington, DC
(202) 488-0823

SEAFOOD   ♿

Open: Daily 9 am-9 pm **Service:** Carry-out only
Entrees: $5.25-$13 **Credit Cards:** All major
Parking: Street

Next time you want to show off authentic local seafood, head for the MAINE AVENUE WHARF, which now sells not just raw ingredients but fried, boiled, steamed and spiced stuff ready to eat. It's one of those colorful corners that makes cities great.

All day and long into the evening, crowds come to gather the makings of an urban picnic. You can buy just-shucked clams and oysters, steamed crabs practically buried in dangerous-looking, red seafood seasoning, and soulful crab cakes. There are mountains of pink, steamed shrimp, with or without spicing. Or you can buy the less local but perennially popular steamed snow or Dungeness crabs, crayfish or lobsters.

> **"All day and long into the evening, crowds come to gather the makings of an urban picnic."**

Blue crabs are the best bet here. They are, after all, what has made mid-Atlantic waterfronts famous in food circles. But if you stopped at crabs, you'd be missing a lot. The stalls serve fish sandwiches with moistly fresh fillets — or whole fish on the bone — dredged in spiced cornmeal, then fried to lacy crispness. You can choose what you like of the season's catch: flounder, trout, whiting, catfish, porgies, rockfish or — the crown jewel of local seafood — soft-shell crabs. All are slapped between two slices of flabby white bread and accompanied by a plastic pouch of tartar or cocktail sauce. There's no place to sit, but for such a great slab of fried fish and an invigorating look at teeming urban life, a few discomforts are a small price.

MAKOTO
4822 MacArthur Blvd. NW
Washington, DC
(202) 298-6866

JAPANESE

Lunch: T-Sat noon-2:30 **Entrees:** $8.50-$21
Dinner: T-Sun 6-10:30 **Multi-Course Meal:** $35 **Closed:** M
Credit Cards: MC, V **Reservations:** Recommended
Dress: Casual; socks required **Parking:** Street

Everything about this restaurant is authentically Japanese, from the slippers at the door where you remove your shoes, to the near-miniature scale of the dining room, to the tables packed with chain-smoking Japanese businessmen.

MAKOTO'S dinner menu has expanded to include a list of teriyaki — chicken gizzard and scallion, chicken midriff along with the usual options — as long as the sushi sheet. À la carte choices could nowadays compose a meal, though the emphasis is still on the 8- to-10-course fixed-price dinner, which is a bargain at $35.

Some of the bloom is off this pristine little restaurant: The menu changes little from season to season, and courses are sometimes repetitious and less exciting than they were in previous years. But I still look forward to MAKOTO'S doll-size banquet of tofu-dressed vegetables teamed with snails in the shell, shaved rare beef in vinegared soy, sashimi and sushi, an odd, starchy chicken galantine, a still-life of salmon and crab with delicious slender garlic shoots, monkfish liver, your choice of grilled beef or fish (mine is always yellowtail), noodles in a heady broth and a most refreshing grape ice.

" . . . precision pacing and careful orchestration of flavors and textures."

Even though MAKOTO doesn't have quite the enthusiastic inventiveness it once had, the overall effect is of precision pacing and careful orchestration of flavors and textures.

MAMA WOK AND TERIYAKI
595 Hungerford Dr, Rockville, MD
(301) 309-6642

CHINESE/JAPANESE

Open: Daily 11:30 am-10 pm
Entrees: $4-$11 **Credit Cards:** MC, V **Reservations:** No
Dress: Casual **Parking:** Free lot **Metro:** Rockville

Rockville is the suburb to head for if you want Chinese food somewhere other than downtown, and each of its culinary stars has its fan club. There's Seven Seas, with its huge menu offering Japanese sushi and teriyaki, low-fat Chinese dishes, vegetarian entrees and seafood kept live in several tanks. Nearby is Four Rivers, whose sign says it's Szechuan, though the menu reveals that its kitchen cooks in several dialects. Up the road is Richland, with its home-style cooking.

Often enough, my fondness leans to MAMA WOK & TERIYAKI — maybe because it's such a diamond in the rough. It, too, is obviously a mix of Japanese and Chinese dishes, and like Seven Seas it has tanks with live fish, Dungeness crabs, clams and oysters, plus shrimp in season. Its mainstay seems to be bargain-priced cafeteria lunches — $1 soups, $4 to $6 entrees. And at lunchtime the neighbors come for a quick lunch and fill up on mounds of fried and glistening Chinese standards.

But the self-service I like is picking a fish or a giant crab from the tank and then discussing with the staff what method of preparation would best suit the creature. While clams might not taste very different here than at restaurants without holding tanks, there's no crab sweeter than a Dungeness that was alive five minutes ago. In season I'd **" . . . a diamond in the rough."** certainly look for live shrimp. And in addition to whatever fish are swimming around in the tank, I couldn't bypass already-cut-up black cod, or sablefish. This silkiest, richest of pure white fish is steamed to near-melting, its pan juices spooned over rice.

The dining room is starkly plain. If you have leftovers, you pack them up yourself with containers stacked on the service counter. You can be sure, at MAMA WOK, that what you're paying for is not atmosphere or service, but simply the food.

MARKET LUNCH

225 7th St. SE, Washington, D
(202) 547-8444

AMERICAN//SEAFOOD/BARBECUE

Breakfast: T-Sat 7:30-11 **Lunch:** T-Sat 11-3
Entrees: $2-$10 **Credit Cards:** No; cash only
Dress: Casual **Reservations:** No
Parking: Street **Metro:** Eastern Market

Walking through markets makes me hungry, and MARKET LUNCH serves just what a stroll through Eastern Market makes me crave. At breakfast time it has ham and eggs and grits and pancakes. At lunch it serves two grades of crab cakes — a good, spicy, shredded crab version and a better all-lump luxury version — along with fried fish and shrimp. Here's one of the rare opportunities to order fried perch — small fish having fallen out of favor these days — and fried shrimp that's hand-breaded and long on flavor.

In season you'll find soft-shell crabs and corn on the cob, while year-round there's terrific creamy potato salad and slaw, and decently tangy cucumber salad. But all is not seafood here. MARKET LUNCH is one of the best in-town sources for authentic, North Carolina barbecue, smoky and vinegary, piled thickly on a huge soft bun with a layer of cole slaw. It's strong, sloppy and wonderful.

"Market Lunch is one of the best in-town sources for authentic, North Carolina barbecue."

Service is friendly, but the lines run long, so you're expected to rattle off your order without hesitation, eat quickly at one of the tables or counters and relinquish your seat for the next customer. MARKET LUNCH isn't for lingering. It's for a quick hit of old-time atmosphere and down-home food.

MARRAKESH
617 New York Ave. NW, Washington, DC
(202) 393-9393

MOROCCAN   ょ

Dinner: Daily 6-11 **Full-Course Dinner:** $22
Credit Cards: No; cash or check only **Dress:** Casual
Reservations: Required on weekends
Parking: Valet (fee) **Metro:** Gallery Place-Chinatown
Entertainment: Belly dancer nightly

Even Chuck E. Cheese couldn't host many more birthday parties than MARRAKESH. This Moroccan pleasure palace is a warehouse-size space converted into one of the city's most ornate dining rooms. Sofas are arranged in clusters around low brass tables, so it makes sense to go with a group.

The festivity starts well before you're seated. A valet parks your car — at a price — then you knock on a wooden door that's opened by a costumed host, who ushers you through a curtain to the dining room. The place vibrates with color, from the intricately painted ceiling to complex patterns on the sofas and pillows. All waiters are in costume, and they begin their service by washing your hands from an etched metal ewer.

The meal is seven courses, served communally and eaten with the hands (spoons are served only with the couscous). Three salads begin the parade, with bread for scooping them. Next comes *bastilla*, the chicken-egg-almond pie wrapped in phyllo and dusted with powdered sugar. Chicken — cooked whole and drenched in lemon and green olives — follows. For the meat course you must make a communal choice among lamb with honey and almonds, lamb with chickpeas and onions or beef kebabs. Vegetarian couscous follows, then a bowl of fruit and, finally, small, nut-filled phyllo turnovers and mint tea. Somewhere in the middle a belly dancer provides a change of pace. The wine flows (budget watchers should exercise caution about that). The music plays.

Like the decor, the food is a barrage of ornate tastes. This is rich food, heavy perhaps, and no dish is outstanding. But it is all good. Maybe MARRAKESH makes you feel like a tourist. Maybe this is a Moroccan version of fast food. But with a seven-course interplay of lemon, olives, cumin, onions and honey, what could be bad?

MARROCCO'S
1120 20th St. NW, Washington, DC
(202) 331-9664

ITALIAN   ♿

Lunch: M-F noon-5 **Entrees:** $7-$15
Dinner: M-Th 5-10:30, F-Sat 5-11 **Entrees:** $10-$21
Closed: Sun **Credit Cards:** All major
Reservations: Recommended **Dress:** Casual
Parking: Complimentary valet **Metro:** Dupont Circle

In an area with so many Italian restaurants that any one would find it hard to stand out, MARROCCO'S has a vocal fan club. The reason: its service, the work of a gracious family and staff. What is less known about MARROCCO'S is that its salads are far above ordinary.

Its Caesar salad is fine — prepared tableside with fresh eggs, anchovies and bold doses of seasonings. But a fine Caesar salad is not hard to come by. Even better are the cold appetizers that qualify as salads, the roasted peppers with *bagna cauda* and the artichokes with walnuts. Both are dishes that are frequently dreadful for their lack of fresh ingredients; MARROCCO'S does them right.

The peppers are fresh red bell peppers, roasted until limp and flavorful, sliced and topped with whole anchovies, garlic and oil. Simply wonderful. Even better are the artichokes, also fresh — only the

". . . its salads are far above ordinary."

hearts, cooked until just firm. They're dressed with olive oil and chopped walnuts — an unexpectedly delicious contrast to the artichokes — plus finely diced bell peppers, onions and celery, bits of herb and little enough seasoning that the artichokes dominate.

The pastas, the meats, the fish that are the mainstays on the menu are perfectly fine, but none such a pleasant surprise as the salads.

MATUBA
2915 Columbia Pike, Arlington, VA
(703) 521-2811

JAPANESE

Lunch: M-F 11:30-2 **Entrees:** $5-$10
Dinner: Sun-Th 5:30-10, F-Sat 5:30-10:30 **Entrees:** $7.50-$15
Credit Cards: All major **Reservations:** Recommended
Dress: Casual **Parking:** Free lot **Metro:** Rosslyn

In both Maryland and Virginia, you're in range of excellent, modestly priced sushi, thanks to the two branches of MATUBA. These busy, efficient little restaurants are almost sushi bargain-basements, considering the variety of specials their menus offer. A small sampler? A large sampler? A box lunch? A tray large enough for a party? Sushi with sashimi? Or tempura? Even if you order à la carte, you can fill yourself without crushing your budget.

There is, of course, more than sushi here. You can find traditional Japanese noodle dishes, grilled meat or fish, and sesame-scented salads. And if you like, you can have raw fish for a first course, before your sushi. That's my choice, since the chopped raw tuna salad, studded with shreds of black seaweed, is one of the spiciest and most scrumptious versions of tuna tartare anywhere.

" . . . almost sushi bargain-basements."

Then check the daily specials for sushi treats: diced raw scallops, soft-shell crabs or fried shrimp formed into a sushi roll, pale pink tuna belly, red clams. And every day there are such rare choices as yellowtail cup, its fish minced and seasoned, then piled on rice and wrapped in seaweed; or rolls of spiced tuna, spiced cod with radish sprouts or raw asparagus with smoked salmon. The greatest treat, though, is a rainbow roll, with diagonal stripes of salmon, yellowtail, tuna and avocado waiting to blend and meld on the tongue. Your eyes will love it, too.

For the Maryland branch of Matuba, which has similar dishes, prices and hours: 4918 Cordell Ave., Bethesda, MD, (301) 652-7449.

MEDITERRANEAN BLUE
1910 18th St. NW, Washington, DC
(202) 483-2583

MEDITERRANEAN   ♿

Dinner: Sun-Th 5-10:30, F-Sat 5-midnight **Entrees:** $7-$15
Brunch: Sun 11-4 **Entrees:** $6-$9 **Credit Cards:** All major
Dress: Casual **Reservations:** Accepted **Parking:** Street

As its name implies, this restaurant on the cusp of downtown and Adams-Morgan has a warm-weather theme. The walls are lined with pictures of impossibly colorful fish taken by a local photographer, and the tables in the front bar room are dark sea blue. It's a fairly plain restaurant except for a couple of immense urns overflowing with dried flowers and two mirrored walls that give it a supper club look.

The menu is short, a mix of Middle Eastern — falafel, hummus, baba ghanouj, *kibbeh* and kebabs — with pastas, salads and a few inventive New American appetizers. Those appetizers are worth trying, yet the kebabs are the centerpiece of this kitchen. On the standing menu, the shrimp or lamb kebabs are terrific. The shrimp, rubbed with peppery spices, are so flavorful that you'd guess they were fresh rather than the usual frozen ones. The lamb kebab is lean and lightly marinated so that the meat is highlighted rather than masked by its seasonings. The chicken breast is well-seasoned, the filet mignon is tender, and each day there's a special kebab.

The kebabs come with a choice of four sauces on the side: a fragrant but tame tomato-basil; a tangy tahini that enhances most kebabs; a honey-mustard that overwhelms them all; and a fiery *harissa* for the adventurous. They are accompanied by broccoli, grill-striped zucchini and yellow squash. More important, the kebabs rest on a mound of utterly delicious pilaf — white rice tossed with a bit of wild rice and minced vegetables, well-seasoned and infused with the kebabs' juices, topped with some toasted pine nuts. The emphasis at MEDITERRANEAN BLUE seems to be on traditional Middle Eastern cooking, and its kebab platters are bound to become a neighborhood staple. But its chef shows a talent for American invention that shouldn't be ignored.

MELATI
3506 Connecticut Ave. NW, Washington, DC
(202) 537-1432

INDONESIAN/MALAYSIAN   ♿

Lunch: T-Sun noon-3 **Entrees:** $6.25-$12
Dinner: M 5-10, T-Th 5:30-10:30, F-Sat 5:30-11, Sun 5:30-10
Dinner Entrees: $7.25-$13 **Credit Cards:** All major
Reservations: Recommended **Dress:** Casual
Parking: Street **Metro:** Cleveland Park

MELATI has two chefs, one Indonesian and one Malaysian. They must be very slim. From what I could see, the kitchen didn't look big enough to hold more than one at a time. In any case, they turn out an astonishing variety of dishes from their two cuisines. What's the difference between the Indonesian and the Malaysian dishes? The Indonesian are spicier, say the waiters, without mentioning that they are also sweeter. To add to the confusion, they're not always spicy — or sweet. Nor are the Malaysian dishes always mild.

It's easy to taste an array of Indonesian dishes, since they are available as a *rijsttafel,* which consists of 10 samplings of the entrees. Beyond rijsttafel, the staff willingly guides you through the labyrinthine menu to the best dishes. My choice would be just to hang around the Indonesian appetizers — particularly the fried ones — and Malaysian soup sections of the menu for the whole meal, adding the pork satay from the Malaysian side, since it's drenched in a fascinating dark soy sauce with bits of fried onions. The Indonesian satays are sweeter and milder, in a barely seasoned peanut paste.

Malaysian curry soup is intricate and luscious, a meal-size portion of fried bean curd, green beans and bean sprouts, with shrimp or chicken and two kinds of noodles. Otherwise, the main dish that stands out for me is the Indonesian spicy fish grilled in banana leaves. The moist fish fillets are thickly coated with a spicy red paste, and the leaves permeate them with fragrance and seal in the moisture. Seafood dishes here combine tropical colors with hot, sweet and sour flavors, and the beef, even if it is chewy, smells as fragrant as a flower garden. MELATI also has a well-chosen and astonishingly low-priced wine list. Here's an Asian restaurant that tempts you to drink something besides beer. But then MELATI is full of surprises.

MELROSE
Park Hyatt Hotel, 1201 24th St. NW
Washington, DC
(202) 955-3899

AMERICAN

Breakfast: M-Sat 6:30-11, Sun 6:30-10:30 **Entrees:** $9-$14
Lunch: M-Sat 11-2:30 **Entrees:** $13-$18.50
Dinner: Daily 5:30-10:30 **Entrees:** $18.50-$24
Pre-Theater: Daily 5:30-6:45, $25 **Brunch:** Sun 11-2:30, $31
Afternoon tea: Th-Sun 3-5, $16-$19 **Credit Cards:** All major
Reservations: Recommended **Dress:** Casual
Parking: Complimentary valet all day **Metro:** Foggy Bottom
Entertainment: Dancing Sat 7-11, pianist at teas and brunch

Its terrace is shielded by bushes and trees, sunken from street level so it's out of the path of fumes. Its outdoor tables are covered by pale canvas umbrellas to let in light but buffer the heat. Its landscaping includes not just decorative greenery and flowers but also an herb garden. And its corner is dominated by a huge, tiered, iron fountain that muffles the cacophony of city traffic and cools the air. Dining outdoors at MELROSE is uncommonly pleasant. Indoors it glistens with marble and brass — less charming but eminently comfortable.

Seafood is chef Brian McBride's specialty, accounting for more than half the menu. Lunch appetizers are soups or salads, the likes of a Thai squid salad, tart with lemon and fragrant with lemon grass, sharpened by shallots. Dinner appetizers are largely seafood: soft-shell crab, elegant Petrossian smoked salmon, shrimp in house-made ravioli or a remarkable preserved tuna — rubbed with salt and spices and cured for 36 hours. Most cleverly, among the lunch entrees, superb Maine scallops have their sweetness emphasized by being threaded on skewers of sugar cane — an adaptation from the Vietnamese grilled shrimp paste. At dinner the lightest — and most Asian-inspired — entree is steamed black bass, in an unnecessarily sweet but vibrantly seasoned broth. Even better is Dover sole, which McBride surrounds with roasted peppers and morels and lays on a bed of *mâche*. Nevertheless, the sleepers on this menu are the pastas: bran pasta with swordfish, arugula pesto and red pepper coulis or angel hair pasta with mascarpone and lobster. For dessert, seasonal fruits are used to advantage — plums show up in a homey crisp, lime in a frozen mousse, berries and mangoes in an airy napoleon. The high prices remind you this is hotel dining, but the personal service has the enthusiasm of a restaurant where the proprietor is closer to home.

MESKEREM
2434 18th St. NW, Washington, DC
(202) 462-4100

ETHIOPIAN   ♿

Open: Sun-Th noon-midnight, F-Sat noon-1 am
Lunch Entrees: $5-$10.50 **Dinner Entrees:** $7-$12
Credit Cards: All major **Reservations:** Recommended
Dress: Casual **Parking:** Street
Entertainment: Ethiopian band F-Sat 11-3 am (no kitchen after 1)

Washington has no Scandinavian restaurants, and almost no Eastern European restaurants, yet it has more Ethiopian restaurants than any other city in the nation. Ethiopian food clearly is enormously popular here. It's spicy, it's cheap and you eat it with your hands. But there's even more to appreciate, as one can tell at our prettiest and most ambitious Ethiopian restaurant, MESKEREM.

On two of its three floors it serves on basket-tables. A table-size tray of *injera* — tangy, fermented pancakes that look like thick napkins — is set atop the basket, and various stewed meats, seafood and vegetables are spooned onto the layer of pancakes. You can order chicken, beef, lamb, shrimp or vegetable stews, hot or

" . . . our prettiest and most ambitious Ethiopian restaurant."

mild, but don't shy away from the hot. They're not fiercely hot, and they feature the distinctive flavor of *berbere,* a haunting red pepper paste. There are also sauteed, diced meats with onions (*tibbs*) and spicy, buttery, raw meat (*kitfo*). A plate of folded injera is served alongside, and you eat communally, tearing off pieces of injera to use as scoops for the stews. It's kind of a soft variation on chips and dip, and equally hard to stop eating. Dollops of lentils, cabbage, collards and green-bean stews provide variety.

MESKEREM, unlike most Ethiopian restaurants here, offers a list of appetizers, including an exceptional shrimp cocktail with a tart, red-pepper dipping sauce, delicate *samosas* and refreshing salads of beets or potatoes. Its list of entrees is more extensive than any other's. And its cooking is lively and not greasy. Like its competitors, it serves locally made honey wine and a flavorful Ethiopian beer, brewed in Northern Virginia by Old Dominion.

MISS SAIGON
3057 M St. NW, Washington, DC
(202) 333-5545

VIETNAMESE

Lunch: M-F 11:30-2:30 **Entrees:** $6-$9
Dinner: M-F 5-10:30, Sat-Sun noon-11
Dinner Entress: $7-$14 **Credit Cards:** All major
Reservations: Recommended **Dress:** Casual **Parking:** Street

L eafy lettuce, sweetly tangy dressings, grilled meats — MISS SAIGON, especially its original Adams-Morgan location with its walled terrace — has everything you could want for summer dining. Indoors, too, both locations are festive, with twinkling little lights in pseudo palm trees, each a pink and green fantasy garden. MISS SAIGON is an unusually charming pair of Vietnamese restaurants, though their kitchens can be erratic.

Not only has MISS SAIGON expanded to two restaurants, but its menu has grown, too. A page of vegetarian specials has been added, and the list of seafood preparations now includes curries, spicy salads, stir-fries served over noodle nests and a fisherman's soup in hot pot.

Caramel pork is a commonplace Vietnamese entree that has always seemed boring to me. At MISS SAIGON, though, the caramel is so intense that it is tangy as well as sweet, almost like China's famous Yunnan ham or even vaguely reminiscent of American country ham with red-eye gravy. The skewered grilled meats, marinated with lemon grass (or lemon juice), garlic and just enough sweetener to turn the edges to a dark brown crunch, are likely to be good, even better when wrapped into a lettuce packet with transparent noodles and raw vegetables, then dipped in a seasoned fish sauce. And "shaking" beef is a chance to witness the happy marriage of French and Asian cooking. Chunks of steak and spiced potatoes are sauteed so that they are crusty and buttery-tasting, a heightened version of steak and french fries.

Service at MISS SAIGON is observant and low-key. Prices are low, particularly at lunch. If you're in either neighborhood, it's worth a try.

Other location: 1847 Columbia Rd. NW, Washington, DC 202-667-1900.

MRS. SIMPSON'S
2915 Connecticut Ave. NW, Washington, DC
(202) 332-8300

AMERICAN   ♿

Lunch: M-Sat 11-4 **Entrees:** $6-$12
Dinner: Sun-Th 4-9:30, F-Sat 4-10:30 **Entrees:** $7-$19
Pre-Theater: Daily 4-6:30, $16 **Brunch:** Sun 10:30-4, $16
Credit Cards: All major **Reservations:** Recommended
Dress: Casual **Metro:** Woodley Park-Zoo
Parking: Free lot; valet (fee) Sat evening

MRS. SIMPSON has had a facelift, and it's a good one, the kind that you hardly notice except that the place somehow looks spiffier. This pretty and dignified Woodley Park mainstay is lined with photos of the woman who won a king right off his throne. And if Wallis Simpson was anything like this restaurant, she was a charmer.

The menu is filled with lightly dressed and seasonally fresh offerings such as grilled vegetables, bright salads, crab cakes, a few pastas, not-too-fussy fish dishes. At dinner as well as lunch, you can eat fully or delicately. And Sunday's champagne brunch is a neighborhood tradition. The food is contemporary but not especially adventurous, and comforting if not notable.

"If Wallis Simpson was anything like this restaurant, she was a charmer."

Seasoning is low-key, sauces are at a minimum. MRS. SIMPSON'S is not trying to make culinary history; it is intent on being hospitable. Thus it is the service that most impresses. MRS. SIMPSON'S is serene and gracious, settled and reliable. It's a restaurant that's maturing handsomely.

MR. YUNG'S
740 6th St. NW, Washington, DC
(202) 628-1098

CHINESE

Lunch: M-F 11-3 **Entrees:** $6-$8
Dinner: M-Th 3-midnight, F 3 pm-2 am, Sat-Sun 11 am-2 am
Dinner Entrees: $7-$16 **Credit Cards:** AE, MC, V
Reservations: Accepted **Dress:** Casual
Parking: Street **Metro:** Gallery Place-Chinatown

There aren't many bad Chinese restaurants, and certainly there are plenty of good ones. MR. YUNG'S often goes that extra mile. First, the waitresses are chatty without being intrusive, free with their opinions and advice when asked, and extremely efficient. The menu is long and interesting, and taped to the front is a list of seasonal specials. Here you can find snow pea leaves, garlic shoots, Chinese watercress, yellow leeks, large mung bean sprouts — all in their season, along with seasonal seafood. And the chef constantly introduces new dishes. I've loved the crispy seafood roll, which is like a Chinese chimichanga.

In all, if you like straightforward, familiar Cantonese cooking, it's here. So is more adventurous cooking. I'd start dinner by sharing a dim sum tray and a sweet-tangy-crunchy mound of jellyfish on a bed of succulent smoked pig feet. I'd certainly include noodles; the choice is wide, but the pan-fried house-made noodles are most unusual. They're fried before they are boiled, and intensely flavored with mushroom. In winter I'd have a clay pot casserole; the taro and chicken is deep and hearty. And I'd choose whatever seasonal vegetables are available to stir-fry with the high-quality shrimp, beef, pork or chicken.

"It's a quietly pleasant place where, if you hit it right, the cooking can be memorable."

MR. YUNG'S is pristine and comfortable, simply decorated in dusty rose. It's a quietly pleasant place where, if you hit it right, the cooking can be memorable.

MORRISON-CLARK INN
1015 L St. NW, Washington, DC
(202) 898-1200

AMERICAN/SOUTHERN

Lunch: M-F 11-2 **Entrees:** $11.25-$14.50
Dinner: M-Th 6-9:30, F-Sat 6-10, Sun 6-9 **Entrees:** $16-$22
Brunch: Sun 11-2, $17 **Credit Cards:** All major
Reservations: Recommended **Dress:** Jacket preferred
Parking: Complimentary valet **Metro:** Metro Center

MORRISON-CLARK is a small inn with a Victorian aesthetic. Lace curtains cover the floor-to-ceiling windows, while draperies, carpeting and soft fabrics conspire to mute any noise that might threaten the peace. Cabbage roses bloom on the upholstery, and an immense arrangement of silk flowers towers over a circular sofa. It is the perfect place to take your grandmother.

One would hope that Grandma has the appetite to enjoy chef Susan McCreight Lindeborg's somewhat Southern and unabashedly rich creations. It would be a shame to miss the "bunny and bourbon," the staff's pet name for the bourbon-sauced rabbit loin stuffed with pecan corn bread. In the spring Lindeborg features garlic grits with spicy shrimp as an appetizer, in fall Carolina Low Country scalloped oysters with Virginia ham. Lindeborg loves hearty foods. Yet she tempers them by degreasing them, lightening their textures and moderating the portions. And all year long the entrees showcase the best of the season's vegetables, so interesting in themselves that they could easily be the main focus. But save room — MORRISON-CLARK'S pastries are casually, subtly beautiful. One day I thought the chocolate-peanut butter mousse cake had to be the best, and I don't even like peanut butter desserts. The next visit, I was swayed by the lemon sesame napoleon with blackberry compote. And the napoleon was in a close contest with the chocolate caramel tart — thick, smooth and buried in praline whipped cream. It's rare that a fruit crisp is outclassed by other desserts, but the cranberry-apple crisp didn't have a chance against such competitors.

Lindeborg's cooking concentrates on flavor, on texture, on the composition in the mouth rather than on the plate. This is not cooking calculated to make the chef look good, but to make the diner feel good.

146

MORTON'S OF CHICAGO
3251 Prospect St. NW, Washington, DC
(202) 342-6258

AMERICAN/STEAKHOUSE

Dinner: M-Sat 5:30-11, Sun 5-10 **Entrees:** $17-$30
Credit Cards: All major **Reservations:** Recommended
Dress: Jacket & tie **Parking:** Complimentary valet at dinner

A great steak exists. It's a matter of breeding, then proper aging, cutting to sufficient thickness and grilling on a hot enough fire to sear the surface. You verify these truths at MORTON'S if you order the porterhouse and ask for it black-and-blue (seared yet near raw) or at least specify you want it crusty if you order it cooked rare or medium rare. The meat is silken and tender, with gutsy, beefy flavor. Even the lamb chops, cut double thick, have a flavor that today's lamb often seems to have lost in its refinement.

MORTON'S menu comes on a cart, a display of raw steaks, veal chop, butterflied chicken, swordfish and giant lobster. So you can see the quality before you order. Notice that the potatoes are Idahos, and don't neglect them. The shredded cake of hash browns is as crisp as potato chips, oozing butter and outrageously compelling. Potato skins are no slouch either. Your eyes should warn you, however, that those "beefsteak tomatoes" have a wintry pallor most of the year.

And MORTON'S hasn't mastered cooking vegetables either. Among appetizers, the shrimp cocktail is big but no better than the usual tasteless crustaceans. I used to love the smoked salmon, but recently it tasted only of salt, not of fish or smoke. Scallops wrapped in bacon with apricot chutney would be a fine prelude to a light entree, but they're a bit much to precede a magnificent steak. Likewise, the warm, oozy chocolate cake or the creamy key lime pie would be welcome after many dinners, but you'd have to be a farm hand to appreciate them after this steak-and-potatoes fare. This is a meal to take slowly: Sink into your curved leather banquette and watch the waiters' spiel repeated around the dining room, observe the suited businessmen and the T-shirted tourists eat like lumberjacks, sip your red wine and ruminate over the role of prime beef in making America a world power.

Another Morton's is at 8075 Leesburg Pike, Vienna, VA, (703) 883-0800, and look for a third, in Washington, at Connecticut Ave. & L St.

MUSIC CITY ROADHOUSE

1050 30th St. NW, Washington, DC
(202) 337-4444

AMERICAN/SOUTHERN   ♿

Dinner: T-Sat 4:30-10, Sun 3-11   **Family-Style Meal:** $13
Late night: T-Sat 10-1 am, $3-$7.50   **Brunch:** Sun 11-2, $13
Closed: M   **Credit Cards:** All major   **Dress:** Casual
Reservations: Recommended   **Parking:** Validated garage
Entertainment: Gospel at Sun brunch, followed by blues

MUSIC CITY ROADHOUSE is an immensely pleasing restaurant, not only because of the music — ranging from jazz to gospel — and the outdoor tables lining the C&O Canal. People go just for the food.

Surely nobody expects to go to a down-home Southern restaurant for a vegetable plate, but that's what I'm tempted to order at MUSIC CITY ROADHOUSE. This big, sprawling barn of a place, with a decor that runs to CAT caps and barbecue signs, serves family-style, fixed-price lunches and dinners (and sensational brunches, as well as à la carte salads and sandwiches) that allow you to order all you can eat of three different meats (say, fried chicken, pot roast, barbecued chicken or ribs) or fish (fried catfish, broiled trout). And with them you get all you can eat of three different vegetables, plus some of the best, richest, creamiest skillet corn bread this side of Georgia. Who could complain?

My problem, though, is that the great greasy fried chicken, the carrot-laden pot roast and the meaty ribs don't leave me enough room for the vegetables. And I can never happily pick only three from the list of six. So one of these days I'm going to order just the vegetable plate (not vegetarian, mind you, since the greens are flavored with pork). Then I can have all of them, and concentrate on those spicy, just-vinegary-enough and truly wonderful cooked

> **". . . family-style, fixed-price lunches and dinners . . . that allow you to order all you can eat."**

greens, the slightly lumpy mashed potatoes with chicken-flavored cream gravy, the sweet potatoes that are light and airy and so delicately sweetened that for once I don't think they should be served as dessert, the sometimes-available black-eyed peas, the slaw and whatever else happens to be on the menu.

MYKONOS
1875 K St. NW, Washington, DC
(202) 331-0370

GREEK

Lunch: M-F 11:30-3:30 **Entrees:** $7-$13
Dinner: M-F 5:30-10:30, Sat 5:30-11 **Entrees:** $10-$19
Closed: Sun **Credit Cards:** All major
Reservations: Recommended **Dress:** Casual
Parking: Complimentary at dinner **Metro:** Farragut West

A t this lively, casual Greek restaurant, first look to the daily specials — especially when they involve stewed or roast lamb. Next consider the Greek Taverna Salad, cut-up romaine combined with tomato, cucumber, onion and black olives, then — this is the important part — tossed with vinaigrette and crumbled feta cheese, so that the dressing and cheese permeate it all. Add a couple of dollars, and you can get it topped with tuna or chicken.

Or forget the standard Greek salads altogether and make a comforting lunch from a combination plate of cold appetizers (the menu prices it for two, but you can order a single portion). This one looks as if the kitchen went to considerable effort, and tastes worthy of it. To spread on your crusty Greek bread there's a mound of *tzatziki* (cucumber with yogurt), another of smoky eggplant puree, and my favorite, the tangy *tarama* (coral-tinged fish roe whipped with bread, lemon, onion and olive oil). A hillock of white beans with onion and a chunk of eggplant buried under diced tomatoes, onions and pine nuts, along with garnishes of tomatoes, purple olives and feta cheese, complete the plate.

NEW HEIGHTS RESTAURANT
2317 Calvert St. NW, Washington, DC
(202) 234-4110

AMERICAN/INTERNATIONAL

Dinner: Sun-Th 5:30-10, F-Sat 5:30-11 **Entrees:** $16.50-$25
Brunch: Sun 11-2:30, $7.75-$11.50 **Credit Cards:** All major
Reservations: Recommended **Dress:** Casual
Parking: Complimentary valet **Metro:** Woodley Park-Zoo

J ust off Connecticut Avenue, NEW HEIGHTS is an elegant, beauti- fully run restaurant where the service is always knowledgeable and accommodating, the wine list is a joy and the furnishings are mag- nificently crafted, right down to the handmade tables. No wonder it's been a launching pad for many Washington chefs.

While certain of its signatures — the black bean pâté, the options of appetizer or entree portions — have stayed through all its years and changes, at NEW HEIGHTS each chef has created a new menu and a new tone. The current chef is Matthew Lake, remarkably young and an adventurer in the kitchen. When he was new at the job he was more restrained, and I wish he had stayed that way. Alternatively, I look forward to his becoming more seasoned. Now he seems to

" . . . a launching pad for many Washington chefs."

be in an interim period of letting his imagination run free, often at the expense of reason. Soft-shell crabs with roasted pineapple and fried plantains has a sticky yellow sauce that tastes vaguely like banana pudding. *Palak paneer* is so overseasoned that it's painful to eat. And croquettes — of rice and quinoa or celeriac — are both leaden and bland. I didn't dare try beet-smoked trout or sea bass with roasted horseradish sauce.

Yet all is forgiven with an appetizer of asparagus-shallot flan that has a silken texture and garden-bright flavor, in a subtle yellow corn sauce. And grouper is outstanding with its earthy dark pureed porto- bello mushroom sauce and hearty goat cheese potato puree, plus a decadent pile of fried onion rings on top. Such inconsistencies are the problem of taking charge too soon, before the mentoring process has run its course. The task is dumped in the lap of the diner, to let the chef know when his ideas don't work. And nobody wants to pay top dollar for the chance to critique an unfiltered imagination.

NIZAM'S
523 Maple Ave. W., Vienna, VA
(703) 938-8948

TURKISH/MEDITERRANEAN ♿

Lunch: T-F 11-3 **Entrees:** $6-$12.50
Dinner: T-Th 5-10, F-Sat 5-11, Sun 4-10 **Entrees:** $13-$17.50
Closed: M **Credit Cards:** All major **Dress:** Casual
Reservations: Recommended **Parking:** Free lot

Even Istanbul has no better *doner* kebab than NIZAM'S (unfortunately, it's not served every night). And if you have only tasted doner kebab elsewhere in Washington, you are probably in for a surprise. Most of the restaurants, carryouts and fast-food stands that serve doner kebab — or gyros, as it is often called — buy it as a big frozen loaf of ground meat. It is cooked on a vertical spit and thinly sliced as the surface browns. But it still tastes like frozen hamburger meat. NIZAM'S starts from scratch, marinating paper-thin slices of lamb and stacking them on the spit to form a giant loaf. As it is served, each portion is a cross section of the thin slices of lamb that have melded together into a juicy, gently herbed and spiced web. It is luscious meat, with crisp edges and juicy texture. And at NIZAM'S you can have it plain or spread over chunks of sauteed pita bread with a bit of thick tomato sauce and dense, rich, tangy yogurt.

"Even Istanbul has no better doner kebab than Nizam's."

If you hit NIZAM'S when it's not doner kebab night, you can compensate with *yogurtlu* kebab, the same mix of bread and sauces with sauteed tenderloin.

The menu goes on to kebabs of swordfish, shrimp, cubed or ground lamb, plus the usual Turkish casseroles. Grilled meat is carefully cooked, but my favorite remains the doner kebab. I'd start dinner with the fine grape leaves stuffed with currants and pine nuts, or the highly peppered baba ghanouj; the *borek* here are heavy. And I'd look into the listing of Turkish wines. Platters are preceded by a salad and accompanied by pilaf — nothing exciting but rather nice. The black-tie service is a little shy and certainly efficient; the dining room is quiet and agreeable, with a few reminders of Turkey. In sum, for a moderate price you can get a meal that's both simple and exotic.

OBELISK
2029 P St. NW, Washington, DC
(202) 872-1180

ITALIAN

Dinner: M-Sat 6-10 **Full Dinner:** $40
Closed: Sun **Credit Cards:** D, MC, V
Reservations: Recommended **Dress:** Casual
Parking: Street **Metro:** Dupont Circle

T he mythic Italian restaurant is right here on P Street. The cooking is so simple, so pure that you might be eating each ingredient in its own garden. The small dining room is gently decorated, with a basket of tomatoes or mushrooms and craggy loaves of bread piled on a table, a few etchings on the walls. Yet, accidental as it all may look, every detail is carefully orchestrated. Notice how the strip of mirror along the wall is above your eye level so you don't spend the dinner staring at yourself? Feel the sense of discovery as you examine the wine list, as if bottles were cajoled from proud, reticent Italian winemakers? That hard-crusted, strong-textured, house-made bread — have you ever found any with better flavor? The fixed-price menu is tiny: only three choices for antipasto, pasta or soup course and entree. But have you ever had a harder time making up your mind?

A literary friend put it thus: OBELISK has artistic integrity. Its meals have a beginning, a middle and an end. There are tiny, mild Italian anchovies with a fluff of fennel salad. Handmade fettuccine, thin as a veil and tossed with just tiny green peas and a hint of ham or maybe some squash blossoms. Sometimes a soup of wild mush-

"The cooking is so simple, so pure that you might be eating each ingredient in its own garden."

rooms, a salad of truly ripe tomatoes or full-flavored asparagus. The first two courses are always the most seductive, though the entrees have an admirable clarity, and with my lightly breaded lamb chops I had baby artichokes, flattened and fried like a flower, better than those I've adored in Rome.

Dessert? I'm tempted to finish with the impeccable cheeses. The sorbet is wan, and seldom do the desserts live up to my expectations, except the understated ones: the biscotti, or a wonderful caramel ice cream. Forget the anonymous name, the American ownership — OBELISK is what every Italian restaurant aspires to be. It's a restaurant that heightens your senses.

THE OCCIDENTAL GRILL
1475 Pennsylvania Ave. NW, Washington, DC
(202) 783-1475

AMERICAN   ♿

Open: M-Sat 11:30 am-11pm, Sun noon-9:30
Entrees: $8-$25 **Pre-Theater:** T-Sat 5:30-7:30, $28
Credit Cards: All major **Dress:** Casual
Reservations: Recommended **Metro:** Metro Center
Parking: Complimentary valet at dinner

A revival of one of Washington's revered historic restaurants, the new incarnation of the OCCIDENTAL GRILL by now has developed a comforting patina. Its walls are covered with photos of the celebrities of its early era, its booths are well-burnished dark wood, and its menu has a clubby feel, though appealingly updated. It features sandwiches and the ubiquitous "lighter fare," as well as serious grilled meats and fish. The quality of ingredients and preparation is high while the style is unfussy. There's a nice balance between meat-and-potatoes tradition and modern experimentation. Take a

"Its walls are covered with photos of the celebrities of its early era, and its menu has a clubby feel, though appealingly updated."

hint from that, and concentrate on meat. The mashed potatoes are à la carte but worth making a meal of — or at least having at the expense of dessert. Potatoes — fried or mashed — often save the day here, especially when the entree falls short. The signature dish at lunch from the beginning, though, has been a glamorous twist on the club sandwich, made with grilled swordfish on brioche. Even with some slips in the kitchen, the OCCIDENTAL GRILL is satisfyingly solid. The broad menu, the intelligent service, the interesting list of American wines and even more interesting microbrewed beers set a mood of comfort and tradition.

OLD ANGLER'S INN
10801 MacArthur Blvd., Potomac, MD
(301) 365-2425

AMERICAN

Lunch: T-Sun noon-2:30 **Entrees:** $14.50-$17
Dinner: T-Sat 6-10:30, Sun 5:30-9:30 **Entrees:** $23-$30
Brunch: Sun noon-2:30 **Entrees:** $20-$25 **Closed:** M
Credit Cards: All major **Reservations:** Recommended
Dress: Jacket required **Parking:** Free lot

Sometimes I wish for a warm, fresh, starlit evening when I'm heading for the OLD ANGLER'S INN. Then I can sit outdoors amid the flowers and trees, listening to fountain and frog sounds while I dine on sauteed scallops in thyme oil, inch-thick swordfish on a bed of near-melting shaved fennel or tuna served raw as a tartare or near-raw as a seared steak with a lemon-grass crust.

Other times I'm hoping for a chilly night when a fireplace will be blazing and I can sit before it on a sofa with a drink while I order my dinner: game, of course, or superb veal cooked as a chateaubriand, with vegetables of the season (my favorites: spring's morels and asparagus). I'll start perhaps with a soup or splurge on sauteed foie gras. No, most likely I'll be unable to resist the little

"The quality of the ingredients plus the magical setting add up to a bargain among luxuries."

appetizer napoleon, its pastry layers of lacy fried potatoes *gaufrette*, its filling a silken, house-smoked salmon and its garnish a dollop of *osetra* caviar, the most flavorful of the sturgeon eggs.

Or maybe I'll order a tasting menu and let the chef show me what he's doing that's most exciting.

Chef Jeffrey Tomchek keeps up with the trends, but he doesn't try so hard to be original that he loses sight of the essentials. His fish, his meats, his vegetables taste primarily of themselves and only peripherally of their elaborations. Nothing too fussy here. Expensive, yes, but the quality of the ingredients plus the magical setting add up to a bargain among luxuries.

OLD EBBITT GRILL
675 15th St. NW, Washington, DC
(202) 347-4800

AMERICAN   ♿

Breakfast: M-Th 7:30-11, Sat 8-11:30 **Entrees:** $5-$10
Lunch: M-Th 11-5, Sat 11:30-4 **Entrees:** $7-$13
Dinner: M-Th 5-1 am, F 5-2 am, Sat 4-1 am, Sun 4-midnight
Dinner Entrees: $8-$17 **Brunch:** Sun 9:30-4 **Entrees:** $8-$17
Credit Cards: All major **Reservations:** Recommended
Dress: Casual **Parking:** Complimentary valet, dinner & brunch
Metro: Metro Center

O nce upon a time Clyde's was the hottest news in town. Now Clyde's has become a conglomerate of restaurants, ranging from the family-oriented Tomato Palace in Columbia to the OLD EBBITT GRILL downtown, to the colonial dowager 1789 in Georgetown.

What's amazing is that this high-intensity chain of restaurants, with its predictable pub fare (fried calamari, Buffalo wings, chili, Caesar salad, the usual pastas, barbecue, crab cakes), comes up with some wonderful seasonable surprises. The few days of halibut season in Alaska mean fresh halibut on the menus at Clyde's and the OLD EBBITT. In the summer, the OLD EBBITT GRILL is probably the only downtown pub serving fresh corn on the cob, local green beans and new potatoes, as well as pies and cobblers made with berries from nearby farms.

"We'd all like to retire on a dollar for every hamburger the Old Ebbitt sells."

Even so, we'd all like to retire on a dollar for every burger the OLD EBBITT sells. What once was Clyde's claim to fame is now the OLD EBBITT'S: a thick, handsome patty of juicy, coarsely ground and loosely packed beef, as crusty outside and as pink inside as you want, on a seeded bun with lettuce, tomato (ripe in season), pickle and utterly indifferent french fries. Ask for the green beans instead.

OLD GLORY
3139 M St. NW, Washington, DC
(202) 337-3406

AMERICAN/SOUTHERN/BARBECUE

Open: M-Th 11:30-11:30, F-Sat 11:30-12:30, Sun 11-11:30
Entrees: $6.50-$16 **Late-Nite:** Sun-Th 11:30-1, F-Sat 12:30-2
Late-Nite Entrees: $5.25-$6.75 **Brunch:** Sun 11-2, $11 buffet
Credit Cards: All major **Reservations:** Accepted for 6 or more
Dress: Casual **Parking:** Street
Entertainment: Blues band Sun-Th at 10 pm

If a restaurant is this noisy, throbbing with rock music and flickering with big-screen TV, and it still manages to attract diners beyond their twenties, it must be serving awfully good food. And so OLD GLORY does, for the most part. It's a two-story, tightly packed barbecue joint, with lean, tender and juicy ribs and brisket that envelop your table in wood smoke, as well as some terrific side dishes.

At most barbecues, the chicken is overcooked, dry and far too smoky to taste like bird. And so it is here. But the buffalo wings are a succulent appetizer. So are barbecued shrimp in the shell. For entrees, the ribs and brisket can't be beat, and the burgers are substantial.

An array of sauces representing eight barbecue regions provides mix-and-match games. And the basket of corn muffins and biscuits tastes of Southern pride. Getting more Southern, mellow collard greens, creamy succotash and barely greasy hush puppies are among the side dishes. The potato salad is worthy of a church picnic, and the mashed potatoes are the real thing. Too bad that the coleslaw and the french fries taste like leftovers.

Few real barbecues have desserts that warrant saving room, but here, too, OLD GLORY exceeds expectations. Apple crisp and cherry-coconut cobbler taste homey and look it, in their Pyrex measuring cups. And cookie-topped chocolate pudding, served in a flowerpot with candy gummy worms peering through, is far more delicious than most practical jokes.

OODLES NOODLES
1010 20th St. NW, Washington, DC
(202) 293-3138

ASIAN

Lunch: M-F 11:30-3 **Dinner:** M-Sat 5-10
Entrees: $6-$8 **Closed:** Sun **Credit Cards:** All major
Reservations: Recommended for 6 or more
Dress: Casual **Metro:** Dupont Circle, Farragut North

Forget trying to spell *fettuccine* or *paglia e fieno*. The word now is noodles. OODLES NOODLES, with branches on 20th Street and in Bethesda, proves the point with noodle dishes from all over Asia, at prices low enough to compete with fast-food.

At the Bethesda branch, with more tables and dishes, appetizers tend to be highlights, and satays may be the best in town. Dough-based appetizers are even more scrumptious: savory pancakes with a well-seasoned meat filling or meaty Japanese dumplings. Spring onion cake is like a pancake, crisp-edged and pleasantly starchy, its dip sweet and fiery. The butterfly shrimp appetizer is the lone disappointment.

I'd be tempted, however, to have soup for both first and second courses. Thai chicken-coconut soup is outstanding, as in an entree of grilled chicken noodle soup. Some Bethesda entrees, though, seem tamed for American tastes. I prefer downtown for such adventurous entrees as Hokkien shrimp noodle soup, *Penang asam laksa* or grilled eel. At either branch, you can expect Thai drunken noodles to be irresistibly fragrant with basil and peppers and Indonesian *nasi campur* to be a small banquet of tangy, sweet-hot glazed shrimp, subtly curried slices of chicken breast, crunchy whole peanuts, crisp little salted fish, diced cucumbers and half a boiled egg around a mound of rice.

Choose your noodles — soft fat Japanese *udon*, thin wiry *ramen*, firm golden egg, fragile filaments of rice vermicelli or wide stark-white rice noodles like the Chinese *chow fun*. And pick your style — mild or spicy; dry, saucy or soupy; Malaysian, Indonesian, Japanese, Thai or Chinese. OODLES NOODLES offers a lot of adventure for under $8.

Oodles Noodles also has a branch at 4907 Cordell Ave., Bethesda, MD, (301) 986-8833

OVAL ROOM
800 Connecticut Ave. NW, Washington, DC
(202) 463-8700

AMERICAN   ♿

Lunch: M-F 11:30-3 **Entrees:** $10.50-$18.50
Light Fare: 3-5:30 **Entrees:** $5.50-$14
Dinner: M-Th 5:30-10:30, F-Sat 5:30-11 **Entrees:** $14.50-$20
Pre-Theater: M-Sat 5:30-7, $22.50 **Closed:** Sun
Credit Cards: All major **Reservations:** Recommended
Dress: Jacket & tie **Parking:** Complimentary valet at dinner
Metro: Farragut West **Entertainment:** Pianist at dinner

The OVAL ROOM'S dining room feels like a nest. Formal but festive, the room invites a game of identifying the caricatures on a mural filling the walls: Kissinger, Streisand and Liz Taylor frolic among past presidents. Everything feels comfortable except the sound level — the low ceilings bounce sound everywhere but across the table.

The menu is a playground for the products of the seasons and the flavors of the world, featuring appetizers of squash pasta with frizzled sage or cured salmon and tuna tartare with *wasabi* and *daikon,* entrees such as grilled shrimp on white bean mousse with diced ham hock or rack of lamb with ratatouille and flageolet beans in a cumin broth. Some appetizers are memorable, especially the velvety chicken-and-pistachio sausage on a bed of white beans with tomatoes. Another, timbale of cured salmon and tuna tartare, is gorgeous, a turban of coral salmon with a band of black seaweed hiding the diced raw fish. Yet fried calamari is pale and limp, and a tart of goat cheese and caramelized onion is sometimes subject to clumsy reheating.

So go the entrees, too. The magnificent veal chop is thick and flavorful, with a rosemary sauce that blends subtly with the wild mushrooms, grilled radicchio and sedately garlicky mashed potatoes. Swordfish is moist and cleanly fresh, on a bed of polenta as creamy as Southern grits, with vinegared greens. Yet from the same kitchen comes rack of lamb overwhelmed with cumin-flavored ratatouille, bland grilled tuna or faintly bitter shrimp with cartilagenous ham hock. Seasonings are sometimes confusing, frequently too strong. But be patient: There's creme brulee at the end. And it's so rich and smooth and cracklingly caramelized that it rights all wrongs.

PAN ASIAN NOODLES AND GRILL
2020 P St. NW, Washington, DC
(202) 872-8889

ASIAN/THAI

Lunch: M-Sat 11:30-2:30 **Entrees:** $6.25-$8.25
Dinner: Sun-Th 5-10, F-Sat 5-11 **Entrees:** $7.25-$9.25
Credit Cards: All major **Reservations:** Accepted
Dress: Casual **Parking:** Street **Metro:** Dupont Circle

When a gust of cold weather reminds you that winter has settled in, PAN ASIAN NOODLES AND GRILL is at its best.

For a pittance you can order a giant bowl of noodles, meat and broth, with mix-and-match choices of rice or egg noodles, chicken or spicy beef broth, sliced beef, pork or wontons with pork. Pay a couple bucks more and you get seafood.

In any case, these are filling meals of warming, aromatic broth heady with fresh coriander and Oriental spices. They're served in spiffy-looking black bowls with red rims, in tune with the neon and lacquered colors of this cheerful, clever little restaurant. Even if the day is not cold enough to shout soup, PAN ASIAN is popular for its plates of noodles topped with every Asian flavor, from Thailand's pad thai (which unfortunately is too sweet) to Canton's *chow fun*. The most addictive, though, is drunken noodles, the wide noodles topped with ground chicken and basil in an aromatic, faintly sweet and fairly spicy sauce. Again, the price is well under $10. And the relative splurges of the menu, the appetizers, include lovely little, grilled skewered bits, crisply fried nuggets and the spring rolls of several nations.

"When a gust of cold weather reminds you that winter has settled in, Pan Asian Noodles and Grill is at its best."

The second location of Pan Asian: 1018 Vermont Ave. NW, Washington, DC, (202) 783-8899.

PANJSHIR
224 W. Maple Ave., Vienna, VA
(703) 281-4183

AFGHAN   ♿

Lunch: M-Sat 11:30-2 **Entrees:** $6-$7.25
Dinner: Daily 5-10 **Entrees:** $10-$13.25
Credit Cards: All major **Reservations:** Recommended
Dress: Casual **Parking:** Free lot **Metro:** Vienna

After years of near-addiction to *aushak*, the leek-stuffed Afghan noodles buried in yogurt, tomato sauce and mint, I discovered PANJSHIR'S *muntoo*, which is a meat-stuffed version of aushak. It became a new love. What all this adds up to is that the same dish can be made many different ways and be wonderful in all its variations, despite the stubborn loyalty we have for our taste memories.

Beyond boiled dumplings, the area's Afghan menus are similar right through dessert. Virtually all offer deep-fried turnovers, usually as appetizers. Entrees are kebabs with seasoned rice, stewed lamb with rice, and (the glory of Afghan cooking) vegetables seasoned with such aromatics as ginger or coriander, moistened with yogurt and tomato sauce, sometimes sweetened with brown sugar or prunes. If you don't order an entree that comes with vegetables, you should include a side dish. And even if you consider pumpkin fit only for pies and jack-o-lanterns, try *kadu* — sautéed pumpkin with tomato and yogurt — lest you miss one of the greatest vegetable dishes ever contrived.

PANJSHIR'S outstanding kebab is lamb chops — called Chopped Kebab on the menu. Marinated for a spicy and vinegary tang, the chops are trimmed well, cut thin and cooked until their edges are crisp. Lamb outshines beef here. If you like a sweet main dish, try *quabili palow* — tomatoey lamb stew with rice topped with glazed carrot shreds, almonds and raisins — or one of the vegetable combinations: apples with prunes and walnuts, brown-sugared turnips, carrots with prunes and walnuts or the wonderful soft and aromatic pumpkin. On the less sweet side is eggplant with tomato sauce, and there's spinach with onion and garlic if you prefer no sweetness at all. All are preceded by a nice crisp green salad and accompanied by typical Afghan bread.

Panjshir also has a branch at 924 W. Broad St., Falls Church, VA, (703) 536-4566.

PAOLO'S
1303 Wisconsin Ave. NW, Washington, DC
(202) 333-7353

ITALIAN   ♿

Open: M-Sat 11:30 am-midnight, Sun 11 am-midnight
Entrees: $7.50-$18 **Credit Cards:** All major **Reservations:** No
Dress: Casual **Parking:** Street **Entertainment:** Jazz Sun noon-3

No matter what else might have gone to pot in recent decades, chain restaurants have improved. In an earlier era, nothing could be more predictable — or boring — than an Italian-American restaurant with branches in the major suburbs. No longer. PAOLO'S is a restaurant of considerable comfort — except for the noise level — and the visual enticements of an open kitchen and a wood-burning oven. Its servers are well trained, and it offers food that is imaginative and made from fresh ingredients. Most important, it has added personality to formula cooking.

I like PAOLO'S at off hours, when the place burbles rather than shouts. And I'm impressed by the attractive listings among the pizzas, pastas and grilled dishes. What's more, PAOLO'S has added a little extra zest to the same old salads that everyone else serves. It's got a Caesar (but with pecorino romano and garlic croutons) and the usual mixed greens (in this case with olives, pine nuts and gorgonzola). Its grilled seafood salads include calamari with hearts of palm, pine nuts and tomato in orange-basil vinaigrette, and grilled salmon and shrimp with olives and dried tomatoes in sherry-herb vinaigrette. While you might think you've seen everything a chicken salad could offer, the grilled-chicken-and-greens toss at PAOLO'S includes eggplant, olives, capers and feta as well.

> **"The main reason for going to Paolo's is for what comes free."**

The main reason for going to PAOLO'S, though, is what comes free: warm, soft, seeded bread sticks and the sensational chickpea-eggplant-olive spread that accompanies them.

For the two other Paolo's branches, in Virginia and Maryland: 11898 Market St., Reston, VA, (703) 318-8920, and 1 W. Pennsylvania Ave., Towson, MD (410) 321-7000.

PATISSERIE-CAFE DIDIER
3206 Grace St. NW, Washington, DC
(202) 342-9083

FRENCH ♿

Open: T-Sat 8 am-7 pm, Sun 8 am-5 **Entrees:** $7-$9
Closed: M **Credit Cards:** All major **Dress:** Casual
Reservations: Recommended for 6 or more **Parking:** Street

A tiny pastry shop on Georgetown's most hidden street, PATIS-
SERIE-CAFE DIDIER is like some sort of gastronomic antique
shop. Pore over the menu and you'll unearth the *madeleines* of
Proust and Mozartian *salzberger knockerl*. There are lunches of savory
souffles or tall, quivery quiches, the authentic kind that the French
would eat. Onion soup starts in-house with onions, left to sweat on the
stove until they sweeten and nearly melt from the heat. CAFE DIDIER
serves the kind of French tearoom food that suggests the old genteel
Georgetown rather than the noisy, modern-day M Street with its Boston
Market and French-from-Texas chain, La Madeleine.

CAFE DIDIER is decorated with a gleaming array of fruit tarts and
creamy cakes, pink tablecloths and pottery vases with a single flower
or a small bouquet. For
breakfast it serves crois-
sants, muffins, scones and
the only honestly buttery,
delicate and flaky Danish I
can find in this town. The
fruit juices are freshly

> **"Pore over the menu
> and you'll unearth the
> madeleines of Proust
> and Mozartian
> salzberger knockerl."**

squeezed. And for lunch there's small selection of salads, cold cuts on
French bread, a hot entree such as a grilled chicken breast, or that
evocative quiche.

It's no bargain, and the portions are, let's say, restrained. But some
might consider that an asset, considering the richness of the food. And
an afternoon break of thick, creamy, old-world, bittersweet hot chocolate and a few airy ladyfingers to dip into it, with classical music in the
background, is an indulgence beyond price.

PEKING GOURMET INN
6029-6033 Leesburg Pike, Falls Church, VA
(703) 671-8088

CHINESE   ♿

Lunch: Daily 11-3 **Entrees:** $5.45-$19.45
Dinner: Sun-Th 3-10, F-Sat 3-midnight **Entrees:** $7.45-$30
Credit Cards: AE, MC, V **Dress:** Casual
Reservations: Recommended on weekends **Parking:** Free lot

D id success spoil the PEKING GOURMET INN? This was once
one of the best Chinese restaurants in Virginia, and in the Bush
administration it was in the spotlight as a favorite presidential
retreat. Now it seems like a standard pack-em-in-and-feed-em-quick
Chinese restaurant, even if it does still grow its own Chinese leeks and
feature them in several dishes.

Two dishes still show what this restaurant used to be. Salt-baked
shrimp are large and juicy, crisped in a hot pan with lots of garlic.

"Did success spoil the Peking Gourmet Inn?" String beans with pork and chili are lightly cooked and strongly seasoned, just as they should be. Crispy beef with sesame seeds is still crunchy, but it is all sweet and no heat. The saddest change is that PEKING GOURMET chicken, which once was glorious, is
now soggy and gluey. The skin on the Peking duck is crisp and fat-
free, but the meat is dry and overcooked. Even the dumplings are thick
and gummy, and it's hard to find a dumpling that isn't lovable.

Yet the PEKING GOURMET INN has weathered decades, expansion,
fame and loss of fame. I wouldn't be surprised if it got itself back in
shape again.

PERRY'S
1811 Columbia Rd. NW, Washington, DC
(202) 234-6218

AMERICAN/JAPANESE

Dinner: Sun-Th 6-10:30 (Sushi bar 10:30-11:30), F-Sat 6-12:30 am
Entrees: $10-$17 **Brunch:** Sun 11:30-2:30, $16
Credit Cards: All major **Reservations:** Accepted
Dress: Casual **Parking:** Street **Metro:** Woodley Park-Zoo
Entertainment: Drag show at Sun brunch

PERRY'S comes into its own in the spring when the roof deck first opens, since it has the largest open-air dining space in Adams Morgan. A silly little fountain burbles, tiny lights stretch across the space like a starry tent, and the Columbia Road vistas are glamorized by the altitude. It's a wonderful place to enjoy an urban evening, though the fly in the ointment is that you have to walk up a narrow, grubby staircase to reach the roof and drink your water from plastic cups.

Even inside — also a climb from the street — PERRY'S has a party atmosphere, for it was once a disco, updated for a funky '90s look. There's something for everyone: Twenty-and-thirty-somethings consider it their hangout, and forty-pluses have kept returning through its various incarnations since they were barely adults.

Sushi is the mainstay of PERRY'S, even if it is not made with the usual precision of most Japanese sushi bars. Where else can you eat sushi on a rooftop? And where else can you follow it with a meal of sesame-crusted tuna with mango salad or barbecued chicken with *wasabi* potato salad, not to mention pizza, tomato basil spaghetti or herbed ravioli? Yep, it's fusion food.

The cooking is experimental, adventurous and rustic. The best of it is *yakitori* of crusty-edged, smoky mixed seafood, piled with salad greens and dressed with a chile-lime vinaigrette. Crisply fried wonton skins filled with seafood mousse are a pleasant appetizer, too. And either could serve as a light meal, particularly following sushi. The kitchen hasn't the finesse to warrant splurging on the bigger-ticket items — grilled shrimp with black beans or that raw-inside tuna. This is a restaurant most suited to casual meals of two or three modest dishes.

PESCE
2016 P St. NW, Washington, DC
(202) 466-3474

AMERICAN/SEAFOOD

Lunch: M-F 11:30-2:30, Sat noon-2:30 **Entrees:** $11.25-$16
Dinner: M-Th 5:30-10, F-Sat 5:30-10:30, Sun 5-9:30
Dinner Entrees: $12.50-$21 **Credit Cards:** All major
Reservations: Accepted for lunch, 6-plus at dinner **Dress:** Casual
Parking: Valet (fee) at dinner Th-Sat **Metro:** Dupont Circle

It's no longer true that Washington is a city without good seafood restaurants. And PESCE is one reason. This small, casual restaurant-and-market is owned by chefs Roberto Donna and Jean-Louis Palladin. They don't actually cook there, but they see that the kitchen gets top-quality ingredients, and that's what really counts in seafood.

The place is crowded, clattery, jovial and simply decorated with colorful wooden fish and little else. PESCE is the casual, decently priced seafood restaurant we all wish we had in our neighborhood. The menu, which changes twice a day, is on a blackboard. It's the food that counts here.

What makes PESCE crowded is impeccable fish, grilled or sauteed, with seasonings ranging from near-nothing to Thai curry. High-quality pastas are topped with seafood. Rarities such as fresh grilled sardines, razor clams or cod cheeks show up among the appetizers. The newly fashionable skate wing is all the more succulent — and rare — for being cooked on the bone. And the more familiar luxuries such as lobster and soft-shell crabs are done with flair. Ordinarily, teaming pineapple, coconut and mango with soft-shells

"Pesce is the casual, decently priced seafood restaurant we all wish we had in our neighborhood."

sounds like a criminal act, but in PESCE'S kitchen, the fruits are fresh and ripe, and the crabs are only enhanced. Similarly, the risotto is properly made and infused with dark mushroom juices, the vegetables are bright and at their peak, and the wine list is intelligently chosen. One caveat: The chef has an inclination to overdose his creations with olive oil, so ask him to go light.

PHO CALI/THE QUALITY SEAFOOD PLACE
1621 S. Walter Reed Dr., Arlington, VA
(703) 920-9500

VIETNAMESE/SEAFOOD

Lunch: M-Sun 11-3 **Entrees:** $4.50-$10
Dinner: Sun-Th 6-10, F-Sat 6-11 **Entrees:** $7-$10
Credit Cards: All major **Reservations:** Recommended
Dress: Casual **Parking:** Free lot

P HO CALI, also called the QUALITY SEAFOOD PLACE, has an outdoor deck that looks a little like a miniature golf course but more entertaining. The real entertainment, though, is the 10-page menu divided into separate categories for crab, clams, scallops, oysters, squid, shrimp and fried fish combinations. Yes, there also are meat dishes, and one page is devoted to *pho* — Hanoi beef soup with such toppings as brisket, flank, soft tendon or tripe.

If there is one thing to remember about PHO CALI, it's soft-shell crabs. I've also loved the clams, tender despite their steaming, enveloped in a thickened sauce, tangy and spirited with onions and whole dried red peppers that can be fished out once they've lent their flavor. The sauce is worth scooping up with the shells or pouring over rice. The crispy fried whole fish is a tour de force, brought to the table looking as if it were still swimming. There's so much more, even steamed hard-shell crabs in the summer. And the waitresses are candid, chatty, irreverent — and efficient.

"If there's one thing to remember about Pho Cali, it's soft-shell crabs."

166

PHO 75
1711 Wilson Blvd., Arlington, VA
(703) 525-7355

VIETNAMESE	&#11104;

Open: Daily 9 am-8 pm **Entrees:** $4.25-$5
Credit Cards: None; cash only **Reservations:** No
Dress: Casual **Parking:** Free lot **Metro:** Court House

I wouldn't dream of suggesting this is the best *pho* restaurant in the Washington area — there are too many for me to be sure. But I can't imagine one better, and I believe it's the oldest. Most important, any list of my favorites has to include one place that serves a proper Vietnamese noodle soup.

PHO 75 is about as charming as your high school cafeteria: big and bare, with long tables and clattering dish carts. Its menu offers one dish and one dish only, pho, that long-simmered beef broth perfumed with Asian spices, the most identifiable one being star anise. But on that simple base is built a sumptuous one-dish meal. The broth — a giant "regular" bowl or an even more immense one — is packed with thin rice noodles, thickly floating sliced scallions and leaves of coriander, and further stuffed with the beef, cuts ranging from thinly sliced top round that cooks in the bowl to tendons or tripe.

Alongside comes a plate of bean sprouts, green-chili slices and lime wedges, and on the table are squeeze bottles of sweet-spicy bean sauce and hot red chili sauce. You create a soup to your own taste, adjusting the seasonings as you go along, and wind up feeling full, healthy and oh so comforted. And at under $5. You jack up the price a bit with a beverage, perhaps fresh lemonade or the dark, rich, condensed-milk iced coffee that's strong enough to keep you awake for a week. You pay at the counter as you leave, after bidding goodbye to your tablemates in Vietnamese, Spanish, English, babytalk or whatever else these varied and faithful diners happen to speak.

Pho 75 has three other locations in the Washington area: 3103 Graham Rd, Unit B, Falls Church, VA, (703) 204-1490; 771 Hungerford Dr., Rockville, MD, (301) 309-8873;and 1510 University Blvd. East, Langley Park, MD, (301) 434-7844

PINES OF ROME
4709 Hampton Lane, Bethesda, MD
(301) 657-8775

ITALIAN   ♿

Lunch: M-Sat 11:30-4 **Entrees:** $5.25-$10
Dinner: M 4-10, T-Th 4-11, F-Sat 4-11:30, Sun noon-10
Dinner Entrees: $6-$12 **Credit Cards:** All major **Dress:** Casual
Reservations: No **Parking:** Street **Metro:** Bethesda

One of the oldest — and most modestly priced — Italian restaurants in the Washington area, PINES OF ROME is a haven for families. I've never seen so many children in a restaurant that didn't serve fast food. And when the 6 p.m. seating is over and the families with small children leave, the second seating arrives — with more, if older, children.

The reason is obvious: The food is inexpensive, the dining room is red-check-oil-cloth casual, the cooking is plain and the menu is long. There's something for everyone. Sure, the service is perfunctory, but it is fast. Yet, sadly, the food can be dismal. If you order something that is supposed to be simple, however, you'll probably get what you expect but far more of it. Portions are huge.

"I've never seen so many children in a restaurant that didn't serve fast food."

Everyone swears by the white pizza at PINES OF ROME; surely it's better than the red-sauced pizza, with its plain canned tomatoes. I also can confidently recommend the white beans, which are nicely seasoned and served warm as an appetizer.

Look for the day's roast meat, and certainly order it if it's pork. Maybe it will be cooked too long and have turned stringy, but it's homey meat, darkened and flavorful from its pan juices. Otherwise, consider this a spaghetti-and-meatballs kind of kitchen — or spaghetti carbonara if you love fried onions and chunks of fried bacon. Skip the seafood and concentrate on heavy, old fashioned red sauce and red meat. Wash them down with an inexpensive bottle of wine poured into tumblers, and enjoy this rustic place even if its charms are no longer culinary.

PIZZERIA PARADISO
2029 P St. NW, Washington, DC
(202) 223-1245

ITALIAN

Open: M.-T 11 am -11 pm, F-Sat 11-midnight, Sun noon-10
Entrees: $5-$10 **Credit Cards:** D, MC, V **Reservations:** No
Dress: Casual **Parking:** Street **Metro:** Dupont Circle

We've grown suspicious of designer pizzas that foist soy sauced, stir-fry vegetables or *fajita* chicken on a defenseless round of dough. But what PIZZERIA PARADISO serves is creative without stepping beyond the bounds of tradition — or good sense. Amend that: Cooking mussels with their shells on top of a pizza is pretty silly. Otherwise, the vegetable and cheese toppings, the salami with black olives and hot peppers, four cheeses with parsley and garlic, even *bottarga* — roe — with egg, garlic and parsley are reasonably Italian. And, of course, you can compose your own combination.

Paradiso keeps its eye on what's important: the dough, flavorful on its own and baked in a wood-burning oven; and the quality of the toppings, which include fresh vegetables, **"I've even seen devotees eating their pizza-to-go right on the front steps."** real Parma ham and buffalo mozzarella, forceful cheeses. The rest of the menu is even simpler, just a few straightforward salads and sandwiches, including a most memorable roast lamb — pink, crusty and infused with garlic — layered with roasted vegetables that are almost a ratatouille, spinach leaves and mustardy dressing on a golden-crusted, house-baked roll. I could even pass up the pizza for this. And the lemonade is so good it could divert you from a beer.

The problem with PIZZERIA PARADISO is that its small, cheerful, town house dining room is always crowded. The solution is carryout; I've even seen devotees eating their pizzas-to-go right on the front steps.

THE PRIME RIB
2020 K St. NW, Washington, DC
(202) 466-8811

AMERICAN/STEAKHOUSE   ♿

Lunch: M-F 11:30-3 **Entrees:** $10-$16
Dinner: M-Th 5-11, F-Sat 5-11:30 **Entrees:** $16-$27
Credit Cards: All major **Reservations:** Recommended
Dress: Jacket & tie **Metro:** Farragut West
Parking: Complimentary valet at dinner
Entertainment: Pianist at lunch, with bassist, too, at dinner

I've finally grown to appreciate THE PRIME RIB. My heart's been won over by the black walls with their gilt trim, the little silk-shaded table lamps and the pianist playing even at lunch. As I sink into a soft leather armchair, I realize I've overcome my resistance to this macho scene. At last THE PRIME RIB'S plain cooking looks good.

Steakhouses are so predictable. The quality depends more on their buying the best and less on who's on kitchen duty. Some things here have changed: There's more fish on the menu. But some things are un-wavering: The martinis never did contain any vermouth, and the roast beef and crab always have been excellent. In light of such long-lived reliability, however, I can overlook the outrageous overselling: the "made to order" fish soup that's just a salty, too-herbal broth with a lot of celery and a little fish; the "fresh peas and carrots" that could only have been fresh several stages earlier in the food distribution system. I'm here for the restaurant's namesake. The surprisingly flavorful, out-rageously thick cut of prime rib woos me with its simplicity: no "au jus," no excess fat, just shavings of horseradish (that are "fresh" but could be fresher). It's some of the best roast beef I've tasted in years.

This is a meat place, and it does well those things that we identify with meat. While the browned and herb-dusted French rolls are shameful, given our recent wave of good bakeries, the mashed potatoes are sen-sational, the potato skins more so. Creamed spinach doesn't quite meet the competition at other steakhouses, but in the right season the thick slices of tomato sprinkled with balsamic vinegar and fresh basil are an ideal side dish. The wine list does honor to beef. And if somebody at your table is averse to red meat, the crab imperial is one of the better versions in this crab-happy town, and the blackened swordfish is as thick and as juicy as a steak.

PROVENCE
2401 Pennsylvania Ave. NW, Washington, DC
(202) 296-1166

FRENCH

Lunch: M-F noon-2 **Entrees:** $12-$23.50
Dinner: M-F 6-10, Sat 5:30-11 **Entrees:** $16.50-$29
Closed: Sun **Credit Cards:** All major
Reservations: Recommended **Dress:** Casual
Parking: Complimentary valet at dinner **Metro:** Foggy Bottom

A s warm and bright as a Van Gogh sun, PROVENCE serves the light, fragrant, olive-oil cuisine that suits our dietary guidelines these days. The menu is long, and the appetizers far outnumber the entrees. Then along comes the waiter with a daunting recitation of specials — certainly more than one can remember in one round. So the sense is of abundance. And while the cooking wavers, much of it is as seductive as it sounds. The grilled lobsters, the salads of seasonal greens with anchovy and garlic, maybe topped with grilled fish; the pastas stuffed or sauced with rabbit — this is sophisticated cooking with an endearing directness, none of the tortured urbanity of Parisian food. Only the *boudin blanc* has struck me as too refined.

Much here is designated as young: young spinach, young squid, and not too long ago the tiniest chops of young lamb. Then there are the hearty country dishes, none better than a risotto of mushrooms with red wine and sauteed snails. The specials lean towards fish, and they are the entrees I'd be inclined to choose after a rich first course of risotto or rabbit ravioli, lobster or foie gras. Grilled rockfish accompanied by chunks of sauteed artichoke, or swordfish with the tang of olives, anchovies or sorrel — they're pure PROVENCE.

Ah, but I'm caught. Diners complain of long waits on busy evenings. And dishes that have stayed on the regular menu sometimes taste tired: the fabulous wheatberry soup is gray and unexciting, whereas it once was dark and mysterious. Yet the specials, recited rather than printed, tend to be more expensive than those dishes with prices revealed, and that makes me feel manipulated (as does the overpriced wine list). So the restaurant is a risk, and an expensive one. Still, it could be the cheapest option available in the search for the flavors of the South of France.

QUEEN BEE
3181 Wilson Blvd., Arlington, VA
(703) 527-3444

VIETNAMESE

Lunch: Daily 11-3 **Entrees:** $5-$7.50
Dinner: Daily 3:30-10 **Entrees:** $5.50-$9
Credit Cards: AE, MC, V **Reservations:** Accepted for 6 or more
Dress: Casual **Parking:** Street **Metro:** Clarendon

Every neighborhood has a favorite Vietnamese restaurant by now, and a few neighborhoods such as Clarendon have a half dozen favorites. Still, you can't beat QUEEN BEE, which is among the oldest and still holding its own. Its menu is extensive, its service is efficient, its prices are low and its cooking is reliable (if you ignore some oversalting here and there). It's a cavernous restaurant that frequently has a line waiting for tables.

Nobody makes better *cha gio*, the crisp, rice-paper wrappers with a savory stuffing of ground pork, vegetables and thin vermicelli. Appetizers also include meaty or vegetarian summer rolls, skewered beef or shrimp and wonderful, plump, roasted quail. Entrees include everything from noodle soups to stir-fried and sauced meats or seafood.

But my favorites are the grilled dishes. Vietnamese cooking at its best, so far as I'm concerned, is bits of pork, marinated with soy sauce, scallions and sometimes honey, cooked over charcoal until the edges are crisp and served with thin white noodles or, even better, rice-flour cakes. The cakes are made of a slippery and slightly

"It's menu is extensive, its service is efficient, its prices are low and its cooking is reliable."

chewy wad of steamed rice-flour dough, here studded with bits of scallion. The contrast of crisp, sweet-salty meat and bland dough is irresistible, particularly when you wrap it with marinated carrots and cilantro in lettuce and dip it in the faintly fishy clear sauce. Wash it down with sparkling fresh lemonade, Vietnamese beer or creamy-rich and intense iced coffee, and you'll have found one of Asia's best meals for under $10.

172

RT's
3804 Mount Vernon Ave., Alexandria, VA
(703) 684-6010

AMERICAN/CREOLE/SEAFOOD

Lunch: M-Sat 11-5 **Entrees:** $6-$14
Dinner: M-Th 5-10:30, F-Sat 5-11, Sun 4-9 **Entrees:** $13-$20
Credit Cards: All major **Reservations:** Recommended
Dress: Casual **Parking:** Street

Okay, so the expansion of RT's to a second location (or a third, if you count the Warehouse in Old Town Alexandria) hasn't done it any good. The Acadian peppered shrimp, last time I tried it, was all pepper and no salt, and the shrimp didn't taste fresh enough. Our party left two, whereas we usually fight over the last nibble. The she-crab soup was crabby, creamy and nicely spirited, even if it wasn't as luscious as we'd last found it. The shrimp cakes were crumbly, and the shrimp in the "Jack Daniel's" shrimp with lump crab meat had a bleary, watery taste (though its rich, pale-pink sauce was worth dunking and swabbing to the last smidgen). Maybe RT's was having a bad-shrimp day. After all, the smothered catfish was luscious under its spicy *etouffe* sauce. And always, when the fish of the day is coated with pecans and livened with creole mustard sauce, you really don't need to know about anything else.

"While RT's shows signs of slipping, its Louisiana specialties remain seasoned as they should be."

While RT's — at both locations — shows signs of slipping, its Louisiana specialties remain seasoned as they should be. So the talent is still there. Both restaurants have a homey style, but since the Alexandria outpost is older and smaller, it is all the more neighborly.

The second RT's location, which has somewhat different hours and prices, is at 2300 Clarendon Blvd., Arlington, VA (703) 841-0100.

RAKU
1900 Q St. NW, Washington, DC
(202) 265-7258

ASIAN

Open: M-T 11:30 am-midnight, F-Sat 11:30-2 am, Sun 11:30-10
Entrees: $4-$8.50 **Credit Cards:** MC, V **Reservations:** No
Dress: Casual **Parking:** Street **Metro:** Dupont Circle

RAKU'S New Wave Asian diner is designed to be replicated, from downtown to Bethesda, then around the country. It signals a shift from the pasta to the noodle era, from casual abundance to studied austerity, from the group to the individual. Most of the seating at RAKU is not at companionable tables but at loners' counters. Single diners perch on backless stools, peering through green lacquered bamboo poles to the street scene, sipping cold sake or designer tea, eating a bowl of noodles or three tiny skewers of *yakitori* — nothing that invites sharing. Forget the menu; I love the stone floors and the mossy, sponged-looking wall panels, the *shoji* screens and the Japanese videos.

The cooking is assembly-line fast food. Morsels of chicken are skewered and grilled as yakitori or arranged on a bowl of broth with Japanese *udon* noodles and a handful of vegetables. Rich, yellow, coconut curry broth is ladled over thin rice noodles with a few shrimp and vegetables (Bangkok noodles) or over thicker, wiry egg noodles with chicken and pretty much the same vegetables (Chiang Mai noodles). Those same egg noodles form the base of Kowloon noodles. Or if the meat is changed to sliced beef and *kim chee* is stirred in to fire up the chicken broth, it becomes Korean chili beef.

The chicken broth tastes real, and the vegetables are crunchy-fresh. The ingredients cooperate rather than clash. Still, there's no escaping the fact that this is mass cooking. *Dim sum* taste as if they've been cooked in a crockpot. And the shrimp paste is starchy. What work best are skewers, of Nonya pork, diced shark meat rubbed with Thai green curry paste, the little chicken morsels or flat slabs of squid. And the most popular dish — deservedly so — is Hunan chicken salad. As for dessert, the sorbets are the class acts on the list.

RED HOT & BLUE
1600 Wilson Blvd., Arlington, VA
(703) 276-7427

AMERICAN/BARBECUE   ♿

Open: Sun-Th 11 am-10 pm, F-Sat 11 am-11 pm
Entrees: $5-$11.50   **Credit Cards:** AE, MC, V
Reservations: Accepted for 15 or more
Dress: Casual   **Parking:** Street   **Metro:** Rosslyn

While it's spinning off branches as fast as a pig produces piglets, RED HOT & BLUE'S original Arlington location always seems to attract a crowd. So expect to wait and not to linger at the table. What are worth waiting for are not just the ribs but also the side dishes. The ribs come wet or dry, and while I usually like the dry — heavily sprinkled with spices rather than sodden with sauce — I don't like the grittyness that comes from pouring on the spices at the end; they should be cooked on the ribs.

So I opt for wet ribs, basted with a thick, sweet-hot sauce that has enough tang to balance the sugar. If you hit it right, the ribs will be crusty and chewy, lightly perfumed with smoke, but sometimes they are overcooked so they are falling off the bone and soft rather than crusty. The accompanying coleslaw is fine, the meaty barbecued beans are nicely spiced, and the beer is icy. Go whole hog and add a loaf of onion rings, thin and crunchy and freshly made.

RED HOT & BLUE also serves pulled chicken, barbecued beef brisket and pulled pig, which is a refined version of North Carolina chopped barbecue with big, soft, lean chunks of smoked pork butt brushed with barbecue sauce. Again, I miss the crustiness, but the

"What are worth waiting for are not just the ribs but also the side dishes."

pulled pig is a generous sandwich served with potato salad. RED HOT & BLUE has hit the right chord in this city that's been whining for good barbecue, and now that it's going national, maybe Washington will become known as a barbecue capital.

Red Hot & Blue's other locations: 208 Elden St., Herndon, VA, (703) 318-7427; 16809 Crabbs Branch Way, Gaithersburg, MD, (301) 948-7333; 677 Main St., Laurel, MD, (301) 953-1943; and 200 Old Mill Bottom Rd. (Rte 50 & Exit 28), Annapolis, MD, (410) 626-7427.

RED SAGE
605 14th St. NW, Washington, DC
(202) 638-4444

AMERICAN/SOUTHWESTERN

Lunch: M-F 11:30-2 **Entrees:** $11.75-$14.50
Dinner: M-Sat 5:30-10:30, Sun 5-10 **Entrees:** $16-$31.50
Chili Bar: Sun-Th 11:30 am-11:30 pm, F-Sat 11:30 am-12:30 am
Chili Bar Entrees: $7.75-$10 **Credit Cards:** All major
Reservations: Recommended for dining rooms; none for Chili Bar
Dress: Casual **Parking:** Street **Metro:** Metro Center

The trick to enjoying RED SAGE, so far as I'm concerned, is not to treat it like a Big Deal. As a serious restaurant, worthy of a big-bucks grilled swordfish or rack of lamb, it has too many flaws. Although the dining rooms are dramatic and colorful, with luxurious little Western details that somehow added up to millions spent on the construction, the place is noisy and clattery, too large to be personal. And the haute Southwestern food, brilliant though its colors and concepts may be, shows more flair than finesse.

Yet while a $70 dinner may be disappointing, a $20 lunch or a $15 bar meal can be great fun. I like RED SAGE when I can eat with a minimum of ceremony — a bowl of chili or a glamorized burrito at an upstairs bar table at off hours, a quick lunch at the counter of the downstairs bar. RED SAGE, despite its (inflated) reputation and its dinner prices, is not a Temple of Gastronomy. It is a sprawl of a

"While a $70 dinner may be disappointing, a $20 lunch or a $15 bar meal can be great fun."

restaurant that cooks to dazzle the eye and wake up jaded taste buds. It is a smashingly vivid site that tourists flock to see, and it adds spice and color to the downtown locals' lunch scene.

RESTAURANT NORA
2132 Florida Ave. NW, Washington, DC
(202) 462-5143

AMERICAN

Dinner: M-Th 6-10, F-Sat 6-10:30 **Entrees:** $20-$25
Closed: Sun **Credit Cards:** D, MC, V
Reservations: Recommended **Dress:** Casual
Parking: Valet (fee) **Metro:** Dupont Circle

For some diners, NORA, with its Organic American Cuisine, is a respite from chemicals, a culinary statement about wise methods of farming. For others, it is merely a quietly attractive and very good luxury American restaurant. For me, it is somewhere in between. Nora Pouillon paid attention to organic ingredients long before most of today's' chefs ever heard the term. And she still seeks out farmers and purveyors of high commitment. But if she once was ahead of the pack, the pack has now caught up. Such quality is now widely available.

So one must admire NORA for more than its ingredients to make its steep prices worthwhile. I find the dusky, quiet dining room a solace, a museum of American quilts and a haven of unfussy comfort. The staff is knowledgeable and smoothly professional. The menu is not particularly long, but ranges from India to California, from austere to rich. Two appetizers illustrate: Quail is poised on spicy lentil *dal* with mango sauce and antennae of *pappadum*; ancient India meets contemporary America, and they have a fine time together. And a clay casserole of mussels is bathed in garlic, leeks, peppers and white wine; modern farmed mussels meet Portuguese tradition in a delicious mingling.

NORA is a magnet for complaints: Prices are too high (I agree, particularly for appetizers, desserts and wines). Cooking is erratic (true, as in strong and juiceless lamb and an underflavored lemon tart with knife-resistant crust). Service is indifferent (a problem I, recognized as a critic, have not encountered). Still, NORA'S standards are high, and more often than not you're charmed and sated by the likes of huge, perfect scallops teamed with celery root puree and fat, flavorful asparagus or apple and blueberry crisp that tastes intensely of fruit and not too much of sugar. At the end, there's some of the best coffee in town.

RICHLAND
865-B Rockville Pike, Rockville, MD
(301) 340-8778

CHINESE

Lunch: M-Sun 11-3 **Entrees:** $5-$7
Dinner: Sun-Th 3-10, F-Sat 3-11 **Entrees:** $7-$14
Credit Cards: AE, MC, V **Reservations:** Recommended
Dress: Casual **Parking:** Free lot **Metro:** Rockville

Given RICHLAND'S shopping-strip location, its big, boxy dining room decorated with gilded fans, and the plates of *moo goo gai pan* and shrimp fried rice on the tables, you'd think this was just another updated Chinese restaurant left over from the '50s. But its reach is much wider, from bargain combination plates to the esoteric. The dinner menu goes on for pages — with eight duck dishes, for example. Entrees you can count on are shredded pork with bean curd strips, lamb with green onions or garlic sauce, and steamed fish that's cooked only until it's barely gelatinous. Even better are sauteed baby shrimp on a bed of spinach, and eggplant with garlic sauce.

But what makes RICHLAND a standout is its appetizer list, at least 30 items, among them a Chinese pizza that is similar to the white pizza Italian restaurants sell for four or five times the price. The greatest treat is the *dim sum*, available at dinner as well as at lunch: *shao my*; spicy, tangy dumplings; and my favorite, deep-fried radish cake, with bits of ham and scallion, wrapped in crisp, flaky dough reminiscent of Italian *sfogliatelle*. The pan-fried radish cake is far less interesting. Hot appetizers also include other fried items — egg rolls, spring rolls, shrimp toast, chicken wings — as well as more steamed dumplings, spareribs and kebabs. Cold appetizers provide contrasts in crunch, tang and lightness. Spicy pickled cabbage is outstanding, and there are bean curd sheets rolled around black mushrooms and cut into handsome slices that look like mushroom strudel. Finally, there's stewed duck in spicy salt water, its flavor reminiscent of France's *confit*.

RICHLAND serves large portions at low prices in a comfortable dining room, which is enough to make it a solidly successful suburban Chinese restaurant. But it is more. Its service is solicitous and its cooking is highly competent. And it provides excellent dim sum at any time of day.

178

RIO GRANDE CAFE
4919 Fairmont Ave., Bethesda, MD
(301) 656-2981

AMERICAN/SOUTHWESTERN

Lunch: M-F 11-3 **Entrees:** $5-$10
Dinner: Sun-Th 3-10:30, F 3-11:30, Sat.11:30-11:30
Entrees: $6.50-$17 **Brunch:** Sun 11:30-3 **Entrees:** $6.25-$8
Credit Cards: All major **Reservations:** No **Dress:** Casual
Parking: Street **Metro:** Bethesda

As soon as I open the door to RIO GRANDE CAFE — any RIO GRANDE CAFE — I'm pushed and pulled. The noise pushes me to seek a quick escape, while the tortilla machine pulls me in to satisfy a craving for its unbeatable flour tortillas.

Its walls painted with fancy graffiti in hot colors and its servers unfailingly cheerful, RIO GRANDE CAFE is always a festival. At lunch, long tables are filled with office parties. At dinner, children and parents, singles and couples celebrate a birthday, or just the end of the workday. Big margaritas, huge baskets of chips, platters large enough to see you through two meals — everything is bigger than life.

And almost everything is good. The chips are thin and delicate, though the same could be said of the salsa, and that's not a compliment. The fajitas are a fabulous pile of crusty grilled skirt steak (or chicken for the timid) to wrap in those warm, puffy tortillas. The tamales and enchiladas have solid character, the chiles rellenos are flavorful as well as moderately fiery. And the accompanying red rice and pork-studded beans are good enough to serve proudly as a meal.

Beyond the down-to-earth Tex-Mex dishes, there are such elegances as quail, frog legs and a big, luxurious, lime-sharpened, cilantro-fragrant seviche of shellfish and orange roughy. Grilled shrimp are merely ordinary, though, and crispy tacos, especially chicken, taste like chain-restaurant cooking. Still, few are the disappointments in this gregarious trio of Tex-Mex restaurants.

Other Rio Grande Cafe branches: 4301 N. Fairfax Dr., Arlington, VA, (703) 528-31311, and 1827 Library St., Reston, VA (703) 904-0703.

ROCKLANDS
At Carpool, 4000 Fairfax Dr.
Arlington, VA
(703) 528-9663

AMERICAN/BARBECUE

Open: Sun-M 11:30-10, T-W 11:30-11, Th-Sat 11:30-midnight
Entrees: $4-$15.75 **Credit Card:** AE **Reservations:** No
Dress: Casual **Parking:** Free lot

One look at the large, glossed-up gas station/pool hall that serves as the Virginia outpost of ROCKLANDS barbecue and you're sure the food's got to be terrible. Quite the contrary. This warehouse-sized space, furnished with countless bar stools and a kind of TV lounge behind pool tables, serves some of the best barbecue in three states, which you might guess if you notice the wood stacked up ready for the smoker. And there's a wonderful array of salads and side dishes that would be worthy of a white-tablecloth temple of gastronomy.

There are two ROCKLANDS: In addition to this pool hall and carry-out, the original carryout, with a few stools and counter space, serves the Glover Park area. At both, the food is remarkable for the price and the setting. The greatest challenge is grilled fish, and here the $6.25 swordfish or salmon sandwich is juicy, smoky, fresh and slathered with a tangy pink sauce on a soft golden roll. A great fish sandwich. The lamb is tender and moist, delicate meat with the flavor of the grill. And ribs are smoky through and through, crusty and just chewy enough.

As for the salads, few upscale restaurants make a better Caesar. None makes a more delicious applesauce, and the corn pudding, macaroni and cheese or mashed potatoes are worthy of the Deep South. Potato salad, coleslaw, green beans and black beans with corn are out of the modern, lighter repertoire. The jalapeno cornbread, brownies and cookies are just plain homey. If you doubt that ROCKLANDS cares about every detail: There's freshly made lemonade — without too much sugar.

The original Rocklands is located at 2418 Wisconsin Ave. NW, Washington, DC, (202) 333-2558.

THE ROOF TERRACE RESTAURANT
The Kennedy Center
New Hampshire Ave. NW & Rock Creek Parkway
Washington, DC
(202) 416-8555

AMERICAN   ♿

Lunch: M-Sat 11:30-2 **Entrees:** $13-$16
Dinner: T-Sat 5:30-9 **Entrees:** $22-$29
Brunch: Sun 11:30-3, $26 **Credit Cards:** All major
Reservations: Recommended **Parking:** Garage (fee)
Metro: Foggy Bottom (with free shuttle bus)

Dining beneath the immense crystal chandeliers of the Kennedy Center's luxury restaurant is no more expensive than tickets to the Concert Hall or Opera House, and with chef Carolyn Flinn in the kitchen and Mike Williams doing the pastry, the show can be as good. The setting — high ceilings and window walls overlooking the Potomac — is pure grandeur. The furnishings are lush with dignity. And the service, given that this is a restaurant where nearly everybody has a curtain to make, is remarkably attentive.

Mindful of the scheduling complexities of such a restaurant, the chef wisely has limited the menu to seven appetizers and seven entrees, including one special of the day. That's the dish to pick, in my experience. Good timing brought me the freshest swordfish, lightly cooked, on a mound of richly cheesy and properly creamy risotto. Otherwise, the menu is fairly traditional: a steak, crab cakes, roast chicken, a vegetarian dish and rack of lamb. That's the most expensive entree, and not nearly as good as the fish. The sauce is vague and saline, the vegetable ragout, which has been the summertime accompaniment, is murky and the lamb is not lean enough. Appetizers include a too-salty, hand-cured gravlax with three kinds of caviar, carpaccio and seasonal salads. And for both courses you'll find a pasta that nicely shows off the vegetables of the season.

The season is even more beautifully celebrated in fruit tarts. There's also creme brulee, a hot fudge sundae or double chocolate cake. The star of this list, though, is a puckeringly wonderful lemon tart with lemon lavender ice cream. It will wake you up for the show to come.

ROXANNE
2319 18th St. NW, Washington, DC
(202) 462-8330

AMERICAN/SOUTHWESTERN

Dinner: Sun-Th 5-11, F-Sat 5-midnight **Entrees:** $8-$15
Brunch: Sat-Sun 11:30-4 **Entrees:** $7-$13
Credit Cards: All major **Reservations:** Recommended
Dress: Casual **Parking:** Street
Entertainment: Karaoke Sat 10:30-midnight

Downstairs it's PEYOTE CAFE. Up a few steps is ROXANNE, which feels more like a restaurant and less like a bar. And on the roof is ON THE ROX. This restaurant may have three names, but it has evolved into one kitchen with mix-and-match menus. Thus ROXANNE now serves the hits from PEYOTE CAFE, some of the best Tex-Mex dishes in town. It's not typical Tex-Mex cooking, but what you might expect if you crossed Tex-Mex with a really good diner and let a contemporary chef lighten the results.

Start with shrimp rubbed with tingly hot spices and grilled, then draped over a vivid salad of oranges and olives. Persuade someone at the table to order the calamari, fried to a crunch and combined with diced vegetables that taste like a kind of sautéed salsa. Among entrees, the chicken dishes are irresistible, particularly since they come with world-class mashed potatoes ladled with chili gravy, and, depending on your particular chicken choice, terrific chunky applesauce and

". . . what you might expect if you crossed Tex-Mex with a really good diner and let a contemporary chef lighten the result."

corn on the cob or a dull zucchini stir-fry. The only entree that makes me vary my chicken routine is salmon enchiladas, because the salmon has a lovely crustiness and bursts with juiciness. This is Tex-Mex cooking with more flavor than heat.

ROXANNE completes its appeal with excellent chips and salsa and such universal desserts as warm, white-chocolate bread pudding with ice cream and a drizzle of fudge. And even if the food were only half as good, the personable service would be an attraction.

RUPPERTS
1017 7th St. NW, Washington, DC
(202) 783-0699

AMERICAN   ♿

Lunch: Th only 11:30-2:30 Entrees: $16-$30
Dinner: T-Th 6-10, F-Sat 6-11 **Entrees:** $16-$30
Closed: Sun-M **Credit Cards:** All major
Reservations: Recommended **Dress:** Casual
Parking: Street **Metro:** Mount Vernon, Gallery Place-Chinatown

The first white tablecloths on Seventh Street? An entry hall full of flowers, just across the street from a soup kitchen and a parking lot? Who thought you could find a $50 dinner on this forlorn strip of downtown? Times are changing, and RUPPERTS is helping them do it.

Here's what serious young American chefs are accomplishing: They're tracking down the first pearly, soft-shell crabs and wild ramps of spring, the figs and wild mushrooms of fall. They're inventing combinations never before considered, and the good chefs, like RUPPERTS', are combining them with logic as well as style. Apples and parsnips in a soup — tree and earth, sweet-tart and a pleasantly bitter resonance. Shad roe and grits — the South revisited, graininess of fish eggs and of ground corn. This food is not about sauces. It's about vegetables dominating and extolling the meat and the fish: shredded parsnip mysterious and delicious with tiny lettuces and idyllic asparagus, all a bed for grilled red snapper. Grilled sweetbreads and mashed potatoes (with oil — no butter or cream is used here) mingle with turnip greens and a surprise of puckery grilled rhubarb. With all this, three kinds of crusty, just-baked bread. And afterward, the absolute in vanilla ice creams, served on a cornmeal waffle with warm seasonal fruit, such as tart rhubarb puree. A dessert to make you count the days until spring.

RUPPERTS is full of surprises, the least happy being the uptown prices for simple cooking in a marginal downtown location. It's surprising, too, to find the waiters in jeans-and-shirtsleeves casualness, given the starched environment. There are precious touches: an hors d'oeuvre served in the bowl of a spoon, after-dinner cookies no bigger than a sequin. Still, the basics are top quality, right down to the Quartermaine's coffee and made-from-scratch cocoa. More than anything else, RUPPERTS is a fashion show for seasonal produce.

SABANG
2504 Ennalls Ave., Wheaton, MD
(301) 942-7859

INDONESIAN	♿

Lunch: M-F 11-3 **Entrees:** $4-$6.50
Dinner: M-Th 3-10, F 3-11, Sat noon-11, Sun noon-10
Dinner Entrees: $7-$12.50 **Credit Cards:** All major
Reservations: Recommended on weekends
Dress: Casual **Parking:** Street **Metro:** Wheaton

For its sheer decorativeness, SABANG is worth a trip. Mythical creatures painted with gilt guard the entrance, fanciful furniture makes for a palatial waiting area, and batik room dividers transform the vastness to human scale. SABANG is candlelit and colorful, and its service is gracious.

The menu runs to a dozen pages, and some of the distinctions are awfully subtle. So the easiest way to cope with the diversity is to order a *rijsttafel*; there are four choices, their differences not so much in number of dishes but in luxury of ingredients. The most expensive — super

" . . . a hint of the real thing at modest prices in dramatic surroundings."

rijsttafel — concentrates on seafood. And it might be the least satisfactory, since the seafood tends to be overcooked. And there is a vegetarian rijsttafel, which might be a good bet since SABANG knows how to preserve the vegetables' brightness and crunch.

In case you are ordering dish by dish, the satays are one of this kitchen's best efforts. *Rendang* — a kind of spicy pot roast — is incendiary and very good. And while the hot-and-sour soup is pure fire and tartness with no underlying flavor, the crab and asparagus soup, often available as a special, is made with fresh ingredients and therefore miles ahead of most Chinese restaurant versions. Much of the food lacks complexity, and much of it tastes similar. But the chef is not afraid of chilies. So it may not be star-quality Indonesian cooking, but it gives you a hint of the real thing at modest prices in dramatic surroundings.

SAIGON GOURMET
2635 Connecticut Ave. NW, Washington, DC
(202) 265-1360

VIETNAMESE   ♿

Lunch: Daily 11:30-3 **Entrees:** $5-$7
Dinner: Daily 5-10:30 **Entrees:** $8-$13
Credit Cards: All major **Dress:** Casual
Reservations: Recommended on weekends
Parking: Street **Metro:** Woodley Park-Zoo

It's one of the prettiest of Washington's Vietnamese restaurants, with pink linens and upholstery and large watercolors of shore birds against sea-green walls. And it has the space for sidewalk dining. While the menu breaks no new ground, what sets the food apart is its bright colors, crisp textures and fresh flavors. Even more refreshing is the calm and helpful service. In case there's anyone left who isn't familiar with the ways of Vietnamese dining, the waiters explain how to use the rice paper and which dipping sauce belongs with which dish. And if you order a whole fish, the waiter will deftly bone it at the table.

If you judge a Vietnamese restaurant by its *cha gio*, this one is a star. The plump fried rice-paper rolls are crisp, flaky and filled with a meaty and fragrant pork-seafood-noodle mixture. Meats and seafood grilled on small bamboo skewers benefit from quality ingredients and a hot charcoal fire. Pork is the best of the grilled options, from appetizers through entrees. As an appetizer, it is sweet and spicy, with crisply caramelized edges and a smoky flavor, topped with bits of onion that have been fried until they are thoroughly crunchy.

Among the entrees is a particularly delicious grilled pork with rice crepe. Seafood choices are mostly routine, except when pork comes into play. Shrimp Saigon Style is fragrant slices of pork and whole shrimp simmered in a thin red sauce that looks hot but is actually quite mild. More zesty — and messy — is Salty Shrimp With Shell; and this kitchen tends carefully to the cooking of its whole fish.

For dessert, bananas dipped in batter and fried, then flamed with a mixture of rum, honey and sesame seeds, make for a grand morass of crunchy, creamy sweetness. And the kitchen concocts the ultimate banana split: banana flambe with rich, sweet-sharp ginger ice cream.

SAIGON INN
2928 M St. NW, Washington, DC
(202) 337-5588

VIETNAMESE   ♿

Lunch: Daily 11-3 **Entrees:** $4-$9
Dinner: Sun-Th 3-11, F-Sat 3-midnight **Entrees:** $8-$15
Credit Cards: All major **Reservations:** Recommended
Dress: Casual **Parking:** Street

When you think of a $4 lunch, you think of minuscule portions, limited choices, drab surroundings and waiters rushing to get you fed and out the door. None of that is the case at SAIGON INN. Its lunch is as generous as any that a $250-an-hour lawyer would proudly submit on his expense account. Even before you've spent any money you're treated like a most welcome guest. Your water is refilled promptly. Your tea — jasmine, the waitress notes proudly — is not only refilled, but immediately replaced if it's not to your liking. The waiters and waitresses are immensely good-natured.

What this bargain lunch consists of is a spring roll and a plate with samples of three entrees chosen from a long list. Rice comes along too, and tea, of course. Dinner isn't exactly expensive either. I have just one warning about this menu, and it's one worth keeping in mind at most inexpensive Asian restaurants: As a general rule, the more expensive dishes aren't worth the splurge.

Remember that at low-price restaurants like this, seafood is rarely a highlight. The ingredients are costly even when they are mediocre, and they are highly perishable. So a $10- to $20-a-person restaurant can't afford to stock top-quality, fresh seafood. Grilled meats, particularly pork, are what Vietnamese kitchens tend to do best. Unlike most Vietnamese restaurants, SAIGON INN makes its spicy dishes — those designated with a star on the menu — just short of explosive. If you like them tamed, say so.

But a dish-by-dish evaluation here of SAIGON INN isn't necessary. A $4 investment lets you sample three entrees at a time; then you return for a full portion of what you liked.

A second Saigon Inn can be found at 2614 Connecticut Ave. NW, Washington, DC, (202) 483-8400.

SALA THAI
2016 P St. NW, Washington, DC
(202) 872-1144

THAI

Lunch: M-F 11:30-2:30 **Entrees:** $6-$8
Dinner: M-Th 5-10:30, F 5-11, Sat noon-11, Sun noon-10:30
Dinner Entrees: $7.25-$13 **Credit Cards:** All major
Reservations: Accepted **Dress:** Casual
Parking: Street **Metro:** Dupont Circle

Downtown Thai restaurants are a treasure, many of them serving elegant food in casual surroundings at easygoing prices. And SALA THAI was the first to venture to Dupont Circle. This downstairs cafe is brightly furnished with laminated tables and spiffy folding chairs. Its menu is extensive, and the waiters warn you if you are ordering dishes that are similar.

There is no stinting on the chilies in this kitchen. If the waiter tells you a dish is hot, watch out. But under the heat is a frenzy of intriguing flavors — this is invigorating food. The hot-and-sour chicken-coconut soup tingles with peppery and cool flavors.

"If the waiter tells you a dish is hot, watch out."

Among the most familiar entrees are a faintly sweet and homey pad thai that is as good as any you'll find. The curry of the day is intricate and aromatic, though its sauce has sometimes been too thin to cling well to the meat or seafood.

If you are inclined to splurge a bit, the shrimp fried in eggroll wrappers — Pinky in the Blanket — is enough to share as an appetizer or even to serve one as an entree. Above all, however, check out the list of daily specials outside the door (the seafood dishes are meant to compete with Pesce next door). That's where you'll find the newest, the freshest, and often the best buys.

SAM & HARRY'S
1200 19th St. NW, Washington, DC
(202) 296-4333

AMERICAN/STEAKHOUSE   ♿

Lunch: M-F 11:30-2:30 **Entrees:** $9-$20
Dinner: M-Sat 5:30-10:30 **Entrees:** $18-$30
Closed: Sun **Credit Cards:** All major
Reservations: Recommended **Dress:** Casual
Parking: Complimentary valet at dinner **Metro:** Dupont Circle

As far as I'm concerned, there are two great steakhouses in town: Morton's and SAM & HARRY'S. And even though Morton's steaks have the edge — slightly juicier, more precisely cooked — I'd be hard-pressed to choose between them. First, SAM & HARRY'S wins hands down on environment. It's an exceedingly comfortable, clubby restaurant, handsome in a strong, silent kind of way. Both restaurants know how to care for a diner, but the last waiter who served me at SAM & HARRY'S was one of the best I've found anywhere. Then there's the food: If SAM & HARRY'S steaks don't quite match those at Morton's, nearly everything else is better.

SAM & HARRY'S serves crab cakes as an appetizer, so luscious, so clearly tasting of crab yet creamy, that I'd be glad to have them as an entree and, again, as dessert. Other appetizers are also fine — a salmon tartare that blossoms upon being mixed with the onions, capers and riced egg on the plate; well-browned veal sausage; a sumptuous house salad with blue cheese and corn as well as the usual raw vegetables, and a properly tangy Caesar.

In addition to steaks, the entrees include lamb chops of magnificent flavor. However, there are a couple of disappointments — lusterless fish and double-thick pork chops that would be better off cooked with a little moisture than grilled. Compensation comes in the à la carte vegetables, as SAM & HARRY'S serves outlandishly delicious fried onions, creamed spinach that puts its steakhouse competitors to shame and several potato dishes that tempt one to order them all. Finally, a world-class list of California wines (no bargain, except during the restaurant's summer sales) reminds us what a serious restaurant this is.

188

SAM WOO
1054 Rockville Pike, Rockville, MD
(301) 424-0495

KOREAN/JAPANESE/CHINESE   ♿

Lunch: M-F 11:30-2, Sat noon-5 **Entrees:** $6.50-$8.50
Dinner: Daily 5-11 **Entrees:** $9-$20
Credit Cards: AE, MC, V **Reservations:** Accepted
Dress: Casual **Parking:** Free lot **Metro:** Rockville, Twinbrook

Rockville Pike looks resolutely all-American, but one of its shopping strips contains a surprising ethnic outpost, a Korean restaurant whose patrons, when I walked in one Saturday evening, were all Koreans.

SAM WOO is a large, blond-wood restaurant with grills in the middle of the tables for barbecuing and a long menu with Japanese as well as Korean dishes. And both are done well. The sushi is as fresh as most in Washington, and the barbecued meat, marinated with garlic, soy sauce and a hefty dose of sugar, is succulent. And like all the other Korean dishes, Sam Woo accompanies entrees with half a dozen little servings of condiments — *kim chee*, fried tofu, shredded *daikon*, marinated bean sprouts, spinach and seaweed — plus miso soup and rice.

"Beef is the star, particularly short ribs."

Beef is the star, particularly short ribs. Other barbecued dishes include thinly sliced beef, pork, chicken, tongue and puffer fish. There's a raw beef dish of julienned meat tossed with soy, sesame seeds and too much sugar for my taste, but the meat itself is lean and excellent.

The menu goes on and on, including several versions of *bibimbap*, a huge bowl of rice with meat and vegetables to be mixed at the table with brick-red pepper paste. There are even bigger bowls of noodles with soup topped with everything from dumplings and rice cakes to beef bones and scallions. Several of the main dishes are also available as appetizers, including interesting rice-flour pancakes with meat or lentils. It's an exotic collection.

SARINAH SATAY HOUSE
1338 Wisconsin Ave. NW, Washington, DC
(202) 337-2955

INDONESIAN

Lunch: T-Sat noon-3 **Dinner:** T-Sat 6-10:30
Entrees: $6-$23 **Closed:** M **Credit Cards:** All major
Reservations: Recommended on weekends
Dress: Casual **Parking:** Street

You'd never know this Indonesian restaurant started life as a French garden cafe. It evokes the jungle, with skylit greenery and dazzling jungle birds, flagstone floor and batik cloths. The menu offers an abundance of choices, with three dozen entrees, enough to create your own *rijsttafel* if you have enough companions. If you are only a small group, you can order a set *rijsttafel* of more than a dozen dishes. On your own, though, you can pick from such appetizers as crunchy pancakes of fried tofu, *tempe* or corn cakes, or variations on an egg roll.

Among entrees I haven't found a standout, but when they are eaten family style, each contributes its assets to make a scintillating meal. The cooked vegetable salad with peanut sauce, *gado gado*, is a little bland; the same peanut sauce serves better as a foil for the explosively hot and spicy grilled chicken. Makasar beef satay is **". . . plenty of charm, low prices and more-than-decent cooking."** spicy too, but heavy on the sugar; mild fried rice and gentle chicken in coconut sauce balance the satay's sweetness. The star of the entrees is a fried whole fish in "special spiced sauce." The sauce is a touch sweet, more perfumed and spiced than sugared, and the crunchy exterior hides fresh, moist flesh. Dutch beer is a good foil for the riot of seasonings that makes an Indonesian meal.

SARINAH has plenty of charm, low prices and more-than-decent cooking. It's an oasis of calm in Georgetown.

190

SAVORY
7071 Carroll Ave., Takoma Park, MD
(301) 270-2233

AMERICAN

Open: M-Th 7 am-9 pm, F 7 am-midnight, Sat 9 am-midnight,
Sun 9 am-4 pm **Entrees:** $6-$10 **Credit Cards:** MC, V
Reservations: No **Dress:** Casual
Parking: Free lot **Metro:** Takoma Park
Entertainment: Blues, jazz, folk music Sat 8-11 pm

SAVORY sometimes looks like a nursery school, other times a community center, in some ways a library and certainly a fancy grocery. Sunlight and bright colors contribute to the nursery school feel, and its open stairway makes it a neighborhood meeting ground. Families sprawl upstairs, downstairs and outdoors, everywhere except for the all-important adults-only bottom floor with its sofas and cafe tables. For solitary loungers, a rack holds as many different magazines as a major library.

Dishes are displayed in glass-front cases where diners order, collect utensils and choose bottled beverages from the cooler. The food's as close to homemade as restaurant food gets. And just like at home, when family members eat at different times, the food is reheated to order in a microwave. The cooking is not only home-style but in home-sized portions. Thus the Swiss chard and gruyere tart — translation: quiche — might be sold out while you hesitate and be replaced by a mushroom tart or chorizo in cornmeal crust. If you see something you want, make a quick decision and order right away — and that goes for the desserts, too. On the other hand, you might have just carried off the last portion of white bean salad when it's replaced with Sri Lankan eggplant, which you may much prefer. There's always a pasta, ranging from light and delicious penne with tomatoes, carrots, onions, celery and lots of lemon peel to flavor its moist hunks of chicken, to a kiddy bowl of plain, buttered, silly pasta shapes. This kitchen roams the world, picking up fajitas from Texas and mahi mahi with fresh pineapple from the Pacific.

For dessert, expect seasonal fruits baked into pies and cobblers, berry tarts, biscotti or cream-drenched cakes. Most are house-made. Choice too difficult? Keep in mind that everything is available for carryout.

SEASONS

Four Seasons Hotel
2800 Pennsylvania Ave. NW, Washington, DC
(202) 342-0810

AMERICAN/FRENCH

Breakfast: M-F 7-11, Sat-Sun 8-noon **Entrees:** $11.50-$17
Lunch: M-F noon-2:30 **Entrees:** $12.75-$21
Dinner: Daily 6-10:30 **Entrees:** $17.25-$34
Afternoon Tea: Daily 3-5, $13.25 **Brunch:** Sun 10:30-1:45, $45
Credit Cards: All major **Reservations:** Recommended
Dress: Casual **Parking:** Complimentary valet

Hotel restaurants often are at a disadvantage. It can be hard to rev up a bureaucratic staff to go beyond minimally doing its job. Yet, at SEASONS, the staff seems — pardon the pun — well seasoned, yet not jaded. An advantage hotel restaurants have is the space and budget for luxurious decoration. SEASONS, in burgundy and forest green, is a cross between a staid country club and an urban park. An indoor garden is backed by a window wall overlooking Rock Creek Park, as if both garden and park were one. A few curved banquettes create coves of privacy that feel almost like picnic areas, separated not by trees and hills but by carpet and potted plants.

Overall, I like the food at SEASONS better than at most luxury hotels. It may sometimes fall short of expectations, but it isn't silly or overcomplicated. Its full, rich flavors don't clash. It seems designed to satisfy more than to impress. In the American way, the menu ranges from old-fashioned East European chicken noodle soup to **"... a cross between a staid country club and an urban park."** Asian tempura, and several of the dinner entrees are pastas. The menu lists healthful "alternative cuisine" and offers vegetarian entrees. In short, this is a hotel menu, which means you can get just about anything you want to eat, at any price the hotel wants to charge.

But the meals that most draw me to this soothing luxuriance are afternoon tea — the pastries are designed to make you salivate with your eyes — and Sunday brunch, which revels in grand simplicity. And in case your romantic dinner at SEASONS develops into planning for a wedding, this hotel's banquets are even better than the restaurant meals — in fact, they may be the best in town.

192

701
701 Pennsylvania Ave. NW, Washington, DC
(202) 393-0701

AMERICAN/INTERNATIONAL   &

Lunch: M-F 11:30-3 **Entrees:** $8.50-$18.50
Dinner: M-T 5:30-10:30, W-Th 5:30-11, F-Sat 5:30-11:30, Sun 5-9:30
Dinner Entrees: $13.50-$22.50 **Pre-Theater:** Daily 5:30-7, $22
Credit cards: All major **Reservations:** Recommended
Dress: Casual **Parking:** Complimentary valet at dinner
Metro: Archives-Navy Memorial
Entertainment: Pianist M-Th dinner, jazz trio F-Sat evening

Shakespeare and caviar — that's what I call a spectacular evening. Instead of preceding the theater with a dinner heavy enough to make me doze through the second act, I'd rather splurge on an invigorating and luxurious snack at 701, which is a comfortable walk from the downtown stages. Cocktail dining tempts me here.

The dining room is spacious, quiet and comfortable. A pianist makes it even more festive. The service borders on royal. And the menu allows you to choose anything from twin mini hamburgers to the most sophisticated contemporary cooking.

I settle into one of the downy soft armchairs at a table in the lounge. I examine the page-long list of vodkas (heather and honey or explosively orange? Polish or Russian? Maybe one plain and dry, then a peppered version, and for dessert a bright pink, house-made berry vodka?). They're all served on ice, as they should be.

As is the caviar. You can go all-out with *osetra* (my preference) or *beluga,* or pull your punches deliciously with salmon caviar. Each is served with tiny blini and brioche toast, dollops of sour cream, chopped onion and capers (which I spread on the breadstuffs only after I've scraped up the last of the caviar, unwilling to dilute the taste of caviar with condiments). And since you can hardly fill up on caviar, order something else from the appetizer list — tuna tartare built into an architectural marvel or maybe mussels in a light winey tomato broth. Then again, those mini bacon cheeseburgers sound seductive, too. Then off to the theater? Actually, maybe not. This little meal is drama enough.

1789
1226 36th St. NW, Washington, DC
(202) 965-1789

AMERICAN

Dinner: Sun-Th 6-10, F-Sat 5-11 **Entrees:** $18-$32
Pre-Theater: Sat-Sun 5-6:45 pm, $25 **Credit Cards:** All major
Reservations: Recommended **Dress:** Jacket required
Parking: Complimentary valet

G randmother visiting? Out-of-town CEO? Japanese industrialist or Swedish poet? 1789 looks like American history and serves the kind of modern American cooking that shows why we now are considered competition for the French and the Italians.

Dining is on two floors, but my favorite is the main downstairs room, with etchings and old maps of Washington on walls, silk-shaded brass oil lamps and tiny bouquets of flowers on tables. With federal furnishings and a working fireplace, it's the most formal room. Yet even the least of 1789's small dining rooms is handsome and cozy. And the service benefits from waiters who've been around countless years.

The menu is of modest length — seven or eight offerings for each course — and particularly shows the seafood-cooking skill of chef Ris Lacoste, who spent most of her career as sous-chef to Bob Kinkead in Nantucket and Washington. Dishes change daily, and most reflect the seasons, though the menu also includes such year-round stalwarts as filet of beef (albeit with mustard, tarragon and malt scotch), rack of lamb and grilled chicken breast. There's also formidable seafood, perhaps fresh shrimp with grits and Smithfield ham or tuna, seared as an appetizer or cut thick and glazed with hoisin sauce as an entree. The crab cakes are creamy and garnished with something surprising such as thumb-sized fresh artichokes and oranges. And fish fillets are attractively but sedately seasoned. Seafood stew especially shows Lacoste's poise in updating traditional dishes. Its clams, mussels, shrimp, chunks of fish and crab meat are in a broth flavored bouillabaisse-style, with croutons spread with the classic rouille, yet it has a spicy bold American flavor.

Here's a restaurant where the entrees are every bit as good as the appetizers, and the breads are outstanding. Thank goodness the desserts are the least exciting course, since I'm usually too full to do them justice.

SHAMSHIRY
8607 Westwood Center Dr., Vienna, VA
(703) 448-8883

PERSIAN   ♿

Open: Daily 11:30 am-11 pm **Entrees:** $6-$10
Credit Cards: All major **Reservations:** Accepted for 6 or more
Dress: Casual **Parking:** Free lot

The first thing you see in this Persian kebab restaurant is a window overlooking the grill. Metal skewers of meats and fish rotate over flames: chunks of salmon (among the best kebabs), long, nubby, sausage shapes of *kubideh* (ground beef), filet mignon threaded as flat strips or rolled around onions and herbs, plain marinated chicken in addition to fiery-herbed tandoori, and the star of the lineup, Cornish game hen "marinated in Grand Fathers original recipe."

These skewers and rice are most of what you need to know about SHAMSHIRY. It offers no entrees besides kebabs. It serves no alcoholic beverages; nearly everybody drinks tea or *doogh*, an astringent combination of yogurt, club soda and dry herbs. Appetizer choices consist simply of raw or pickled vegetables, but a sufficient beginning to the meal is the basket of flat bread, with a dish of green herb paste peppery enough to clear any winter stuffiness. Try this fiery condiment, but only after you've buffered the bread with a thin veneer of butter.

White rice, served with beef dishes, achieves greatness when you order a raw egg yolk on the side, to stir in so that the egg coats all the grains as the heat cooks it. Also stir in as much butter as you dare, and sprinkle on the dark, brown, powdered *sumac* that's in a shaker on the table. The other rice variations are recommended with chicken dishes. Sweet rice is perfumed with sugared orange peel and crunchy with pistachios and almonds. Cherry rice is topped with syrupy preserved cherries, and barberry rice is studded with tart dried red currants. Finally, the unpromisingly named "veggie rice," which comes with the salmon and can be ordered with other kebabs, is tinted an intriguing greenish beige and seductively flavored by dill and soft, delicious fava beans. Though decorations are simple, the dining room feels like a Persian dinner party; on some Saturday nights when there's taped Persian music and tables are filled, you might feel like the guest at a Persian wedding.

SHOLL'S COLONIAL CAFETERIA
1990 K St. NW, Washington, DC
(202) 296-3065

AMERICAN

Breakfast: M-Sat 7-10:30, Sun 8-3
Lunch: M-Sat 11-2:30, Sun 10:30-3
Dinner: M-Sat 4-8 **Entrees:** $2.25-$5.25
Credit Cards: None; cash only **Reservations:** No
Dress: Casual **Parking:** Street **Metro:** Farragut West

Hamburgers just won't do when you've got a craving for an old-fashioned chopped steak. That's when you've got to go to SHOLL'S, the enduring cafeteria where the juicy little chopped steak is my favorite entree. There's more that draws me back, though, from the 50-cent cucumber-sour cream salad to the freshly cooked vegetables — firm broccoli, meltingly soft cabbage, well-browned french fries and corn on the cob in season. The mashed potatoes, however, taste as though they're from a box.

But the puddings don't, and they include rice with raisins, baked custard and occasionally tapioca. The pies have fresh fruit spilling out of them, and the doughnuts, biscuits and rolls are made in-house. Some of the salads look tired, and much of the food is overcooked, but if you use your eyes and trust your instincts, you'll generally eat well. This is the plainest food imagin-

> **" . . . the enduring little cafeteria where the juicy little chopped steak is my favorite entree."**

able, at prices that couldn't be lower. Thus the unadorned beige dining room is a second home to locals both marginal and mainstream, as well as busloads of teen-age tourists. Their guides know that SHOLL'S is invaluable as a source for healthy, well-balanced, seasonal meals at fast-food prices.

SKEWERS
1633 P St. NW, Washington, DC
(202) 387-7400

MEDITERRANEAN

Lunch: M-Sat 11:30 am-5 pm **Entrees:** $7-$17
Dinner: M-Sat 5-11, Sun 3-11 **Entrees:** $11-$17
Credit Cards: All major **Reservations:** Recommended weekends
Dress: Casual **Parking:** Street **Metro:** Dupont Circle

A few steps above street level, this is one of Dupont Circle's long-running bargain restaurants. The list of appetizers has expanded beyond the original tabouleh, hummus and baba ghanouj to nearly two dozen *mezze*, including carrot puree with *harissa* spice, *kibbeh* of meat or vegetables and two additional versions of hummus and of eggplant salads. Yet the entree list remains simple — kebabs on rice, kebabs on fettucine, kebabs on salad or kebabs with romaine and crisped pita topped by yogurt and pine nuts, plus a few pastas.

The primary draws at SKEWERS are its homey environment and its modest prices. The dining room has a cheerful, palm-tree theme, and the service is personable, even if it is not very efficient.

Given the basically simple menu, though, SKEWERS has surprisingly erratic cooking. At one meal the filet mignon kebab might be spicy and juicy while the chicken and shrimp are bland and limp. Baba ghanouj and tabouleh might taste fresh and lively, while stuffed grape leaves and hummus have no taste at all. The trick is to order a *mezze* — an appetizer combination for two or four people — which offers an assortment of little dishes and a basket of warm pita. It's enough for a light meal, and it allows you to hedge your bets.

SOUTH AFRICAN CAFE
1817 Columbia Rd. NW, Washington,
(202) 332-0493

SOUTH AFRICAN   ♿

Dinner: T-Th 5-11, F-Sat 5-1 am, Sun 5-11 **Entrees:** $9-$14
Lunch: Sat noon-3 **Entrees:** $7-8
Brunch: Sun. 11:30-3 **Entrees:** $7-$9
Closed: M **Credit Cards:** All major
Reservations: Recommended **Dress:** Casual
Parking: Street **Entertainment:** Quartet F-Sat 10 pm-1am

The first South African restaurant in Washington, this one's a bit ramshackle, my image of a bus stop cafe in an underpopulated town. The kitchen isn't much bigger than the galley of a day-sailor, a squeeze for the one chef, one dishwasher and one manager to maneuver around each other. No wonder it takes a half-hour (at best) to get appetizers. Dinner here demands patience and congenial company.

The chef has a way with seasonings, and it shows best in appetizers. *Peri peri* wings are six pieces, rubbed with dark, fiery spices and broiled until crackly. Beef kebabs, even as appetizers, are enough for an entree. For vegetarians there are skewered mushrooms, broiled whole on a three-pronged "devil's fork." Vegetables (mostly cabbage) or beef make the fillings for samosa — smaller and thinner than the Indian version — or for patties, typically Jamaican, short-crusted pastries. Beef comes also as a sausage — hearty, lean and savory. And there's sweet-sour pickled fish, firm and chewy, with a vinegar tang and curry-yellow tint.

Making a meal of appetizers is a good idea here, perhaps the *peri peri* wings, or the sausage, which come as entrees as well. Otherwise, the best are the lamb curry — sweetly mild — and a seafood stew, herbed and lemony, pulsating with garlic. Anyone who loves extracting morsels of meat from bones will appreciate the straightforward oxtail stew, but even an Englishman raised on frozen fish and overcooked meat ought to find fault with the fish and chips and the mixed grill. Nor are the *bobotie* and chicken curry as good as they should be. The coffee is good, deserving of a homey sweet to accompany it: sweet potato cake with cream cheese frosting, "tipsy tart," milk tart, custard pie, apple crumb tart or bread pudding with rum sauce The desserts aren't elaborate or sophisticated, just good, family-style baking.

SOUTHSIDE 815
815 S. Washington St., Alexandria, VA
(703) 836-6222

AMERICAN/SOUTHERN   ♿

Open: M-Th 11:30-10:30, F-Sat 11:30-11, Sun 2:30-10:30
Entrees: $5.50-$14 **Brunch:** Sun 11:30-2:30, $5.75-$7
Credit Cards: All major **Reservations:** Accepted for 6 or more
Dress: Casual **Parking:** Free lot

Bring a big appetite to SOUTHSIDE 815, because the best of its dishes are the heavy, rich, homey Southern classics. The Low Country Shortcake says it all: It's layers of corn bread, mashed potatoes, oysters and chicken drenched in succotash gravy.

Okay, so you want something lighter? There's a thick, grilled tuna steak, flavored with lemon and pepper. But be warned: As good as the tuna is, it pales beside its vegetable accompaniments of peppered and vinegared Southern greens, wildly rich cream grits and those drive-you-crazy mashed potatoes. Another of the potential stars on this menu is Charleston Chicken, the breast topped with shrimp, corn and sausage in sherry butter. The sandwich choices are equally interesting, from the catfish po' boy to the pulled pork to the burger with fried oysters.

With all this, you surely don't need an appetizer. But there are oysters three ways, which means with heady seasoned spinach (Rockefeller), creamy crab (Virginia) and bacon (Maryland). It's enough for two to share, as are the crab and corn drop fritters and the sweet potato biscuits smothered with crab, Virginia ham and cream gravy. Likewise, you ought to share a side dish of fried green tomatoes. The only trouble is, the kitchen is no longer reliable as it was in SOUTHSIDE 815's early days. You can hope to catch it on a good day.

"Bring a big appetite to Southside 815, because the best of its dishes are the heavy, rich, homey Southern classics."

STAR OF EUROPE
5125 MacArthur Blvd. NW, Washington, DC
(202) 244-3106

PORTUGUESE

Lunch: M-F11-5 **Entrees:** $4-$10
Dinner: M-Th 5-11, F 5-midnight, Sat-Sun 4-midnight
Dinner Entrees: $9-$17 **Pre-Theater:** Sun-Th 5-7:30 pm, $11
Credit Cards: All major **Reservations:** Recommended
Dress: Casual **Parking:** Street
Entertainment: Pianist F 9:30 pm-1am

West of Wisconsin Avenue, Washington is surprisingly short of restaurants; along MacArthur Boulevard, dining out has generally been limited to a standard pizza or pasta at Listrani's or an ethereal nine-course dinner at the Japanese Makoto. Now there's STAR OF EUROPE, a cross between a tea room and a Portuguese restaurant, with enough Italian dishes to give Listrani's pause.

STAR OF EUROPE is a pleasant restaurant, with pink tablecloths and a second-floor balcony for dining in good weather. Family-run and eager be accommodating, it's a decent place for a quiet lunch or dinner if you're in the neighborhood.

The lunch menu is routine, mostly sandwiches and salads, with chicken salad the specialty. But if you want something Portuguese, it can be ordered at lunch anyway. At dinner, the menu is weighty with Portuguese seafood stews, kebabs, sauteed meats with a Portuguese touch and even a kale-potato-chorizo version of fettuccine bolognese. Chorizo plays a substantial role in STAR OF EUROPE'S ethnic dishes. Seasoning does not, however, and even the *caldo verde* — kale, potato and chorizo soup — is likely to beg for salt and more.

The dish with the most gusto is the traditional combination of pork and clams, though here it is untraditionally sautéed (and not degreased) rather than stewed. Thus, the few little clams in their shell taste like a garnish rather than an integral flavor; even so, the pork is juicy and the potatoes are irresistibly crusty. Somehow that huge portion just disappears, despite its imperfections.

STRAITS OF MALAYA
1836 18th St. NW, Washington, DC
(202) 483-1483

MALAYSIAN   ♿

Lunch: M-F noon-2 **Entrees:** $7-$15
Dinner: Sun-Th 5:30-10, F-Sat 5:30-11 **Entrees:** $10-$15
Credit Cards: AE, MC,V **Dress:** Casual
Reservations: Recommended weekends
Parking: Street **Metro:** Dupont Circle

S ome say Singapore has the world's best food, and STRAITS OF MALAYA encourages me to believe that. Its cooking hints of China and India, with the tropical fragrances of coconut and ginger, *galanga* and lemon grass, chilies and tamarind, plus strong overtones of cilantro. Dine on these highly perfumed, family-style dishes on the roof terrace, and you'll feel closer to Singapore than to Washington.

STRAITS OF MALAYA'S menu can be daunting, even though the entrees are almost all based on chicken or shrimp. You can order many dishes in vegetarian versions, with or without tofu, and seasoned highly or gently. And the staff will guide you to the best dishes.

Among entrees, don't miss *poh pia*. It's served with pancakes a la mu shu pork, but the similarities pretty much end there. Its vegetables — including jicama — are crunchier, and the spicing — incorporating dried shrimp — is more exotic, while the dark sauce for smearing on the pancakes is far more pungent than hoisin. The noodle dishes — *cha kway teow, bee hoon* and Singapore rice noodles — are a pleasant balance to the hotter, creamy, coconut-based curries, such as the pink-sauced shrimp or the more familiar yellow chicken curry. A consistent favorite is small Chinese eggplants curried with chunks of carrots and chicken. And the *nasi goreng* — Indonesian fried rice — is one of those dishes you can't resist nibbling to the last morsel.

As for appetizers, be sure to try the crisp, fried, beef-stuffed curry puffs and the *rojak*, an unusual salad made with jicama, cucumbers, carrots and pineapple coated with a savory shrimp paste marinade. Then there are the flat scallion-and-cilantro shrimp pancakes with a bright red peanutty hot sauce, the fried tofu with a similar sauce, five-spice roll (an exotic cousin of meat loaf) and the meal-in-itself soup called *laksa*.

SUPORN'S
2302 Price Ave., Wheaton, MD
(301) 946-7613

THAI   ♿

Lunch: T-Sun 11:30-3 **Dinner:** T-Sun 5-10
Closed: M **Entrees:** $7.50-$10 **Credit Cards:** D, DIS, MC,V
Reservations: Recommended on weekends **Dress:** Casual
Parking: Free after 6 pm **Metro:** Wheaton

Thai salads teach us how densely flavor can be packed in a pile of greens. Thai cooks use fresh herbs as abundantly as Americans use lettuce. They add lime juice full force instead of diluting it with oil. They sprinkle on hot pepper the way most of us use salt. Then they elevate the mix with charcoal-grilled beef, seafood, ground chicken or pork and add a flavorful crunch with peanuts or toasted ground rice. One of the smallest Thai restaurants in the Washington area offers the longest list of salads.

SUPORN'S lists more than a dozen variations under its salads category and more in the appetizer section. In fact, the best is an appetizer of *yum pla krob*. Its green base is a ruffled leaf of lettuce topped with shredded mint and cilantro leaves, then strips of onion and scallion and crunchy fried shards of sweet-salty dried fish. It's sprinkled with peanuts and dressed with lime and hot pepper.

You also can get the same greens and flavorings with sweet-savory slices of anise-scented Chinese sausage and cucumbers, with canned tuna and shreds of ginger instead of onion, plus whole, tiny, incendiary red peppers. And there are tangy and minty salads with grilled beef, chopped meats or seafood. Shredded papaya also appears in two salads, one accompanied by a barbecued chicken leg and fat, glutinous rice. It's a meal disguised as a salad.

As for more familiar Thai salads, they, too, are irresistible interplays of tart and hot, sweet and nutty, fragrant and mild. Of course, SUPORN'S also serves the full range of Thai entrees, from noodle soups to stir-fries, but they're not as notable as the salads.

SUSHI-KO
2309 Wisconsin Ave. NW, Washington, DC
(202) 333-4187

JAPANESE

Lunch: T-F noon-2:30 **Entrees:** $6.50-$17
Dinner: M-F 6-10:30, Sat 5-10:30, Sun 5-10 **Entrees:** $7.50-$18
Credit Cards: AE, MC, V **Reservations:** Accepted
Dress: Casual **Parking:** Valet (fee) at dinner

Yes, it's a sushi bar. And it's a Japanese restaurant serving the typical tempuras, teriyakis and noodles, all of them competent. But above all, SUSHI-KO is a playground for chef Kazuhiro Okochi's ideas in raw and cooked fish and in everything Japanese from grilled tofu to sake ice cream.

This small, two-story restaurant often has a waiting line, and no wonder. The sushi is exacting, the tempura is just fine, and the chef's specials are invariably exciting. In soft-shell crab season they include jumbo soft-shells, fried tempura style. Tuna tartare is particularly dazzling, topped with a quail egg yolk and fish roe, drizzled with a brick-red sauce, all of which tastes wonderful stirred together on the plate. Snapper carpaccio is a pretty turban of raw fish with dabs and swirls of flavored oils decorating the plate and ultimately perfuming the fish. Sometimes you can find thumb-sized octopus in a fragrant marinade, crisped on the grill and tossed with salad greens. And the succulent collar or jaw of yellowtail is tinged with dark teriyaki sauce and extraordinarily juicy after its grilling. Most dashingly, raw fish might be diced, seasoned and piled on crisp rice crackers as a kind of Japanese napoleon.

There are all the usual sushi choices, too, as individual pieces, six-piece rolls or cone-shaped hand rolls. In addition, special ingredients — tuna belly, fresh rather than processed salmon roe, smoked mussels — are available as sushi, and Kaz Okochi modernizes everyday sushi with basil on the tuna or mango puree decorating the salmon. Table service is gracious, but the most fun is sitting at the sushi bar and watching your meals being constructed. The ordinary sushi is as good as it gets in Washington, but the chef's fancies are even better. The best dish I've found lately is a surprisingly companionable combination of raw tuna and artichoke puree. Like many of Okochi's creation's, it's a simply brilliant idea.

SWAGAT
2063 University Blvd E., Adelphi, MD
(301) 434-2247

INDIAN

Lunch: M-F 11:30-3, Sat noon-5
Dinner: M-Th 3-9, F 3-10, Sat 5-10, Sun 5-9
Entrees: $6-$7 **Brunch:** Sun noon-5, $9
Credit Cards: All major **Reservations:** Recommended weekends
Dress: Casual **Parking:** Free lot

The furnishings have a kind of shopping-center layout, with row after row of leatherette booths and a stainless-steel buffet table in the center. But the walls bring India to center stage. They're rough-textured wood, hung with a gallery of vibrant photographs of India. SWAGAT has transported South India to suburban Maryland. The menu is, of course, vegetarian, and the restaurant serves no alcohol. Yet those restrictions seem less limiting than inspirational. One dish I'd be sure to order is *khasta kachori*, an appetizer of tiny, one-bite, puffed fried breads filled with a creamy-spicy-crunchy mix of chopped onions, chutney and yogurt. As for *samosas* and *bhajias*, those usually leaden fried appetizers, SWAGAT has lightened them.

Where else do you see five different versions of *paneer*, those cubes of house-made cheese so spongy and bland that they intensify a curry's other ingredients? *Vindaloo* curry is an explosion — not simply of chilies but of flavor, with a jolt of vinegar. At the other end of the spectrum, spinach with corn is equally complex but far more subtle. The only consistent flaw is that the solid ingredients are shortchanged; the paneers need more cheese, the other curries perhaps more cauliflower or potato or carrot. Mostly, they are sauces to spoon over rice.

Swagat's *dosas* are a good yard long, rolled with the usual turmeric-yellow potato filling or mixed vegetables or paneer — or as a sandwich rather than a roll. *Uttapam* is a thicker pancake, crisp on the surface and soft inside, studded with vegetables and served flat. *Idlis* are stark little pillows of plain steamed rice batter, a blank canvas for the accompanying coconut or coriander chutneys. If the menu seems hopelessly confusing, there's an easy solution: SWAGAT serves buffets at lunch, brunch and some dinners, so you can preview what you might like to order à la carte next time.

T.H.A.I.
4029 S. 28th St., Arlington, VA
(703) 931-3203

THAI

Lunch: Daily 11:30-4 **Entrees:** $6-$9.75
Dinner: Sun-Th. 4-10, F-Sat 4-11 **Entrees:** $8-$15
Credit Cards: All major **Reservations:** Recommended weekends
Dress: Casual **Parking:** Free

Thai restaurants are no longer homey eateries; the new ones are designer environments even hotter than the food. T.H.A.I., a spin-off of Busara, is fun from the first moment, a mingling of whimsy and high-tech decorations, a bit like a three-dimensional cartoon. Also like its sibling, T.H.A.I.'s service is genuinely nice.

Despite its colorful backdrop, though, the food is merely standard Thai, which is good enough if you happen to be in the neighborhood. Among

"T.H.A.I. is one of those gifts most distinguished by its wrapping paper."

the appetizers, the tart-hot ground chicken dish, *larb*, is tops. Autumn rolls, long and thin variations on an eggroll theme, look dramatic even if they don't taste any better than usual. Dried beef is a more interesting appetizer, appealingly chewy and salty.

If most of the entrees are ordinary, the seafood dishes don't even achieve that distinction. There's one exception. Crispy whole flounder is rubbed with dark, fragrant spices and decorated with vibrant vegetables, boned with a flourish at the table and about as festive as this menu gets. And the restaurant has been revamping its kitchen and upgrading its menu. So far, though, T.H.A.I. is one of those gifts most distinguished by its wrapping paper.

TABARD INN
1739 N St. NW, Washington, DC
(202) 331-8528

___

AMERICAN   ♿

___

Breakfast: M-F 7-10, Sat-Sun 8-10 **Entrees:** $2.50-$7.50
Lunch: M-F 11:30-2:30 **Entrees:** $8.50-$14
Dinner: Sun-M 6-10, T-Sat 6-10:30 **Entrees:** $14-$23
Brunch: Sat-Sun 11-2:30 **Entrees:** $8.75-$10.50
Credit Cards: MC, TM, V **Reservations:** Recommended
Dress: Casual **Parking:** Street **Metro:** Dupont Circle

Since it is perennially one of the most charming restaurants in town, the TABARD INN gets a lot of leeway from those of us who have loved it over the years. Its walled garden is peaceful, the sofas and fireplaces in the anteroom are inviting, and the dining room itself — with its kind of '60s church-pew-and-flea-market conglomeration of furnishings — is endearing. Still more: Tabard Inn grows some of its own vegetables and herbs, and serves its own potato and other vegetable chips, obviously maintaining a commitment to fresh, seasonal ingredients.

On the other hand, it changes chefs from time to time, and the cooking is erratic. Prices are high, and lately they haven't been warranted. For nine months the TABARD INN ran without any executive chef, trying a co-op kitchen structure. Then it promoted the pastry chef to executive chef, and it's been working at improving the organization and consistency. That sounded like good news, since my fondest memory in recent years has been TABARD'S fruit crisps. But the dishes — particularly entrees — still don't live up to the top prices it asks. The menu is strong on fresh fish, enchanted with fresh herbs, given to creativity and committed to vegetables. The TABARD serves contemporary American food in an endearing yesteryear setting.

> **"The Tabard serves contemporary American food in an endearing yesteryear setting."**

TABERNA DEL ALABARDERO
1776 I St. NW, Washington, DC
(Entrance on 18th Street)
(202) 429-2200

SPANISH   ♿

Lunch: M-F 11:30-2:30   **Entrees:** $10-$18
Dinner: M-Th 6-10, F-Sat 6-11   **Entrees:** $15-$26
Pre-Theater: M-Sat 6-8 pm, $30   **Closed:** Sun
Tapas: Served throughout the day, $5-$8
Credit Cards: All major   **Reservations:** Recommended
Dress: Jacket & tie   **Parking:** Complimentary valet at dinner
Metro: Farragut West

It's comforting to sit in a Spanish restaurant and hear nothing but Spanish spoken at the tables around you. But that's not the only reason TABERNA DEL ALABARDERO breeds confidence. This formal, Old World restaurant has grown more solid over the years, and more interesting as well. Much of its menu is predictably continental, but it's been adding more distinctly Iberian dishes. And now it offers four paellas — one with pasta instead of rice, one black with squid ink — though they are still available only for two people.

Except at the tapas bar. And that's what particularly draws me to this restaurant, for a quick or late lunch, an unstructured dinner or an evening snack. The curved bar is decorated with a parade of dishes, so you choose by viewing them or from a menu: crisp brown ham and cheese croquettes; crunchy, cold vegetable-stuffed mussels; half-moon, beef-filled empanadas; small, open-face Serrano ham or smoked salmon sandwiches; paella portioned appetizer-size, and much more.

The cold seafood salad is a mild and elegant seviche, with sumptuous shrimp and raw, marinated scallops in a bright, crisp mixture of chopped onions and peppers. There are salads of artichokes and ham, or vinegared octopus. Hot tapas include extraordinarily succulent leg of duck, long-cooked into the softness and crispness of a French *confit*, its juices soaking into sliced potatoes. Fresh sardines are grilled, the wonderful Spanish ham is sautéed with artichokes or stuffed with cheese into crumb-coated, rolled breast of veal. And every day a family-style stew, sometimes as homey as just leeks with potatoes, simmers at the ready for tapas or full entrees.

TAKO GRILL
7756 Wisconsin Ave., Bethesda, MD
(301) 652-7030

JAPANESE   ♿

Lunch: M-F 11:30-2 **Entrees:** $6-$9
Dinner: M-Th 5:30-10, F-Sat 5:30-10:30, Sun 5-9:30
Dinner Entrees: $10.50-$16
Credit Cards: AE, MC, V **Reservations:** No
Dress: Casual **Parking:** Street

At most Japanese restaurants there's a long sheet of sushi to accompany the menu. At TAKO GRILL there are two long sheets, the second one for *robatayaki* — charbroiled foods — a first for Washington. It may be no surprise that clams and mushrooms can be grilled, but potatoes, *gingko* nuts and rice balls should attract the jaded.

What draws me to TAKO GRILL, though, is the broiled yellowtail jaw, which isn't on the menu but is often available; it's the richest fish you can imagine. I'm also fond of the custard-soft, long, narrow, peeled eggplants with ginger sauce, though they look like something the chef served by mistake.

TAKO GRILL doesn't shortchange the sushi either. The selection is extensive, and you can order by the piece. And now the restaurant has strengthened its weak link: It's redecorated and increased its size. Surely the days of waiting in line are gone.

208

TARA THAI
4828 Bethesda Ave., Bethesda, MD
(301) 657-0488

THAI

Lunch: M-F 11:30-3, Sat noon-3:30 **Entrees:** $5-$8
Dinner: Sun-Th 5-10, F-Sat 5-11 **Entrees:** $7-$19
Credit Cards: All major **Reservations:** Recommended
Dress: Casual **Parking:** Street **Metro:** Bethesda

Fire and ice. TARA THAI weaves the theme subtly. Its walls are murals of icy ocean depths and sea creatures, dark marine blue with the suggestion of sunlight filtering through. Glass dividers show underwater scenes etched in their surfaces like ice sculptures. Sprays of orchids and zebra-striped banquettes suggest the tropics and warmth, but they are lit by the cold glow of electric-blue neon. This is a breezy backdrop for chili-hot Thai cooking.

Some dishes are outstanding, and since even ordinary Thai cooking is pretty good, you can't go too wrong. Generally, at Thai restaurants I'd be delighted to make a meal of appetizers, and entrees usually are hardly more filling than first courses. Not here. Entrees are often standouts, and typical portions are hefty. To start, look for any appetizer with lemon grass or lime. Mussels with lemon grass and chili sauce are small yet plump, fragrant and tangy. Lime also comes into play with *larb gai*, the tart, hot, ground-chicken dish, and with green-papaya salad with grilled shrimp, or *yum talay*, a platter of warm shellfish and salad greens.

In choosing an entree, the underwater murals provide a hint: Order a whole fish. And while familiar Thai entrees are available, TARA THAI also breaks away from the usual, offering grilled tiger shrimp — as large as prawns —under a fragrant blanket of ground chicken and crab. There's home-style braised beef with a puree of green onions and chili, and a soup called *tom klong*, identified as "a long lost recipe" of monkfish, shiitakes, lemon grass, chilies and tamarind. Never have I seen a more interesting selection of Thai desserts: coconut ice cream with jackfruit and berry sauce, ice creams of Thai coffee or *pandan* leaves with lotus seeds, tropical sorbets, and two kinds of sticky rice — one with mango, another prepared as a pudding with taro root.

Tara Thai has a second branch at 226 Maple Ave., Vienna, VA, (703) 255-2467.

TEASM
2009 R St. NW, Washington, DC
(202) 667-3827

ASIAN

Open: M-Th 8 am-10 pm, F 8 am-11 pm, Sat 9 am-11 pm
Sun 9 am-10 pm **Entrees:** $6-$7.50 **Credit Cards:** AE, MC, V
Reservations: No **Dress:** Casual
Parking: Street **Metro:** Dupont Circle

A few steps away from Connecticut Avenue's bustle yet serenely Japanese in spirit, this converted town house is a shrine to tea. It serves two dozen varieties, plus carefully chosen self-service foods to accompany them, from breakfast through dinner. You can carry them out or eat them at backless stools — upholstered in subtly beautiful Japanese fabric — and silky wood tables.

The cooking, much of it done in a *tandoor* oven, is simple: three kebabs, two flatbreads, three sandwiches, four stir-fries, two bento boxes, three salads and a few side dishes and desserts. Then there's breakfast — the time to discover *chai*, a bracing, spiced tea concoction with a pleasantly bitter finish ameliorated by milk and sugar. The tea-smoked salmon — on a sandwich or in scrambled eggs at breakfast — is velvety and gently saline, hinting of tea bitterness and sugar for balance. It's a luscious change from smoked salmon or gravlax. I also like the hamburger, spiked with fresh ginger, lean and cooked through evenly rather than seared. It's fun to create your own combination platter with a kebab and your choice of flatbreads (the onion *kulcha* is wonderful), rices, salads and chutneys, *raitas* or pickles. For a nibble or a meal (it comes in two sizes) there's a chicken-noodle salad with cold linguine, raw vegetables and sesame seeds in a vinegary Japanese-style dressing.

The meal that's most Japanese, though, is a bento box. A still life on a tray, it comes with cold salmon or with a refreshing, all-vegetable construction of yam slices, lemony asparagus spears, tofu with ginger and soy, plus a turban of red-peppered, peanut-sauced soba noodles. Cookies, too. For dessert, there are short-crusted individual pies of seasonal fruit, chiffon cake or a rice pudding with coconut cream, lots of raisins and shavings of white chocolate and almonds. They beg to be washed down with the proper brew from a mud-colored little pot.

TERRAMAR
7800 Wisconsin Ave., Bethesda, MD
(301) 654-0888

NICARAGUAN/LATIN AMERICAN   ♿

Dinner: T-Th 5-10, F-Sat 5-11, Sun 5-9 **Entrees:** $12-$21
Closed: M **Credit Cards:** All major
Reservations: Recommended on weekends
Dress: Casual **Parking:** Street **Metro:** Bethesda
Entertainment: Flute and guitar Sat 7-10 pm

B efore TERRAMAR opened, Central American restaurants generally were just storefronts with down-home food. But this stucco-and-tile restaurant that looks like an indoor courtyard has linked elegance with yucca and plantains.

My preference here would be to make a meal of *tapas*, since the extensive list runs the gamut from pretty little pork turnovers dusted with sugar to remarkable tamales filled with pork and rice and explosive rings of chilies. There are lemony, peppered chicken wings and chorizo served with tortillas. There are the familiar (seviche with plenty of tartness and crunch) and the unusual (ripe plantains stuffed with shredded barbecued pork). Some are mini-meals: *Caballo bayo* teams shredded beef with tortillas, sour cream guacamole and a fiery cabbage salad. And most are quite delicious.

"This stucco-and-tile restaurant . . . has linked elegance with yucca and plantains."

If you go on to an entree, consider the *churrasco* — the marinated grilled beef served with piquant herb sauce. Whole red snapper with a spicy tomato sauce is another inviting specialty. Beyond the churrasco, the remaining grilled meats are generally fine. Fish and seafood are less consistent. Even so, the accompanying red beans, rice, sweetly caramelized fried, ripe plantains and long crisp chips of fried green plantains are enticing on their own. In tune with the menu, the wine list is devoted to Spanish and Latin American labels. All this and intensely thoughtful service, too.

3RD & EATS
500 3rd St. NW, Washington, DC
(202) 347-8790

AMERICAN/SOUTHERN   ♿

Breakfast: M-F 7-10:30 **Lunch:** M-F 11-3
Entrees: $2.75-$5 **Closed:** Sat-Sun
Credit Cards: None; cash only **Reservations:** No
Dress: Casual **Parking:** Street **Metro:** Judiciary Square

Y can put your money where your mouth is at 3RD & EATS, doing good while eating well. This small, self-service restaurant,
open weekdays for breakfast and lunch, is a training ground for
the unemployed and a source of funds to aid the poor and homeless.
It's also an awfully nice place to eat.

In fact, few luncheonettes around town serve food that is fresher or
more likely to be made from scratch. And certainly none offers lower
prices. Breakfast be-
gins the day with **" . . . a training ground**
house-made biscuits **for the unemployed and**
that are crunchy and **a source of funds to aid**
flaky enough for the
most persnickety **the poor and homeless.**
Southerner, layered **It's also an awfully nice**
with scrambled eggs, **place to eat."**
American cheese and
bacon or a sausage patty. The blueberry muffins are soft and moist,
thick with berries. The raisin bread is also made in-house, but it tends
to be a little dry; it's better toasted. There are bagels, English muffins,
cereals and just-cut fresh fruit, plus juices and coffees to serve yourself. Regulars have learned to check the lunchtime special when they
stop in for breakfast. Some days it's short ribs, other days ham hocks
with red beans and rice or ham with macaroni and cheese. It could be
stuffed flank steak or stuffed peppers, tuna noodle casserole or spaghetti with meat sauce. There is also a house-made soup each day.

Every day the display case is filled with salads, including a wonderful
home-style chicken salad with raisins, walnuts and celery plus a carefully restrained dose of mayonnaise. Sandwiches are the usual deli
choices — roast beef, corned beef, turkey, ham, tuna, chicken or egg
salad. They are nothing special — the meat is prepackaged and the
bread is squishy. There is always a red-cabbage slaw, and sometimes
the kitchen has time to make potato salad.

THYME SQUARE
4735 Bethesda Ave., Bethesda, MD
(301) 657-9077

AMERICAN

Lunch: M-Sat 11-5 **Entrees:** $9-$13
Dinner: S-Th 5-10, F-Sat 5-11 **Entrees:** $11-$15
Brunch: Sun 11-3 **Entrees:** $7-$8
Credit Cards: AE, MC, V **Reservations:** Recommended
Dress: Casual **Parking:** Street

People no longer ask, "Where's the beef?" They're too busy trying to get their five-a-day servings of fruits and vegetables. Thus the moment has come for such restaurants as THYME SQUARE, where the center of the plate is occupied by Swiss chard and the pizza is topped with spinach, mushrooms and potatoes. Fish is welcome; red meat hasn't been invited.

THYME SQUARE isn't what we used to expect from a meatless restaurant. It's not Earth Shoes and granola. The dining room has a tropical sizzle and a fashionable attitude. The electric buzz from the bar is not a blender but a juicer. You can drink your produce here. There is also a modestly priced, organic wine list, and the beers are interesting.

Yet, where the vegetables work is just where you expect them to work in a meaty mainstream restaurant: at the side of the plate. And THYME SQUARE does a snazzy Caesar salad, whole leaves of perfectly dressed romaine tumbling out of a Parmesan cornucopia. Otherwise, what this restaurant does best is seafood. An appetizer of Thai mussels is sensational, and if you like coconut, the Brazilian fish stew, with its haunting, spicy, opaque broth of tomato and coconut milk, is hefty with shellfish and fin fish, rice and plantain fries. On the other hand, the Chilean sea bass deserves better than its salty, harsh Hunan barbecue sauce. Bear in mind that the seafood here is top quality, and keep it simple. Watch out for sloppy cooking, particularly in such ethnic dishes as pad thai, quesadillas and pizzas. In the great American tradition, you can dine in low-fat style and then proceed to finish your meal with the richest of desserts. A bowl of Thai mussels, a Caesar salad and a lemon berry pie: That's the menu that would draw me back to THYME SQUARE.

"You can drink your produce here."

TIVOLI RESTAURANT
1700 N. Moore St., Rosslyn, VA
(703) 524-8900

ITALIAN   &

Lunch: M-F 11:30-2:30 **Entrees:** $8.50-$12
Dinner: M-Sat 5:30-10 **Entrees:** $13.50-$26
Pre-Theater: M-Sat 5:30-6:30, $16 **Closed:** Sun
Credit Cards: All major **Reservations:** Recommended
Dress: Casual **Parking:** Complimentary garage **Metro:** Rosslyn

Downtown it's rare to find a moderately priced restaurant where you can talk without clashing with your neighbor's conversation. But TIVOLI, two floors above the Rosslyn Metro in Arlington, has all the quiet and comfort of a country inn.

The convenience and comfort certainly account for the abundance of business dining on weekdays, but TIVOLI looks romantic enough for weekends as well. In the paneled and mirrored dining room, pink napkin fans and silver bud vases decorate the tables, rose carpeting muffles noise and a large, glass-enclosed wine cellar in the middle of the room fairly sparkles in the soft but not dim lighting. Sofas and deeply cushioned banquettes suggest you are expected to stay for the evening, unlike the hot new restaurants that schedule rigid, two-hour seatings. The staff takes its job seriously, seating you with a little bow, explaining the menu with enthusiasm, keeping watch over glasses and bread basket. And meeting modern expectations, the bread basket offers herbed focaccia and bread sticks along with the usual slices.

Tivoli's menu is Italian — but not insistently so. Like the continental menus of old, it spreads from risotto to an Italian-named steak with peppercorns, cognac and cream (sounds like good old steak au poivre to me). Cream and butter eclipse olive oil here, and this may be the last place in town to serve veal Oscar, that dear, old-fashioned veal tenderloin topped with crab meat and hollandaise.

TIVOLI isn't going to win stars, but it wins friends with nice cooking, a little on the heavy side but clearly from scratch. The pasta may be a little limp, the sauces may taste oversalted and the desserts may look like assembly-line products, but it doesn't seem to matter much. The cooking is far from the main attraction at TIVOLI.

TOM SARRIS' ORLEANS HOUSE
1213 Wilson Blvd., Arlington, VA
(703) 524-2929

AMERICAN/PRIME RIB

Lunch: M-F 11-3:30 **Entrees:** $5.50-$13
Dinner: M-Sat 4-11, Sun 4-10 **Entrees:** $5.50-$15
Credit Cards: All major **Dress:** Casual
Reservations: Recommended for large parties
Parking: Validated garage **Metro:** Rosslyn

The quantity/price ratio is as good as it gets here. For one low price, you can have all the salad you can eat (with cheeses added at dinner). For $1 more at lunch you can add a half-pound hamburger. For a few dollars more you can have the salad bar with rib roast (on the bone) and potatoes. The surprise is that it's not bad.

All this, of course, is no secret. So even though there are two duplicate salad displays to speed the line, it goes slowly. No wonder. Crowded onto the huge cart of ice are nearly 30 salad fixings, six dressings plus some psychedelic-red vinegar and oil and stacks of bread. You start with a mid-sized glass plate and face two bowls of lettuce nearly the size of bathtubs. As you pile on the usual shredded carrots, mushy tomatoes, finely sliced peppers and onions, broccoli and cauliflower, you come to a few show-stoppers. Hominy, small, brown pea beans, chopped, cooked kale and pickled green tomatoes slow down the line for gawkers. Green and wax beans, corn salad and chickpeas add more familiar variety. But there are no luxury items — no olives or anchovies.

"The quantity/price ratio is as good as it gets here."

The raw stuff is kept fresh, since the turnover is so swift. But most of the rest is canned and bland. On a salad bar, that's easily remedied. Pickled hot peppers can liven up the mix. And for extra crunch, the croutons keep company with fried chow mein noodles. Besides, once you bury your vegetable mound in thick, creamy dressing, everything melds into a generic salad taste anyway.

Mushy canned vegetables? Who cares? I've had a lot worse roast beef dinners at four times the price.

TONY CHENG'S SEAFOOD RESTAURANT & MONGOLIAN BARBECUE
619 H St. NW, Washington, DC
(202) 371-8669 (Seafood)
(202) 842-8669 (BBQ)

CHINESE

Lunch: M-Sat 11-3 **Entrees:** $6-$12 (**BBQ:** $8.50 buffet)
Dinner: M-Th 3-11, F-Sat 3-midnight, Sun 11-11
Dinner Entrees: $8-$25 (**BBQ:** $14 buffet)
Dim Sum: Sun 11-3 **Entrees:** $2.35-$8
Credit Cards: AE, MC, V **Reservations:** Recommended
Dress: Casual **Parking:** Street **Metro:** Gallery Place-Chinatown

Washington hasn't much more than a hint of a Chinatown, but through the years Tony Cheng has populated it with several restaurants. These days, he's concentrating on two restaurants in one building: TONY CHENG'S SEAFOOD RESTAURANT (second floor) and his MONGOLIAN BARBECUE (first floor).

The seafood restaurant is enormous, anchored with a tank of live lobsters and Dungeness crabs. The menu, too, is extensive, going well beyond seafood. At lunch *dim sum* is served; on Sundays it's wheeled around on carts. But if you tried only dim sum, you'd think this was a pretty pedestrian place. In fact, much of the menu would leave that impression. The most worthwhile dishes are seafood, especially fresh shrimp, wrapped in lotus leaves and steamed in spicy soybean paste, and Dungeness crab strewn with scallions, ginger and onions. It's the ingredients that stand out here: whole fish, shrimp with their heads, snails, clams, oysters. And the choices are many. Two pages of dim sum, dozens of noodle dishes, and a wide selection of vegetables keep company with the Chinese restaurant standards.

At the MONGOLIAN BARBECUE, self-service combines with showmanship to produce a favorite meal of the $10-lunch crowd. The salad bar is raised to new heights as customers circle the buffet, piling bowls with sliced raw meats and vegetables that the chefs season and cook on a big grill. The browned ingredients are flipped into a clean bowl, and that's lunch. Back at the table, the mixture is stuffed into sesame-studded rolls or piled on rice. With a free nibble of roasted peanuts and spicy pickled cabbage and a fortune cookie for dessert, the MONGOLIAN BARBECUE can offer a hefty meal tailored to your taste.

TRUMPETS
1603 17th St. NW, Washington, DC
(202) 232-4141

AMERICAN

Dinner: Daily 5:30-11 **Entrees:** $8-$20
Brunch: Sun 11-3, $13 **Pre-Theater:** Daily 5:30-7, $20
Credit Cards: All major **Reservations:** Recommended
Dress: Casual **Parking:** Street **Metro:** Dupont Circle
Entertainment: Dancing W 10 pm-1 am

Tucked behind a gay bar downstairs on 17th Street is a restaurant with one of the most clever and satisfying menus in town. Chef David Hagedorn never runs out of good ideas. Now he's divided his menu into the Low Fat Side and the Don't Ask, Don't Tell Side. And I could happily eat from either list.

This cozy, funky modern dining room caters to diners of every dress code, from glamour to grunge, though mostly it's casual. And the menu encompasses burgers (beef or turkey) as well as a dressed-up shrimp cocktail with pepper vodka that's served in a martini glass, tenderloin of beef and pizza with smoked salmon. Hagedorn's signatures are such witticisms as a carrot and goat cheese turned into corn on the cob, fish and chips in tempura batter puffed up like a sofa pillow and pizza with a portobello mushroom as the crust. Yet he doesn't confuse witty with silly or substitute clever for delicious.

> **A menu with "the Low Fat Side and the Don't Ask, Don't Tell Side."**

I've roamed the menu, from the shish kebab on couscous (terrific North African seasoning but too chewy) to the appetizer plate of baba ghanouj, olives, goat cheese and roasted peppers with irresistible grill-striped pita wedges. But finally I've come home to what would draw me back to TRUMPETS regularly: The Gadsden Blueplate Special. This is Hagedorn's family recipe from his home town in Alabama. Two cornflake-crusted pork chops, slightly Tabasco-spiked and extravagantly juicy, sit atop a soft warm pool of cheese grits littered with crunchy little cuts of fried okra that could convert an okra hater. Maybe I'd alternate this with my TRUMPETS dream meal, which would be a plate of side dishes: the grits, the okra, garlicky fried potatoes, potato fingers and herbed mashed potatoes. Then, I suppose, it would be back to the Low Fat Side.

VIDALIA
1990 M St. NW, Washington, DC
(202) 659-1990

AMERICAN/SOUTHERN

Lunch: M-F 11:30-2:30 **Entrees:** $13.25-$17.50
Dinner: M-Th 5:30-10, F-Sat 5:30-10:30 **Entrees:** $18-$22
Closed: Sun **Credit Cards:** All major
Reservations: Recommended **Dress:** Casual
Parking: Complimentary valet at dinner
Metro: Dupont Circle, Farragut West

Jeff Buben keeps getting better and better. His sunny yellow, below-ground restaurant is comfortable and quiet, smoothly run and elegant — a Washington powerhouse. Yet, much as these amenities account for its success, the food would be enough. His menu is continually refreshing, a matter of seasonal New American dishes with a slight Southern accent. Squint and you'll think you're on a veranda as you sip rosemary-spiked fresh lemonade and eat cream-rich corn bread, truly fine biscuits and yeasty flatbread squares topped with caramelized onions. The wine list, of course, is impressive, too.

For some chefs, asparagus would be enough for asparagus salad. Buben's includes marinated fresh morels and a supporting cast of yellow potatoes and onions dressed with mushroom oil. A chicken club sandwich is not a matter of white bread, mayo and sliced breast meat; it's a kind of summery appetizer napoleon with paper-thin sheets of crisp dough layering the chicken, vegetables and a touch of ham, with red-eye vinaigrette. The Italians team arugula, balsamic vinegar and shavings of parmesan as a salad; Buben is likely to add a grits cake.

These days you can rate Southern restaurants by their shrimp with grits, and VIDALIA'S is top-notch. And Buben can make even farmed salmon taste a little wild — seared and nearly exploding with juiciness. What's more, the entrees seduce you with their side dishes: turnip gratin and swiss chard with walnuts accompanying the liver, onion-dusted chips aside the swordfish club, grits cake nuzzling the seared salmon. This is a restaurant where I might be compelled to order a vegetable plate. It's also a restaurant where I undoubtedly would save room for dessert. The creme brulee is close to perfect, and the season's fruits find their way into cobblers, crisps, shortcakes and tarts.

VIET DELI
2065 University Blvd., Hyattsville, MD
(301) 422-6339

VIETNAMESE

Open: Daily 10 am-9 pm
Entrees: $2-$9 **Credit Cards:** None; cash only
Reservations: No **Dress:** Casual **Parking:** Free lot

VIET DELI, with just a few picnic-style tables and a busy carry-out business, is one the smallest of the region's countless Vietnamese restaurants. It is also undoubtedly one of the cheapest. Think of a sandwich made on a light, crusty submarine roll reminiscent of New Orleans' famous French loaves. Warm the roll and spread it with homemade mayonnaise. Layer it with soft, buttery liver pâté, then spicy jellied ham studded with peppercorns. Lighten it up with raw vegetables — shredded marinated carrots, sliced cucumbers and sprigs of cilantro — to add a colorful note as well. Shake on a little Maggi seasoning or soy sauce. Serve it in a basket. How much would it be worth? At the VIET DELI it's less than $3.

There's more, too. The steamed buns are always sold out by the time I get there, so I start with shrimp rice cakes. I also think highly of the *cha gio* and the cold, refreshing shrimp rolls, with their lettuce and mint crunch and their dark, spicy peanut dipping sauce. As for entrees, the rice crepes, slick white rolls studded with bits of pork and topped with grilled pork, are my first choice, though not everyone likes those slippery crepes. More mainstream are the noodle or rice dishes topped with grilled meat or shrimp. In general, they're all fine, but those with pork are the stars.

Still, VIET DELI isn't as shipshape as it once was, and the service can be slow. So pick your time carefully or be ready to wait.

VILLAGE BISTRO
1723 Wilson Blvd., Arlington, VA
(703) 522 0284

AMERICAN/INTERNATIONAL   ♿

Lunch: M-F 11:30-2:30 **Entrees:** $5-$13
Dinner: M-Th 5-10:30, F-Sat 5-11, Sun 5-10 **Entrees:** $8-$17
Pre-Theater: M-Th 5-7, $13 **Brunch:** Sun 11-2:30, $8-$13
Credit Cards: All major **Dress:** Casual
Parking: Free lot **Metro:** Rosslyn, Court House

Nothing inspires more trust in a kitchen than a long list of seasonal daily specials. At the VILLAGE BISTRO the specials run half as long as the regular menu, and they include rarities the season evokes: shad in the spring (the fish, not just the roe), softshells in summer, roast goose in winter.

From the street, the VILLAGE BISTRO would seem to be just another neighborhood restaurant in a shopping strip that is fraying at the edges. Inside, though, it's dressed with bouquets of flowers and so friendly that after your first few visits the waiter is likely to know your preferences without being reminded. While such personal service may be noteworthy in this chain-restaurant era, the

> **". . . you can wear jeans or jewels and eat Broadway cooking at movie-house prices."**

VILLAGE BISTRO'S quality/price ratio is even more remarkable. At chicken-carryout prices the VILLAGE BISTRO offers a long list of fresh fish and seafood, luxurious choices among the meats, nicely dressed pastas. Except for the uninteresting pizzas, the cooking is a sure-handed and creative mingling of French, Italian, Indian, Middle Eastern and American.

Even so, appetizers are the winners, from steamed clams fragrant with orange and lemon to calamari sauteed with an herbed beurre blanc. Those buttery yet light sauces for seafood and Mediterranean garnishes of olives, arugula and balsamic vinegar or pernod and garlic are the kitchen's signatures, so when in doubt, choose fish. And if you find a disappointment — dry crab cakes, for instance — remind yourself that those generous and elaborately garnished cakes cost little more than a sandwich elsewhere. Here is a place where you can wear jeans or jewels and eat Broadway cooking at movie-house prices.

VINCENZO

1606 20th St. NW, Washington, DC
(202) 667-0047

ITALIAN   ♿

Lunch: M-F noon-2 **Entrees:** $15-$17
Dinner: M-Sat 6-10 **Entrees:** $16-$25
Closed: Sun **Credit Cards:** All major
Reservations: Recommended **Dress:** Casual
Parking: Valet (fee) at dinner **Metro:** Dupont Circle

O ver its decade and a half, VINCENZO has changed its dining rooms, its chefs, its menu, even its name, to Trattoria al Sole, and now back again. Yet at the core it remains the same: a simple, distinguished Italian restaurant that is as close as Washington comes to a trattoria. Its main dining room is long and narrow, covered by an arched skylight, and the walls are the color of Florentine clay. Decorations are few. The service is expert, not stiff in the least.

The menu is simple, mostly fish, and the cooking shows an Italian respect for the intrinsic flavors of the ingredients. A dewy, thick fillet of cod is dressed only with a light coating of bread crumbs and a smear of chopped olives. Stuffed swordfish, the most elaborate offering, is still only garnished with bread crumbs, anchovies, herbs, onions — nothing to mask its taste. In fact, some might find the food a little dull if they are used to more adventurous cooking. This is quiet food. It's so straightforward that when there is a flaw — a too-heavy batter on the fried soft-shells the last time I tried them — it can't slip by your notice. Fortunately, such mishaps are rare.

" . . . an Italian respect for the intrinsic flavors of the ingredients."

Even more important, lately VINCENZO has been serving some of the most exquisite pastas and breads in the city. Chef Frank Ruta was making them, but he's gone now. We can hope Ruta trained the other staff to reproduce his excellent breads, his remarkably light pappardelle and his feathery, teasingly sharp goat cheese ravioli.

VOX POPULI
800 Connecticut Ave. NW, Washington, DC
(202) 835-2233

AMERICAN/INTERNATIONAL   ♿

Breakfast: M-F 8-11 **Entrees:** $5-$10
Lunch: M-F 11-3 **Entrees:** $8-$15
Afternoon Tea: M-F 3-7 **Entrees:** $2.50-$9 **Closed:** Sat-Sun
Credit Cards: AE, MC, V **Dress:** Casual
Reservations: Accepted for parties of 5 or more
Parking: Street **Metro:** Farragut West

In this semi-self-service cafe, music from the 1940s plays and sun streams in through the big cafe windows. Beyond them are the green, pierced-metal cafe tables on the sidewalk and Decatur House across the street. Paris flourishes inside, in the accents of the utterly chic staff, in the floor of small mosaic tiles and the marble tables on ornate iron pedestals, and in the magazines filed in wall holders. Around a central column, clocks are set to times around the world.

The food looks magnificent; even the wines, stored behind the bar in horizontal cubicles, look especially tempting. And if the sandwiches and salads don't taste exactly marvelous, they are all fresh and agreeable. As for the high prices, it's worth a premium to spend a lunch hour in a place stylish enough to be at home on the Rue du Faubourg St. Honoré.

The menu changes daily, but there are always two soups. Pâté is also always available as an appetizer (enough for two) or a light entree. Sandwich fillings are layered with restraint, European style, rather than piled on heavily, American style, so sandwiches are no bargain, and I've been bored by the fillings. So I've mostly eaten salads. Sparkling with bright colors and mounded on huge white platters, they look irresistible: artichokes with green beans and asparagus, couscous with black olives and dried cranberries, cubes of grill-striped chicken with sliced leeks, Caesar dressed to order and topped with shrimp. The salad vegetables are fresh and precisely cooked. Everything in the fruit salad is also fresh, and moistened with its own juices.

VOX POPULI provides a very civilized break for coffee and a croissant in the morning, soup and a small salad at lunch, a glass of wine and a quick sandwich for an early dinner.

WEST END CAFE
Washington Circle Hotel
1 Washington Circle NW, Washington, DC
(202) 293-5390

AMERICAN/MEDITERRANEAN   ♿

Breakfast: M-F 7-10, Sat-Sun 8-10   **Entrees:** $6-$9.25
Lunch: Daily 11:30-2:30   **Entrees:** $7.50-$13
Dinner: Sun-M 5:30-10, T-Th 5:30-11:30, F-Sat 5:30-midnight
Dinner Entrees: $8-$21 **Brunch:** Sun 11-2:30, $8.50 buffet
Credit Cards: All major **Reservations:** Recommended
Dress: Casual **Parking:** Free garage **Metro:** Foggy Bottom
Entertainment: Pianist T-Sat nights

W est End Cafe, with its glass walls curving overhead like a greenhouse, lets you feel the sun, see the sky and eat your smoked salmon in cool comfort. Given Washington summers, it's even better than an outdoor cafe. This creative American restaurant has two dining rooms with a hallway between. The Garden Room has lush greenery and floral upholstery, art deco fashion prints and taped classical music amid sunshine or starlight. The Piano Room, a bar and lounge, is a darker nook, decorated more with sound — a pianist in the evenings — than with light. I've been eating Caesar salad on this site since back when the West End theater showed plays rather than films. And the Caesar is still good, though the West End Cafe has modernized it with baked parmesan crisps.

Over the years, many of Washington's best young chefs have come through this kitchen on their way up the ladder. This is the place where much of the city's New American cooking got its start. Smoked salmon, fried oysters, grilled fish, seasonal soups — they take on new character with each chef. And there's always an array of informal dishes, even at dinner: burgers, pizzas, antipasto samplers, omelets and sandwiches. Vegetarians have plenty to choose from. So dinner can be elaborate or simple, leisurely or quick.

At midday, though there is an à la carte menu, the highlight is a Mediterranean antipasto buffet: an array of salads — asparagus, baby artichokes, couscous with dried fruit. A quiche — a little bland and soggy, though still better than most — adds heft, as do salamis. With serve-yourself soup to start and slices of melon for dessert, the buffet is a three-course meal for hardly more than the price of a sandwich.

WILLARD ROOM
Willard Hotel
1401 Pennsylvania Ave. NW
Washington, DC
(202) 637-7440

AMERICAN/FRENCH

Breakfast: M-F 7:30-10 **Entrees:** $11.50-$26.50
Lunch: M-F 11:30-2 **Entrees:** $9.75-$16.75
Dinner: Daily 6-10 **Entrees:** $17-$29.50
Credit Cards: All major **Reservations:** Recommended
Dress: Jacket & tie preferred **Metro:** Metro Center
Parking: Complimentary valet at dinner

This is simply the most magnificent dining room in Washington, outside of the White House and the State Department. Its carved wood paneling is worthy of a cathedral. The dining room is furnished in mahogany, velvet and silk, with European silver and crystal dessert carts, abundant chandeliers and an immensity of vertical space. The chairs are comfortable enough for a vacation, the tables are large enough for a day's desk work, and the carpets are thick enough to muffle any exchange of state secrets.

The service is as grand as the setting deserves. So is the wine list — and its prices follow suit. The menu, under Alsatian chef Guy Reinbolt, is a fashionable show of phyllo-wrapped entrees, of venison and boar, pheasant and lobster. And the dishes look as if constructed by a large team, with precise dots of sauce ringing the plate, tulip-shaped pastries cosseting the vegetables. A truffled potato risotto one day appeared as if each piece of potato had been carved to mimic a grain of rice.

"This is simply the most magnificent dining room in Washington, outside the White House and the State Department."

The result of this painstaking preparation can be a dish suited more to photography than to gastronomy. Delicious components are smothered in abundance. Some of the garnishes taste as if they were meant only for show. Texture, flavor and even temperature often take a back seat to shape and color. The sublime and the clumsy share the same plate. There's talent here. Sometimes one needs to dig for it.

XING KUBA
2218 Wisconsin Ave. NW, Washington, DC
(202) 965-0665

AMERICAN/SOUTHWESTERN/CARIBBEAN/ASIAN

Lunch: M-F 11:30-2:30 **Entrees:** $6-$8
Dinner: Sun-Th 5:30-10:15, F-Sat 5-11:15 **Entrees:** $13-$20
Brunch (dim sum/tapas): Sat-Sun 11:30-3, $3.25-$5
Credit Cards: All major **Reservations:** Recommended
Dress: Casual **Parking:** Street

XING KUBA, an exotic-looking little restaurant that fuses the flavors and techniques of Asia, New Mexico and Havana, is one of those rare places where the entrees tend to be better than the appetizers. Not all of the menu's first courses come up short: Potato-leek chowder studded with roasted corn and bacon, swirled with red pepper *coulis*, is so thick and fragrant, so full of satisfaction, that I'd gladly order a bowl and consider that dinner .

Search through your menu for a sheet of specials: That's the ticket to dining well here. One night it included an appetizer of tiny scallops in the shell, baby clams and small, free-spirited, non-farmed mussels, all steamed together with Asian-Cajun seasonings. Grilled swordfish, an entree among the specials that night, was crusted with pumpkin seeds and coriander — swordfish with remarkable flavor, tangy on its seared surface and steamy inside.

". . . one of those rare places where the entrees tend to be better than the appetizers."

Entrees on the regular menu also can play in this league. Sesame-herbed sautéed shrimp is coated with flavors that tingle and bloom and fill your senses, riding on a spicy Thai peanut sauce. Salmon with a pine nut-plantain crust doesn't taste exotic; it just tastes nutty, crunchy and wonderful. Chilean sea bass, seared in a wok and served with papaya-mango salsa, slithery transparent noodles and succulent Asian greens, is perfectly cooked and happily married. Yet meat dishes don't have the flair of the fish here. The dessert tray features one particularly outrageous and glorious confection. It's a flat wedge of crushed chocolate cookies sandwiching coconut that tastes real and fresh, and finished off with a buttery chocolate glaze. If Oreos had been invented by some brilliant 10-year-old tropical chef, this is what they'd be. And I'd demand one every night after I'd licked my soup bowl clean.

GUIDE LISTINGS

Finding
what you want . . .
the food, the features,
the atmosphere, and
all the right places

226

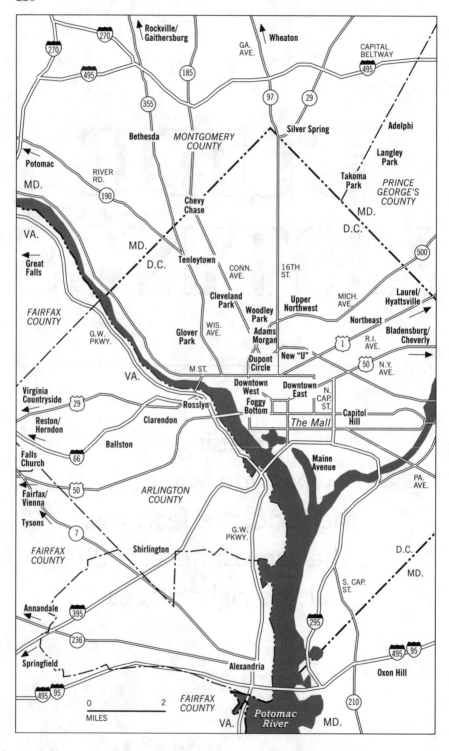

WHERE THEY ARE

DISTRICT OF COLUMBIA

ADAMS MORGAN
Cashion's Eat Place
Cities
Felix
Grill from Ipanema
I Matti
La Fourchette
Meskerem
Miss Saigon
Perry's
Roxanne
South African Cafe

CAPITOL HILL
Anatolya
B. Smith's
Cafe Berlin
Capitol City Brewing
   Company
Capitol View Club
Dubliner
La Colline
Louisiana Cafe
Market Lunch

CHEVY CHASE
Arucola
Chadwick's
Cheesecake Factory
Clyde's of Chevy Chase
   (Maryland)
La Ferme (Maryland)

CLEVELAND PARK/
TENLEY/WOODLEY PARK
Amazonia Grill
Cafe Deluxe
Coppi's Vigorelli

Ladda
Lavandou
Lebanese Taverna
Melati
Mrs. Simpson's
New Heights
Saigon Gourmet
Saigon Inn

DOWNTOWN - 16TH
STREET AND EAST
A.V. Ristorante
Bacchus
Bice
Burma (Chinatown)
Cafe Atlantico
California Grill
Capitol City Brewing
   Company
Capital Grille
Coco Loco
Coeur de Lion
Dean & Deluca
Full Kee (Chinatown)
Georgia Brown's
Gerard's Place
Haad Thai
Hunan Chinatown
Jaleo
Lafayette
Les Halles
Lespinasse
Luigino
Marrakesh
Mr. Yung's (Chinatown)
Morrison-Clark Inn
Occidental Grill
Old Ebbitt Grill
Pan Asian Noodles and Grill

Red Sage
Rupperts
701
3rd & Eats
Tony Cheng's (Chinatown)
Willard Room

DOWNTOWN - WEST OF 16TH STREET
Aroma
Bombay Club
Dean & Deluca Cafe
Galileo
Greenwood
Kinkead's
Le Lion d'Or
Legal Sea Foods
Marrocco's
Morton's of Chicago
Mykonos
Oodles Noodles
Oval Room
Prime Rib
Sam & Harry's
Sholl's
Taberna del Alabardero
Vidalia
Vox Populi

DUPONT CIRCLE
BeDuCi
Bistro 2015
Brickskeller
Brighton-on-N
Bua
C.F. Folks
Cafe Parma
City Lights of China
Gabriel
Il Radicchio
I Ricchi

Jockey Club
La Tomate
Lauriol Plaza
Luna Grill & Diner
Mediterranean Blue
Obelisk
Pan Asian Noodles and Grill
Pesce
Pizzeria Paradiso
Raku
Restaurant Nora
Sala Thai
Skewers
Straits of Malaya
Tabard Inn
Teaism
Trumpets
Vincenzo

FOGGY BOTTOM/WEST END
Aquarelle
Asia Nora
Goldoni
Jin Ga
Melrose
Provence
Roof Terrace

GEORGETOWN
Balalayka
Bistro Francais
Bistrot Lepic
Cafe Milano
Cafe Riviera
Chadwick's
Citronelle
Clyde's
Dean & Deluca Cafe
Enriqueta's
Hibiscus Cafe

Houston's
Il Radicchio
Japan Inn
La Chaumiere
Miss Saigon
Morton's of Chicago
Music City Roadhouse
Old Glory
Paolo's
Patisserie-Cafe Didier
Saigon Inn
Sarinah Satay House
Seasons
1789

GLOVER PARK
Austin Grill
Busara
Germaine's
Le Caprice
Rocklands
Sushi-Ko
Xing Kuba

NEW U
Coppi's
Cafe Nema

NORTHEAST
Ellis Island
Levi's

MAINE AVENUE WATERFRONT
Le Rivage
Maine Avenue Wharf

PALISADES
Makoto
Star of Europe

UPPER NORTHWEST-EAST OF ROCK CREEK
Fio's
Hitching Post

MARYLAND
BETHESDA
Austin Grill
Bacchus
Cafe Bethesda
Capitol City Brewing
Cottonwood Cafe
Delray Garden and Grill
Houston's
Il Ritrovo
La Miche
Le Vieux Logis
Matuba
Oodles Noodles
Pines of Rome
Raku
Rio Grande Cafe
Tako Grill
Tara Thai
Terramar
Thyme Square

BLADENSBURG
Cielito Lindo

CHEVERLY
Fratelli

CHEVY CHASE
Clyde's of Chevy Chase
La Ferme

LANGLEY PARK/ADELPHI/ HYATTSVILLE
Ledo
Pho 75

Swagat
Viet Deli

LAUREL
C.J. Ferrari
Red Hot & Blue

**SILVER SPRING/WHEATON/
TAKOMA PARK**
Crisp & Juicy
Sabang
Suporn's
Savory

OXON HILL
Levi's

POTOMAC
Old Angler's Inn

**ROCKVILLE/
GAITHERSBURG**
Bombay Bistro
Cafe Bethesda North
Crisp & Juicy
Houston's
Kosher Express
Mama Wok & Teriyaki
Pho 75
Richland
Red Hot & Blue
Sam Woo

**VIRGINIA
ALEXANDRIA**
Afghan
Bilbo Baggins
Casablanca
Chadwick's
Generous George
La Bergerie
Le Gaulois

Le Refuge
RT's
South Austin Grill
Southside 815

**ANNANDALE
/SPRINGFIELD**
Austin Grill
Generous George
Hee Been

ARLINGTON/CLARENDON
Atilla's
Bangkok Siam
Blue-N-Gold
Cafe Dalat
Cafe New Delhi
Crisp & Juicy
Lebanese Taverna
Matuba
Pho 75
Pho Cali
Queen Bee
RT's
Red Hot & Blue
Village Bistro

BALLSTON
Bistro Bistro
Food Factory
Rio Grande Cafe
Rocklands at Carpool

FAIRFAX/VIENNA
Bombay Bistro
Nizam's
Panjshir
Shamshiry
Tara Thai

FALLS CHURCH
Bangkok St Grill
Duangrat's
Galaxy
Panjshir
Peking Gourmet Inn
Pho 75

GREAT FALLS
L'Auberge Chez Francois

RESTON/HERNDON
Bistro Bistro
Rio Grande Cafe
Red Hot & Blue

ROSSLYN
Il Radicchio
Tivoli

Tom Sarris' Orleans House

SHIRLINGTON
Bistro Bistro
Capitol City Brewing
  (scheduled to open)
Carlyle Grand Cafe
T. H. A. I.

TYSONS
Busara
Legal Sea Foods
Morton's of Chicago

VIRGINIA COUNTRYSIDE
Ashby Inn
Inn at Little Washington
L'Auberge Provencal

WHERE TO GET BREAKFAST

Aquarelle
Bistro 2015
Cafe Riviera
Cafe Nema
California Grill
Citronelle
Coeur de Lion
Dean & Deluca
Dubliner
Gabriel
Jockey Club
La Colline
Lafayette
Lespinasse
Luna Grill & Diner

Market Lunch
Melrose
Old Ebbitt Grill
Patisserie-Cafe Didier
Pho 75
Savory
Seasons
Sholl's Colonial
  Cafeteria
Tabard Inn
Teaism
3rd & Eats
Vox Populi
West End Cafe
Willard Room

WHAT FOOD THEY SERVE: BY CUISINE

AFGHAN
Afghan
Panjshir

AMERICAN
Aquarelle
Ashby Inn
Austin Grill/South
Austin Grill
B. Smith's
Bilbo Baggins
Bistro Bistro
Bistro 2015
Blue-N-Gold
Brickskeller
Brighton-on-N
C. F. Folks
Cafe Bethesda
Cafe Deluxe
California Grill
Capitol City
  Brewing Company
Capital Grille
Capitol View Club
Carlyle Grand Cafe
Cashion's Eat Place
Chadwick's
Cheesecake Factory
Citronelle
Clyde's
Coeur de Lion
Cottonwood Cafe
Dean & Deluca Cafe
Dubliner
Ellis Island
Eye Street Cafe
Felix
Georgia Brown's
Greenwood

Hitching Post
Houston's
Inn at Little
  Washington
Jockey Club
Kinkead's
Lafayette
Legal Sea Foods
Levi's
Louisiana Grill
Luna Grill & Diner
Maine Avenue
  Wharf
Market Lunch
Melrose
Mrs. Simpson's
Morrison-Clark Inn
Morton's of Chicago
Music City
  Roadhouse
New Heights
Occidental Grill
Old Angler's Inn
Old Ebbitt Grill
Old Glory
Oval Room
Perry's
Pesce
Prime Rib
RT's
Red Hot & Blue
Red Sage
Restaurant Nora
Rio Grande Cafe
Rocklands
Roof Terrace
Roxanne
Rupperts

Sam & Harry's
Savory
Seasons
701
1789
Sholl's
Southside 815
Tabard Inn
3rd & Eats
Thyme Square
Tom Sarris' Orleans
 House
Trumpets
Vidalia
Village Bistro
Vox Populi
West End Cafe
Willard Room
Xing Kuba

AMERICAN /BARBECUE
Levi's
Market Lunch
Old Glory
Red Hot & Blue
Rocklands

AMERICAN /CREOLE-CAJUN
Blue-N-Gold
Louisiana Cafe
RT's

AMERICAN /SOUTHERN
B. Smith's
Georgia Brown's
Levi's
Morrison-Clark Inn
Music City
 Roadhouse

Old Glory
Southside 815
3rd & Eats
Vidalia

AMERICAN /SOUTHWESTERN
Austin Grill/South
Austin Grill
Cottonwood Cafe
Houston's
Red Sage
Rio Grande Cafe
Roxanne
Xing Kuba

AMERICAN /STEAKHOUSE
Capital Grille
Les Halles
Morton's of Chicago
Prime Rib
Sam & Harry's
Tom Sarris' Orleans
 House (prime rib)

ASIAN
Asia Nora
Bangkok St. Grill
Germaine's
Oodles Noodles
Pan Asian Noodles
 & Grill
Raku
Teaism
Xing Kuba

BRAZILIAN
Amazonia
Coco Loco
Grill From Ipanema

BURMESE
Burma

CARIBBEAN
Cafe Atlantico
Hibiscus Cafe
Xing Kuba

CHINESE
City Lights of China
Full Kee
Hunan Chinatown
Mama Wok &
  Teriyaki
Mr. Yung's
Peking Gourmet Inn
Richland
Sam Woo
Tony Cheng's

ETHIOPIAN
Meskerem

FRENCH
Bistro Francais
Bistrot Lepic
Cafe Riviera
Citronelle
Gerard's Place
Jockey Club
L'Auberge
  Provencal
L'Auberge Chez
  Francois
La Bergerie
La Chaumiere
La Colline
La Ferme
La Fourchette
La Miche
Le Caprice
Lavandou
Le Gaulois

Le Lion d'Or
Le Refuge
Le Rivage
Le Vieux Logis
Les Halles
Lespinasse
Patisserie-Cafe
  Didier
Provence
Riviera
Seasons
Willard Room

GERMAN
Cafe Berlin

GREEK
Mykonos

INDIAN
Aroma
Bombay Bistro
Bombay Club
Cafe New Delhi
Swagat

INDONESIAN
Melati
Sabang
Sarinah Satay House

INTERNATIONAL
C. F. Folks
Cities
New Heights
Restaurant Nora
701
Village Bistro
Vox Populi

IRISH
Dubliner
Ellis Island

ITALIAN
A.V. Ristorante
Arucola
Bice
C.J. Ferrari
Cafe Milano
Cafe Parma
Coppi's
Fio's
Fratelli
Galileo
Generous George
Goldoni
I Matti
I Ricchi
Il Radicchio
La Tomate
Ledo
Luigino
Marrocco's
Obelisk
Paolo's
Pines of Rome
Pizzeria Paradiso
Tivoli
Vincenzo

JAPANESE
Hee Been
Japan Inn
Jin Ga
Makoto
Mama Wok &
   Teriyaki
Matuba
Perry's
Sam Woo
Sushi-Ko
Tako Grill

KOREAN
Hee Been

Jin Ga
Sam Woo

LATIN AMERICAN
Cafe Atlantico
Crisp & Juicy
Gabriel
Terramar

LEBANESE
Bacchus
Lebanese Taverna

MALAYSIAN
Melati
Straits of Malaya

MEDITERRANEAN
BeDuCi
Cafe Nema
Eye Street Cafe
Gabriel
Il Ritrovo
Kosher Express
Mediterranean Blue
Nizam's
Skewers
West End Cafe

MEXICAN
Cielito Lindo
Coco Loco
Enriqueta's
Lauriol Plaza

MOROCCAN
Casablanca
Marrakesh

NICARAGUAN
Terramar

PAKISTANI
Food Factory

PERSIAN

Shamshiry

PORTUGUESE

Star of Europe

ROTISSERIE CHICKEN

Crisp & Juicy

RUSSIAN

Balalayka

SEAFOOD

Greenwood
Hitching Post
Kinkead's
Legal Sea Foods
Maine Avenue
  Wharf
Mama Wok &
  Teriyaki
Market Lunch
Pesce
Pho Cali
RT's
Tony Cheng's

SOMALIAN

Cafe Nema

SOUTH AFRICAN

South African Cafe

SPANISH

Gabriel
Jaleo
Lauriol Plaza
Taberna del
  Alabardero

THAI

Bangkok Siam
Bangkok St Grill
Bua
Busara
Duangrat's
Haad Thai
Ladda
Pan Asian Noodles
  & Grill
Sala Thai
Suporn's
T.H.A.I.
Tara Thai

TURKISH

Anatolya
Atilla's
Nizam's

VIETNAMESE

Cafe Dalat
Delray Garden
  and Grill
Galaxy
Germaine's
Miss Saigon
Pho 75
Pho Cali
Queen Bee
Saigon Gourmet
Saigon Inn
Viet Deli

CHEAP EATS: DINNER ENTREES
STARTING UNDER $10

AV Ristorante
Afghan
Anatolya
Aroma
Arucola
Atilla's
Austin Grill
　/South Austin Grill
Balalayka
Bangkok Siam
Bangkok Street Grill
Bistro Francais
Bombay Bistro
Bombay Club
Brickskeller
Bua
Burma
Busara
C.J. Ferrari's
Cafe Dalat
Cafe Deluxe
Cafe Nema
Cafe New Delhi
Cafe Parma
Capitol City Brewing
　Company
Carlyle Grand Cafe
Chadwick's
Cheesecake Factory
Cielito Lindo
City Lights of China
Clyde's of Chevy Chase
Clyde's of Georgetown

Coppi's
Crisp & Juicy
Dean & Deluca
Delray Garden and Grill
Dubliner
Ellis Island
Enriqueta's
Eye Street Cafe
Fio's
Food Factory
Fratelli
Full Kee
Gabriel
Galaxy
Generous George
Germaine's
Grill From Ipanema
Haad Thai
Hee Been
Hitching Post
Houston's
Hunan Chinatown
I Matti
Il Radicchio
Il Ritrovo
Kosher Express
La Fourchette
Ladda
Lauriol Plaza
Le Gaulois
Lebanese Taverna
Ledo

Levi's Luna Grill & Diner
Maine Avenue Wharf
Mama Wok & Teriyaki
Market Lunch
Matuba
Mediterranean Blue
Melati
Meskeram
Miss Saigon
Mrs. Simpson's
Mr. Yung's
Occidental Grill
Old Ebbitt Grill
Old Glory
Oodles Noodles
Pan Asian Noodles and Grill
Paolo's
Peking Gourmet Inn
Pho 75
Pho Cali
Pines of Rome
Pizzeria Paradiso
Queen Bee
Raku
Red Hot & Blue
Red Sage (chili bar)
Richland
Rio Grande Cafe
Rocklands
Roxanne
Sabang
Saigon Gourmet
Saigon Inn
Sala Thai
Sam Woo
Sarinah Satay House
Savory

Shamshiry
Sholl's Colonial Cafeteria
Skewers
South African Cafe
Southside 815
Star of Europe
Suporn's
Sushi-Ko
Swagat
T. H. A. I.
Tara Thai
Teaism
Tom Sarris' Orleans House
Tony Cheng's
Trumpets
Viet Deli
Village Bistro
West End Cafe

RESTAURANTS WITH FIREPLACES

Ashby Inn
Coeur de Lion
(afternoon tea room)
La Chaumiere
Le Gaulois
Old Angler's Inn
1789
Tabard Inn

WHERE LATE-NIGHTERS GO

The following hours apply mainly to weekends, though more than a few restaurants also keep late hours during the week.

3 AM TO 4 AM
Bistro Francais
Brickskeller
Full Kee

1 AM TO 2 AM
Cafe Milano
Cafe Nema
Cafe Parma
Capitol City Brewery,
  Arlington
Chadwick's
Dubliner
Coppi's
Music City Roadhouse
Meskerem
Old Glory
Mr. Yung's
Il Ritrovo
Old Ebbitt Grill
Raku
South African Cafe

MIDNIGHT TO 12:30 AM
A.V. Ristorante
Afghan
Austin Grill - Glover Park
Austin Grill - Bethesda
B. Smith's

Blue-N-Gold
Busara - Bethesda
Cafe Atlantico
Capitol City Brewing
  Company (DC)
Cheesecake Factory
Clyde's of Chevy Chase
Generous George
Georgia Brown's
Grill From Ipanema
Hibiscus Cafe
Hitching Post
Houston's
Ledo
Il Radicchio
Jaleo
Lauriol Plaza
Les Halles
Louisiana Cafe
Mediterranean Blue
Paolo's
Peking Gourmet Inn
Perry's
Pizzeria Paradiso
South Austin Grill
Roxanne
Saigon Inn (M St.)
Savory

Star of Europe
Tony Cheng's
West End Cafe

11 PM TO 11:30 PM
Amazonia Grill
Atilla's
Austin Grill
  -Springfield
Bangkok Siam
Bice
Bistro Bistro
Bombay Club
Burma
Busara Tysons
C.J. Ferrari's
Cafe Berlin
Cafe Deluxe
Capital Grille
Carlyle Grand Cafe
Casablanca
Cashion's Eat Place
Cities
City Lights of China
Clyde's of Georgetown
Coco Loco
Cottonwood Cafe
Crisp & Juicy
  -Silver Spring
Duangrat's
Ellis Island
Enriqueta's
Fratelli
Galaxy

Germaine's
Hee Been
Hunan Chinatown
I Matti
La Fourchette
La Tomate
Lavandou
Le Gaulois
Le Rivage
Lebanese Taverna
Legal Sea Foods K St.
Luigino
Luna Grill & Diner
Marrakesh
Marrocco's
Melati
Miss Saigon
Morton's
Mykonos
New Heights
Nizam's
Occidental Grill
Oval Room
Pan Asian Noodles and
  Grill
Pho Cali
Pines of Rome
Prime Rib
Provence
RT's
Red Hot & Blue
Richland
Rio Grande Cafe
Rupperts

Sabang
Saigon Inn - Conn Ave
Sala Thai
Sam Woo
701
1789
Shamshiry
Skewers
Southside 815
Straits of Malaya

T. H. A. I.
Taberna del Alabardero
Tara Thai
Teaism
Terramar
Thyme Square
Tom Sarris' Orleans
  House
Trumpets
Village Bistro

FOR LIVE ENTERTAINMENT & DANCING
(D) Indicates dancing

Afghan
Amazonia (D)
Atilla's
B. Smith's
Balalayka
Bistro Bistro
Bistro 2015
Blue-N-Gold
Bombay Club
Cafe Nema
Capitol View Club
Casablanca
Cities (D)
Coco Loco (D)
Coeur de Lion (D)
Duangrat's
Dubliner
Felix (D)
Galaxy (D)
Georgia Brown's
Jaleo
Kinkead's

La Ferme
Lafayette
Lespinasse
Louisiana Cafe
Marrakeh
Melrose (D)
Meskerem
Music City Roadhouse
Old Glory
Oval Room
Paolo's
Perry's
Prime Rib
Roxanne
Savory
701
South African Cafe
Star of Europe
Terramar
Trumpets (D)
West End Cafe
Willard Room

FAMILY-FRIENDLY RESTAURANTS

A.V. Ristorante
Afghan
Atilla's
Austin Grill
  /South Austin Grill
Anatolya
Bangkok St. Grill
Bistro Bistro
Cafe Dalat
Cafe Deluxe
California Grill
Chadwick's
Cheesecake Factory
Cielito Lindo
Clyde's of Chevy Chase
Coppi's
Crisp & Juicy
Dean & Deluca
Delray Garden and Grill
Pho Cali
Fio's
Food Factory
Fratelli
Full Kee
Generous George
Greenwood
Hee Been
Houston's
Il Radicchio
Kosher Express
Lebanese Taverna
Ledo
Levi's
Mama Wok & Teriyaki
Market Lunch

Maine Avenue Wharf
Music City Roadhouse
Old Glory
Oodles Noodles
Paolo's
Patisserie-Cafe Didier
Peking Gourmet Inn
Pines of Rome
Red Hot & Blue
Richland
Rio Grande Cafe
Rocklands
Saigon Inn
Shamshiry
Southside 815
Savory
Sholl's
Star of Europe
Swagat
Tara Thai
3rd & Eats
Thyme Square
Tony Cheng's
Viet Deli

ROOMS WITH A (SPECIAL) VIEW

Aquarelle
Capitol View Club
Lafayette
Le Rivage
Roof Terrace

THE SUNDAY BRUNCH BUNCH

Amazonia Grill
Aroma
Ashby Inn
Austin Grill/
  South Austin Grill
B. Smith's
Bilbo Baggins
Bistro Bistro
Blue-N-Gold
Bombay Club
Brighton-on-N
Cafe Deluxe
Cafe New Delhi
Cafe Parma
Cafe Riviera
Carlyle Grand Cafe
Cashion's Eat Place
Chadwick's
Cheesecake Factory
Citronelle
Clyde's of Chevy Chase
Clyde's of Georgetown
Coeur de Lion
Coppi's Vigorelli
Ellis Island
Felix
Fratelli
Gabriel

Georgia Brown's
Grill From Ipanema
Kinkead's
Lafayette
Lauriol Plaza
Louisiana Cafe
Luna Grill & Diner
Mediterranean Blue
Melrose
Mrs. Simpson's
Morrison-Clark
Music City Roadhouse
New Heights
Old Angler's Inn
Old Ebbit Grill
Old Glory
Perry's
Rio Grande Cafe
Roof Terrace
Roxanne
Seasons
South African Cafe
Swagat
Tabard Inn
Thyme Square
Trumpets
Village Bistro
West End Cafe
Xing Kuba

THE GREAT CHEFS

Patrick O'Connell (Inn at
  Little Washington)
Jeff Buben (Vidalia)
Roberto Donna (Galileo)

Bob Kinkead (Kinkead's)
Gerard Pangaud (Gerard's
  Place)
Peter Pastan (Obelisk)

RESTAURANTS WITH PRIVATE DINING ROOMS

Aquarelle
Ashby Inn
A.V. Ristorante
B. Smith's
Balalayka
BeDuCi
Bilbo Baggins
Bistro Bistro
Bistro 2015
Brickskeller
Brighton-on-N
Burma
Busara
Cafe Bethesda North
Cafe Milano
Cafe Riviera
Capitol City Brewing
  Company (Mass. Ave.,
  Arlington)
Capital Grille
Casablanca
Chadwick's Georgetown
Chadwick's Old Town
Cities
Citronelle
City Lights of China
Coco Loco
Coeur de Lion
Delray Garden and Grill
Duangrat's
Ellis Island

Felix
Fio's
Fratelli
Galileo
Generous George
  (Springfield, Annadale,
  Alexandria)
Germaine's
Goldoni
Greenwood
Hee Been
Hibiscus Cafe
Hunan Chinatown
I Matti
Il Ritrovo
Inn at Little Washington
Japan Inn
Jin Ga
Kinkead's
L'Auberge Chez Francois
L'Auberge Provencal
La Bergerie
La Chaumiere
La Colline
La Fourchette
La Miche
Ladda
Lafayette
Le Caprice
Le Gaulois
Le Lion d'Or

Legal Sea Foods
Les Halles
Lespinasse
Levi's - Oxon Hill
Louisiana Cafe
Marrakesh
Marrocco's
Matuba
Mediterranean Blue
Melrose
Mr. Yung's.
Mrs. Simpson's
Morrison-Clark Inn
Morton's Of Chicago
Nizam's
Occidental Grill
Old Angler's Inn
Old Ebbitt Grill
Old Glory
Oodles Noodles
Oval Room
Pan Asian Noodles and
  Grill
Peking Gourmet Inn
Pho Cali
Red Hot & Blue
Red Sage
Restaurant Nora
Roxanne
Sabang
Saigon Gourmet
Saigon Inn
Sam & Harry's
Sam Woo
Seasons
701

1789
Skewers
Star of Europe
Straits of Malaya
Taberna del Alabardero
Terramar
Tivoli
Tom Sarris' Orleans House
Tony Cheng's Seafood
Trumpets
Vidalia
Vincenzo
West End Cafe
Willard Room
Xing Kuba

AFTERNOON TEA

Bice
Coeur de Lion
Lafayette
Lespinasse
Melrose
Seasons
Roof Terrace-The Kennedy
Center- Hors d'Oeuverie
South African Cafe
Teaism
Vox Populi
Willard Room

BUFFETS

These buffets are mostly for lunch or brunch.

Afghan
Amazonia
Aquarelle
Aroma
Ashby Inn
Balalayka (except summer)
Bistro 2015
Bombay Bistro
Bombay Club
Cafe Bethesda North
Cafe Dalat
Cafe New Delhi
Cafe Parma
Coco Loco
Fratelli
Gabriel
Generous George

Georgia Brown's
Hee Been
Lafayette
Le Caprice
Levi's in Oxon Hill, MD
Louisiana Cafe
Marrocco's
Matuba in Arlington, VA
Old Glory
Perry's
Roof Terrace
Sam Woo
Swagat
Trumpets
Vox Populi
West End Cafe
Willard Room

PRE-THEATER BARGAINS

Afghan
Aquarelle
Aroma
Bistro Francais
Bombay Club
Cafe Bethesda North
Carlyle Grand Cafe
Citronelle
Clyde's of Georgetown
Felix
Generous George
Lafayette
Lavandou
Ledo
Le Refuge

Le Rivage
Luna Grill & Diner
Luigino
Melrose
Mrs. Simpson's
Occidental Grill
Oval Room
701
1789
Star of Europe
Taberna Del Alabardero
Tivoli
Trumpets
Village Bistro

WHERE YOU CAN DINE OUTDOORS

Amazonia
Aroma
Arucola
Ashby Inn
Austin Grill Bethesda
Bangkok St. Grill
BeDuCi (Glass-enclosed area)
Bice
Bistro Bistro
Bistro 2015
Bombay Bistro
Bombay Club
Bua
Busara
C.F. Folks
Cafe Berlin
Cafe Bethesda
Cafe Dalat
Cafe Deluxe
Cafe Milano
Cafe New Delhi
Capitol City Brewing
   Company (2 Mass Ave.,
   Arlington locations only)
Carlyle Grand Cafe
Cashion's Eat Place
Chadwick's
Coco Loco
Cottonwood Cafe
Crisp & Juicy
   (Rockville, Silver
   Spring locations)

Dean & Deluca
   (M St., 1919 Pennsylvania
   Ave. locations)
Delray Garden and Grill
Duangrat's
Dubliner
Ellis Island
Gabriel
Galileo
Generous George (Spring-
field)
Gerard's Place
Grill From Ipanema
Il Radicchio (Wisc. Ave.)
Il Ritrovo
Inn at Little Washington
Kinkead's
La Colline
La Ferme
La Fourchette
La Tomate
Ladda
L'Auberge Francois
Lauriol Plaza
Le Caprice
Le Gaulois
Le Rivage
Le Vieux Logis
Lebanese Taverna
Les Halles
Luigino
Luna Grill & Diner

Maine Avenue Wharf
Market Lunch
Marrocco's
Mediterranean Blue
Melrose
Miss Saigon (Columbia Rd.)
Mrs. Simpson's
Morrison-Clark Inn
Music City Roadhouse
New Heights
Old Angler's Inn
Old Glory
Oodles Noodles
Oval Room
Paolo's
Perry's
Pho Cali
Raku
Restaurant Nora

Rio Grande Cafe (VA)
Roxanne
Saigon Gourmet
Saigon Inn (Connecticut
  Ave.)
Savory
701
Skewers
South African Cafe
Southside 815
Star of Europe
Straits of Malaya
Tabard Inn
Taberna Del Alabardero
Tivoli
Trumpets
Village Bistro
Vincenzo
Vox Populi
West End Cafe

TAKING NO CREDIT

A dozen restaurants in this book do not accept credit cards, only cash or, in at least two cases, checks as well. So you won't be caught by surprise when dining at them, they are:

C.F. Folks
Crisp & Juicy
Food Factory
Full Kee
Hitching Post
Kosher Express

Market Lunch
Marrakesh
Pho 75
Sholl's
3rd & Eats
Vie Deli